THE RING

THE RING

SYLVIE LAMBERT

Eagle
Editions

À Dominique Puaud et Maman

FRONTISPIECE

Ruudt Peters,
Ouroboros 'Wunstorf' ring in gold and silver plate and
marcasite, 1995–96. Photograph by Rob Versluys Studio.

TITLE PAGE

Françoise and Claude Chavent,
gold and iron wedding rings made since 1993.

ACKNOWLEDGEMENTS

I would like first of all to thank my publisher for his continued confidence
over these long months of research and work, Madame Claudette Joannis
for her care; my sister Dominique for her advice and suggestions; my whole
family, Natacha, Françoise, Laurence but also Agis, Xam, Alain, Smicky,
Christophe, Karim, Dan, Jo and Bruno for their help and encouragement.

I wish to thank the Houses of Cartier, Van Cleef & Arpels, Boucheron,
Poiray, O.J. Perrin, Ilias Lalaounis, Jean Dinh Van, Uno A. Erre, Niessing,
Bellon, Charles Perroud and Caplain Saint-André for their committed co-
operation.

I would also like to thank all the artists for their support, and sincere
help and commitment throughout this huge and ambitious project. Thanks
should also go to the galleries, museums and jewellery schools, details of
which I give at the end of the book.

A QUANTUM BOOK

Published by Eagle Editions Ltd.
11 Heathfield
Royston
Hertfordshire SG8 5BW

Copyright ©MCMXCVIII
RotoVision SA

This edition printed 2002

ISBN 1-86160-574-9

QUMRING

This book is produced by
Quantum Publishing Ltd
6 Blundell Street
London N7 9BH

Printed in Singapore by
Star Standard Industries (Pte) Ltd.

Contents

Preface   *8*

Foreword   *11*

General introduction   *12*

1. MAJOR PERIODS IN RING-MAKING   *15*

Introduction   *16*

The prehistoric ring   *19*

The ring shape in the 5th century BC   *25*

The Sumerian seal ring   *29*

The Egyptian prophylactic ring   *33*

The Greek allegorical ring   *37*

The Roman ostentatious ring   *43*

The symbolic ring   *49*

The stirrup-shaped ring   *55*

The emblematic ring in the 13th century   *59*

International Gothic and the metaphorical ring in the Renaissance   *63*

Identity and the power of the Name in the 15th century   *67*

Science, faith, love and death in the 16th century   *73*

Between baroque and classicism in the 17th century   *81*

From rococo to neo-classicism in the 18th century   *87*

Neo-classicism, eclecticism and industrialisation in the 19th century   *93*

Art Nouveau as a break from the past: 1895-1914   *99*

Art Deco and the 'reckless' years: 1915-39   *105*

Rings in the 1950s: tradition and creativity   *113*

Conclusion and overall perspective   *118*

2. FINE JEWELLERY AND MASS PRODUCTION   *121*

Designer and mass-produced rings   *123*

Constraints   *131*

    Creation and manufacturing techniques   *131*

    Economics   *132*

    Regulation   *132*

Consequences and strategies   *137*

3. MODERN AND CONTEMPORARY RINGS   *147*

The modern ring: first-generation designers of the 1960s   *149*

    General historical and artistic context   *149*

    Schools and formative influences   *150*

    The geometric and analytical tendency   *150*

    The lyrical and spiritual tendency   *153*

    In summary   *157*

The modern ring: second-generation designers of the 1970s   *161*

    Exhibitions, galleries and museums   *161*

    The geometric and analytical tendency   *163*

        Germany, Austria, France and the Netherlands   *163*

        United Kingdom   *170*

        France, Belgium, Switzerland and Denmark   *173*

    The lyrical and spiritual tendency   *175*

        France   *175*

        Switzerland and the United Kingdom   *177*

        Germany   *177*

        Italy   *179*

        Austria   *181*

        Finland and Denmark   *181*

        Spain and Portugal   *184*

    In summary   *186*

Contemporary rings: third-generation designers of the 1980s and 90s   189

Third-generation designers in context   190

Netherlands   190

Germany   198

Italy   204

Spain   209

Portugal   216

United Kingdom   217

Austria   224

Switzerland   227

Denmark and Norway   234

France   236

In summary   246

4. CONCLUSIONS   251

Avant-garde and towards the year 2000   252

Artistic and aesthetic references   252

Circulation   255

Hermeneutic references   256

Conclusion   260

Glossary   262

Bibliography   263

Books   263

Catalogues   265

Museums and galleries   266

Index   269

Preface

These pages invite us to go on a voyage of discovery which sweeps through history from early antiquity to the present, with many stops in different places, times and cultures, illustrated by a single item of jewellery: the ring. The signet ring of the Near East; the serpent ring of Greece; the Bishop's ring; the fede ring of the Romans, which was echoed several centuries later by the engagement ring of the Breton peasants; the sentimental ring, whose bezel holds hair or inscriptions; the ring-sculpture or the ring-object of the contemporary period, decorated with diamonds, stones, bones, wood or even scrap materials such as rusty iron or broken glass: the list of ring-types is infinitely varied.

Behind these different types and materials, the pictures, photographs or writings of certain individuals often spring to mind. Many Renaissance paintings depict men – goldsmiths perhaps – some of whom are holding one or several rings in their hands, while others may be wearing a chain around their necks on which rings are hung, perhaps souvenirs of their dead wives. Princes, like Francesco d'Este, as painted by Roger van der Weyden, might clasp between their fingers a ring and a hammer, symbols of power and authority.

The ring has often symbolised authority and power for men, whereas it signified the marriage bond and adornment for women. Iconography, however, presents a more complex argument. Coquetry, for example, may be a masculine form of behaviour demonstrated by the wearing of ear-rings and finger-rings. Prominent men in the French Revolution were thus adorned, whether they were soldiers or heads of political parties. These visible signs of the cult of appearance are also found in the concern for elegance of the dandies of the 19th century. In England, Beau Brummel and, in France, the Count of Montesquiou and the Count Boni de Castellane, rejected gaudy jewellery, with the exception of tie-pins or signet rings with coats of arms or initials. Wearing rings on several fingers was, for a long time, a way for a man to get himself noticed, while the romantic portraits by Ingres or Chasseriau have left us the image of women with slender fingers adorned with several rings, as dictated by fashion. Nowadays, sports and music personalities ostentatiously wear rings on several fingers, or a broad ring on the index finger like the rock singer, Iggy Pop.

This study of ring design is certainly a voyage in time, but also a detailed presentation of the techniques of stone-setting and metal-working, the extraordinary precision of 'system' rings and the development of forms – information which bears witness to the constant invention of craftsmen and artists, and their desire to combine dreams with matter.

The presentation of contemporary creative artists sheds light on a subject which has so far been little-known, since, while many works have dealt with the ring over history, few of them have elaborated to such an extent on the forms and variants of the rings designed nowadays. These rings, reflecting a troubled period and, at the same time, freed of constraint, prove to be as much the testimony of an individual as of a time. While aesthetic research is always there – to the extent of presenting rings as sculptures to be looked at rather than to be worn – there is also a dematerialisation of jewellery, reflecting the phenomenon of destructuring in fashion. The ring may also be an object of social protest, though an approach which may seem new is often never far from the traditions of the past. When the French artist Michel Journiac designs rings using human bones, he is linking up with the ancient custom of the *memento mori* of the 16th century.

There are therefore many milestones along the way in this book, which gives us a wealth of knowledge and pleasure at one and the same time.

Claudette Joannis
Head Curator of National Heritage
France

Yet when from her black skin

She drew a little hand which looked like ivory

Coloured with a little purple,

And when the fatal ring,

Fitting so perfectly,

Surrounded her small finger,

Such was the surprise at Court,

It just cannot be understood.

[free translation]

Charles Perrault, Donkey Skin

The Ring of the Way has no beginning and no end.
It is the repeating of experience lived 'here and now'
which bears eternity within it.

Zen Master Taisen Deshimaru

Foreword

This book focuses on a single artistic motif which is also the most widely sold and most widely worn form of jewellery – the ring. It aims to explore the relationship between jewellery and art and fashion, as well as the creative approach of artists and jewellers and, in doing so, to provide a timely addition to existing studies in this field.

Any work of art – whether it be in the field of painting, sculpture or adornment – will teach us something about its time and about ourselves. Artists everywhere have sought to express a wide range of ideas and emotions in their work. In this way, the ring – 'that small, finely-worked object, rendered precious by the materials or the labour that have gone into it, and serving to adorn a specific part of the body'[1] – has also taken on many forms and functions throughout its history.

But while the history of the ring has been documented, its more contemporary dimension has remained unexplored. A study of the historical development of the ring, focusing on the way in which – in every era – it has reflected the aesthetics of its time, is vital in understanding the design of this most precious object.

The second part of the book deals with contemporary fine and mass-produced jewellery and the economic and aesthetic constraints which have influenced its design. Here we focus on the explicit relationship that the ring has with fashion, popular mentality and more contemporary concerns.

Whatever the wishes and intentions of the artists who crafted them over the centuries may have been, rings continue to reflect the search and desire for enriched forms of perception – a game based on symbolic communication, just as much as conceptual thinking. These are the aesthetic experiences and issues which – through a study of concepts (ideas) and form (design) – have shaped the main argument of this book.

The vast and fascinating question implicit here relates to the status people attribute to jewellery in general and rings in particular, perhaps as they seek to transcend it. This book reveals the many ways in which this unique form of adornment has made its mark, at each point in history reflecting the essence of an era.

1 Petit Robert, Dictionaire de la Langue Français

General introduction

The ring is undoubtedly the bodily ornament which has generated the most power, mystery, magic, desire and thought in the general history of adornment. As the 20th century draws to a close, it is appropriate to study the design of this particular item and, *a fortiori*, attempt to review the contemporary creation of rings. [1] The ring is an object which it is possible to think so much and yet so little about. The following statements may all be true, even if they apparently contradict each other: 'That because of its totally free form and non-precious materials, it is unwearable and has, therefore, no value, indeed no reason to exist; that it is no longer worn for a special event or to signify a certain belief, but for the simple desire to please or, above all, to provoke; that it is directed at a minority in any case; that it is not art; that it can be no more than a mirror of fashion in which our society sees its own reflection, inherently linked to the development of a culture in sharp decline; that it does not exist because no one sees it, displays it in museums and galleries, or wears it...' [2]

At first sight, therefore, it does seem difficult to define precisely the aesthetics and artistry involved. It is true that the expression, 'the art of the ring' could have several possible meanings. In the broadest sense, it could refer to all the skills traditionally put into making this small object by the goldsmith or jeweller and, more particularly, it could also apply to all the processes the artist-jeweller uses to express an ideal or a more personal emotion.

Despite the almost total impossibility of defining the current practice of ring-making, it should be possible –

and perhaps more relevant – to stress the rich inter-play of formal and synchronic questions and answers that this particular art generates. If this creative practice can be described as contemporary, it is because it shares the time of the artist and the spectator, who might be the art lover, collector or wearer. Linking a part of the body to the thinking or glances it attracts, this revealing object reflects our lifestyle, culture, society and, on a larger scale, our fears and our world.

Rings have always existed and still exist in every part of the globe, even though current knowledge of this art as practised by certain prehistoric or geographically more distant cultures is slight.

So what then is the future for this object of our time, with its non-traditional forms and diverse materials? The finished ring, like any other work of art, still tries to reach out to a certain audience; even though its market may continue to be uncertain.

Because of the materials used and the manufacturing techniques employed – as well as the free, diverse and surprising forms of modern rings, which are subject to the most varied social and artistic influences – these radically different creations no longer correspond to any traditional shape or style. They disturb, disconcert and upset people.

However, within this creative freedom, one thing lies at the heart of the work undertaken by artist-jewellers: the symbolic and aesthetic scope of rings, their strong reference to fingers, hands and, by extension, the body and its movements. This must be taken into account in order to understand the extent of this artistic experimentation. The essential argument is concerned with visual, sensual and temporal perception – in other words, our relationship with reality – not to mention conceptual challenges.

The contemporary ring is no longer produced in accordance with rules regarding use of materials, techniques, shapes, ideas or motifs. Nowadays, its purpose has changed: it now seeks to portray forms of reality in different ways and achieve the active and sensual participation of its owner.

The ring of today is therefore an experience of the living world, so that at each moment new perceptions take shape. If it can be called contemporary, this is precisely because it seems to challenge every attempt at critical interpretation with each new creation or appearance.

It is therefore quite clear that, while the conception and design of a ring are certainly the product of tradition, its more contemporary experience is genuinely practical; it has its own formal and specific language. The ring is a work of reflection and personal research by every artist-jeweller; it seems always to conform perfectly to both personal and collective spheres of interest and to be linked to a more general search for truth.

In order to understand the semantic changes undergone by rings, it is important to see how their form has progressed in relation to technical developments and in parallel with various social and religious functions; and then to study contemporary artist-jewellers' creations despite industrialisation, which now controls the major share of production. The whole history of forms and techniques demonstrates the strength of the designers' creative investment.

Contemporary artists all share the desire to take account of economic circumstances and to bring something of reality and the personal into the very material of their creations. This reaches the essence of that aesthetic universe which is so close to our beliefs and our dreams and which touches on the truth of life.

1 and 2 For this introduction see especially Christophe Domino *Introduction à l'Art Contemporain* in *L'Art Contemporain*, Centre Georges Pompidou, Editions Scala, Paris, 1994 pp.14–19; Jean-Marc Poinsot, *L'atelier sans mur*, in *L'Atelier Sans Mur*, Vilembanne Art Edition, 1991 pp.9-7; Hugh Honour and John Fleming, *Introduction* in *Histoire Mondiale d'Art*, Bordas, Paris, 1992 pp.10–17, but also the work as a whole for aesthetic research and reflections.

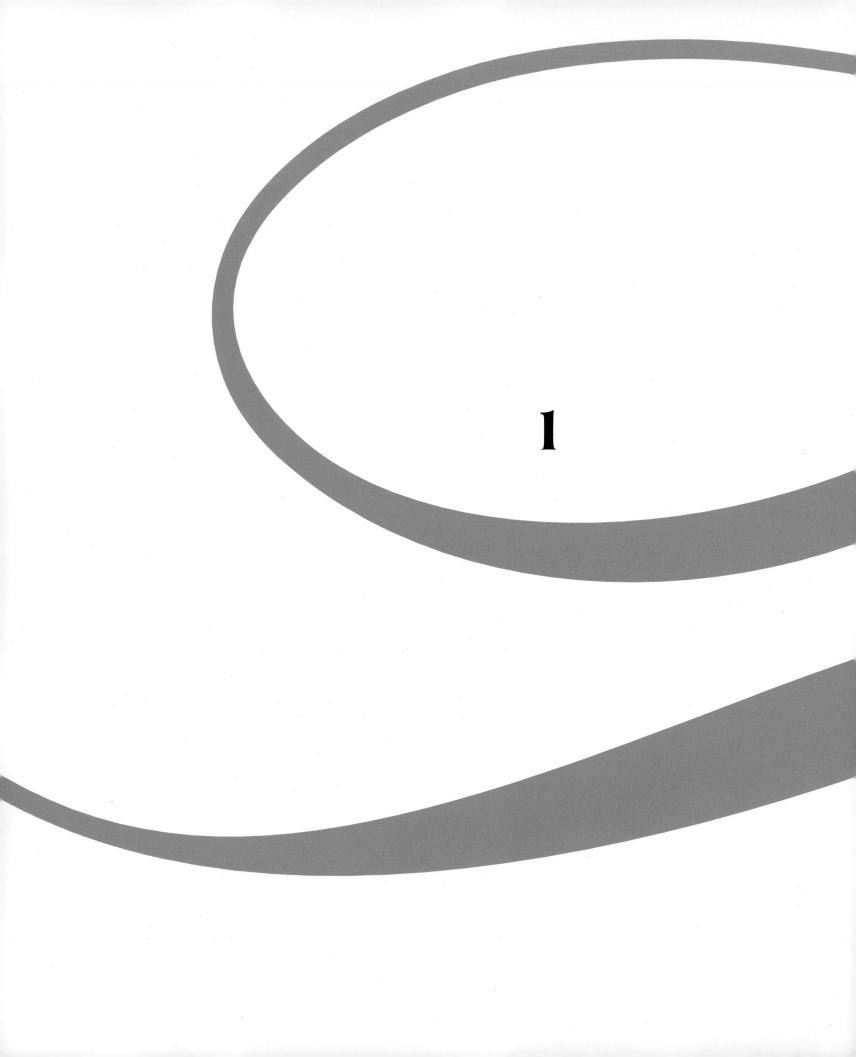

1

Major periods in ring-making

Introduction

Rings are, quite rightly, seen as items of adornment with a decorative purpose and well-defined functions. However, the studies that have been devoted to rings have tended to focus on describing their design or form, in isolation from the rest of history and the history of art. Defined simply as a small object intended to adorn one or several fingers of the hand, the ring automatically acquires limitations as to its use and the part of the body it concerns. That definitely distinguishes it from a statue or a picture, but if the ring is to be fully understood, it needs to be placed within a more general aesthetic context. For archaeologists, rings are precious relics. With the efficient technical resources available today, historians can authenticate this small object with a large degree of certainty and trace its date in history, placing it more generally within a historical and social reconstruction and thereby give meaning to its existence in the organisation of the life and beliefs of a past civilisation.

Simultaneous and more specific analysis of changes in the form of rings and in the materials and techniques used to manufacture them can enable art historians to make rings more understandable and accessible. However, the interest attracted by this specific item of adornment and analysis of its formal development also shows that it can acquire, over the centuries, genuine artistic value compared with the mere usage value it may have had at one time.

Form and function thus seem to be the two vital and almost inseparable poles in the history of this small object. Should rings be perceived and considered as art objects? Current debate and research in the theoretical and historical schools of study recognises that the boundaries of art are relatively vague; moreover, researchers are constantly agreeing to extend them. The initial purpose of art in general, and rings in particular, was not simply a search for immediate aesthetic pleasure; rings have never been created to fulfil the aspirations of a single artist. The concept of aesthetics is recent in this respect, dating from the 19th century and prevalent mainly in the West. Rings have, therefore, always been at the service of the men and women in a society symbolising religion, power, magic or ideology.

Yet paradoxically, even though the pretext for designing a ring has always been social, political, religious, magical – and, more rarely, the subjective expression of a world view – not one of these objects was created without obvious concern to achieve a pleasing appearance. This almost universal and fundamental need of human beings could be likened to a desire to impose order on nature, or to stand out in a crowd. Each individual would then shape, manufacture, decorate or wear a ring in accordance with the prevailing balance of power. In making this choice, people express their personal aspirations while creating the aesthetic ideals of their own social group. There would then be perfect osmosis between aesthetic and moral experience, because the union of these two considerations fosters knowledge, power and sensitivity, making rings an expression of both ethics and art.

The art of rings must be understood as a whole. A ring cannot be understood outside its context; its form is related to the material of which it is made, but also to its social and religious function. Whatever the period it comes from, a ring is part of the building blocks of society and civilisation: its form is dictated by its use. The very way in which individuals craft and wear this precise, precious object reveals his or her nature. The ring is not just a means of communication, nor the materialisation of a common experience, it is also a singular, coded and political representation of our way of living. The ring has always been charged with symbols and signs, whatever the intrinsic value of its material components. Moreover, it is still the piece of jewellery which is the most frequently exchanged, because it is laden with meaning and designed to serve many different purposes. The following chronological study examines the way in which the ring has taken various forms as a result of its social usage and the materials used.

The prehistoric ring

It is difficult to trace the exact date when the ring motif appeared in the history of art, or to describe with certainty the precise circumstances when rings were first created and worn. It is possible, nevertheless, to put forward some hypotheses: while language enabled prehistoric man to communicate orally with his peers, standing upright enabled him to work with his hands and craft his own tools. He could thus provide for his needs and, using objects as intermediaries, make a direct link with reality, or an indirect link with the supernatural. Neanderthal man had perfect mastery of his hands as of 50,000 BC. As an instrument of touch, the source and means of technical mastery in manipulating materials, he cut and polished ivory, stone, bone or wood. By modifying the initial form of an object stemming directly from nature, either by assembling natural materials such as flowers, leaves, stalks and vines, successively removing or cutting up fragments, he created his own tools; his own increasingly precise, regular and symmetrical objects. His understanding of form (and function, whether utilitarian, commemorative or magical) led him to surround himself with artistic creations.

The growing maturity of Homo sapiens (at the period around 40,000 BC, as demonstrated in cave paintings), was also expressed in the production of objects of adornment, which have been found either in settlements or in tombs. Bodies found wearing adornments are relatively few in number and, in most cases, were excavated in the old-fashioned way, at a time when archaeological standards were less rigorous. Brno man (around 30,000 BC), found in

Czechoslovakia, is apparently one of the oldest examples. However, despite all these discoveries and research, it is still currently a delicate matter to ascertain with certainty the real function of the various objects of adornment belonging to the Palaeolithic period. Produced for utilitarian, magical and aesthetic purposes, it seems likely that it was also intended that they should be 'surrounded' by something beyond human reality, something superhuman.

One may, however, argue that jewellery has existed since modern, Cro-Magnon, man came to form small groups, which was no doubt a time when the social cohesion of his immediate circle had become an indispensable element of his lifestyle and economic system.[1] Excavations undertaken in Europe do, in fact, corroborate this statement. Rings, or something very like them, also seem to have been present. What exactly were the items like? Ignoring adornments made of perishable materials (since they obviously do not survive today), there seem to have been two fairly clear categories of natural objects: the first covers items made from objects such as animal teeth and shells, which were perforated and/or grooved; while the second covers objects made of ivory, bone, antler and stone, which were soft, shaped and pierced to varying degrees.

Adornments belonging to the first category were quite small in size (between 3cm and 6cm), could not be used as tools and were usually hung or threaded on to something. When bones and teeth were involved, they were never human in origin, but always came from animals such as stags or reindeer.

The sea has always thrown a variety of shells on to the shore; it is therefore easy to understand today the attraction for Palaeolithic man of picking up such treasures. His choice was dictated by length, thickness, colour, shape, dissymmetry, openness, pattern, plastic harmony and the presence of bulges or notches (Fig. 2). In addition, he favoured certain species and probably collected them 'in order deliberately to make up an ornament which had a meaning and to express an understandable message'.[2] The shapes of these shells acted as signs loaded with symbolic meaning, which were also used for other means of expression: claviform signs were particularly frequent in cave art and it is even thought that they suggested a feminine 'meaning'.[3] These shells also provide a better understanding or knowledge of the social relationships and exchanges that certainly existed between individuals and tribes, even if they were geographically distant.

Animal teeth (usually incisors, as they were the strongest, with long roots and a broad crown), along with shells, are the oldest items of adornment. However, whereas the latter could simply be picked up, teeth needed careful, delicate extraction in order not to damage either the enamel or the root. Those used for adornment were usually perforated, grooved or carved. The shape of teeth kept for adornment was meaningful in itself and more or less pleasing in appearance (Fig. 3): they came from herbivores like reindeer, bison, aurochs, stags and ibexes, or, more rarely, carnivores like bears, wolves and foxes. Animals were right at the heart of human life, feared at the same time as they were the driving force behind the technical development of weapons and tools, a reference point and the focus for symbolic beliefs. Such teeth fashioned into adornments must surely have signified the possession of strength and been the receptacle of a symbolic meaning, which Palaeolithic man would inherit as the owner and wearer. Whether perforated, polished or grooved, they were worn as they were, attached by a strap.

Adornments made from various raw materials such as deer antlers, bone and ivory, soft stones such as lignite or limestone, or harder ones such as certain minerals, were worked to obtain a particular shape. They are classed more generally as pendants. Elongated pendants (between 4cm and 12cm in length), whether narrow or broad, elliptical or cylindrical, display remarkable technical skill. When their surfaces were flat enough, they could be used for graphic expression, made up of incisions and carvings, which could be very harmonious. Ovoid pendants were directly inspired by their original shape: 'So it was indeed the shape itself which revealed the meaning that the artisan wished to give to the object and the carvings that adorn its surface are intended to reinforce the meaning of the shape'.4 Meaning is therefore derived from shape.

Pendants have even been found that evoke the human form: when female, this was suggested and rendered in a stylised way rather than really described; when male, phalluses (often in ivory) were explicitly sculpted in the round. Others (which might have been worked directly from a shoulder blade) evoke animals: deer, and also bison, mammoths, felines and horses. These pendants thereby reflected in the bestiary used in wall painting. In every case, it was the initial form that inspired the representation. The carved themes are recognisable, but cannot be

listed here in their entirety. They come under the heading of stylised graphic expression, which may not even be figurative (linear or geometric) at times. Generally speaking, although stylised, the representation is relatively naturalistic, meaning that the animal is visualised rather than conceptualised: the image is based on what the eye sees and not on what the mind knows or thinks it knows and perceives. These clearly-identifiable animals are represented in a specific way and according to appropriate social conventions. They are executed with a good deal of elegance and astonishing accuracy, resulting from keen observation. In addition, these objects are of a sometimes startling realism, especially when the very shape of the animal seems literally to extricate itself and spring from the matter or raw material.

How can this impression be explained? Palaeolithic man adapted and worked the form of his figures in accordance with the original material that he found and chose to sculpt. It was therefore matter in its raw, natural state that dictated the shape and final representation given to the object. The hunter living continually in contact with nature, on which he was

3 *Perforated tooth (teeth), Musée Archéologique, St Germain-en-Laye.*

completely dependent, drew from it his formal repertory and his whole inspiration. This human action on nature displays a high degree of technological skill as well as very personal aspects. The fine dimensions, the refinement and the extraordinary skill shown in these pieces corroborate the hypothesis that even though the significance of such plastic expression still escapes us, it had an ornamental function and more. All these ornaments designed to adorn very precise parts of the body no doubt assumed identity and social cohesion merely by the fact that their presence was recognised 'by some' and their meaning clear 'to some'. Their shapes and arrangement on the body were thus familiar to members of the same tribe.[5] Their meaning was incorporated in the wearer, while the graphic message was wrapped up in the usual role of adornment, probably with much greater significance.

Smaller perforated pieces have also been found (from 1cm to 1.5cm, made of steatite, reindeer antler or ivory), generally spherical in form and almost identical. They were intended to make up adornments in several sections. In contrast to the pendant, which carried within it its own individuality and significance, these beads (Fig. 4), took on their full meaning when threaded and assembled together. The neck, chest, wrist, ankle and finger could then offer themselves as perfect props.

It should be remembered that, for these past civilisations, all these items of adornment had a commemorative, magical, supernatural and aesthetic, as well as ornamental, significance. According to research,[6] prehistoric man considered animal teeth, horns and claws and polished stones as the receptacles of material and spiritual forces. In addition, they associated ochre, a red paste symbolising blood, with this idea of vital, superior energy, a promise of survival and the source of intense life and creative production. Yet were these adornments painted red all over or just partially? Were they left as they were? Despite the high-tech procedures available to researchers today, it is still almost impossible to know.

It would therefore be difficult to base analysis of these objects on a solely visual interpretation of their form, materials and representation. One must always try to understand them in their social, economic and religious context, as they are indisputably linked to specific functions. What are these exactly?

Ritual certainly. Anthropologists suggest as an explanation for the existence of this motif an obvious relationship either with a magical rite intended to ensure success in hunting, or a cosmic connection related to the different seasons and herd migrations, or a totemic, mythological connection (the outside world as culturally construed by these human hunters). Nevertheless, these ornaments, which must therefore be included within a set of creative practices and beliefs, remain enigmatic. Even though the leading specialists still refuse clearly to identify some of these adornments as finger rings, this could very well have been the case. Pendants or perforated beads could in fact have acted as mobile bezels, with a hole

through which a small thread could be slipped to place or attach around the finger like the Egyptian seal ring.

Palaeolithic man lived in the areas around caves, close to the circle constituted by the fire. Light came from torches made from coniferous trees or small clay lamps burning oil or animal fat. It seems quite logical that, in this world without mirrors, the ornament could enable him both to gain pleasure personally and directly from his appearance and to feel protected and potent in the hostile world around. This provided him with a feeling of strength, glorifying and highlighting that particular part of his body: the hand. This precise part no doubt conveyed for him and his group longstanding knowledge and reliable power, just as much as singular strength.

The Palaeolithic period has left us a large number of hands depicted on cave walls (Fig. 1): sometimes carved, but more often painted or outlined with a cloud of paint. These representations show hands (usually left hands) opened wide, with fingers spread apart, or missing one or several fingers. The portrayal of these hands was obtained either by applying a hand covered in colouring directly on to the wall or by flinging the colouring all around the hand first applied to the wall, which was more common. It is interesting to note that these hands could very well have been made by applying not the palm, but rather the back of the hand to the wall. In this case, the fingers could easily be bent back before being outlined with red ochre or manganese dioxide.

Leroi Gourhan has made a thorough study of these practices of representation:[7] according to him, complete hands or hands with missing fingers should be seen as a kind of code for hunters using symbolic substitutes for animals, or as having entirely feminine significance, directly related to the topographical features of the cave. A signature, sign, symbol of power or possession, an attempt to relate to the divinity or an empirical therapeutic expression, for example, against diseases, 'the hand is a symbol of unambiguous meaning'; its image 'is found throughout the world'.[8] It is clear that, at this stage of discovery and analysis, life in and around the cave must have been a genuinely organised and symbolic world. No object can be understood outside this general framework.

By drawing his hands on the walls of grottoes or adorning them with objects, Palaeolithic man was glorifying precious tools that were essential to his

4 *Bead(s), Musée Archéologique, St Germain-en-Laye.*

survival. He was a nomad with a very short life expectancy of something like twenty-five years. He produced little and lived on the resources of nature. It is against the background of this dependent relationship with nature and precarious living conditions that we must understand and examine these singular hand ornaments, designed and made using the shape of a tooth, claw, shell or piece of wood. They had to be adapted to his fears, his magical and religious beliefs and the values around which his whole social system was organised. As visible signs of the transformation of his bodily image, they needed to be able to accompany him everywhere and thus to mark the various hardships or important events in his life and even beyond his lifetime. When he died, Palaeolithic man was usually buried with his ornaments.

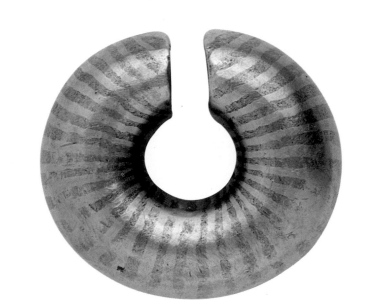

5 *Penannular ear-ring,
2nd millennium BC modelled
on 16th and 15th century BC
Cypriot and West-Asiatic
ear-rings. Ashmolean
Museum, Oxford.*

The ring shape
in the
5th century BC

The major climatic upheavals that occurred around 8000 BC gradually changed the landscape and lifestyle of Mesolithic man. He began to become settled. This fundamentally important phenomenon brought about changes in the way he saw himself in relation to the world. From being a hunter or gatherer, he gradually became a producer, little by little moving towards a sedentary lifestyle and domesticating animals, sculpting stone, modelling clay, producing ceramics and, finally, developing and refining his weaving technique. The growing of cereals, selection of species and domestication of livestock were thus the two major stages in this period. They were to revolutionise settlement patterns (small communities sprang up) and means of production. They thereby altered the relationship between neighbouring or foreign communities and, of course, specialised and accentuated the hierarchy and inequalities within a single community.

As of the 7th millennium BC (the Neolithic period), these more stable living conditions were responsible for an increased population and the development of urban centres of varying sizes in Northern Europe, the Mediterranean Basin, Asia and America. Indeed, when the first concern of Neolithic man was no longer to ensure his daily food supply, precisely because his own crops enabled him to store his produce and meet his own and his community's needs, he could concentrate on and develop his own agricultural methods. He could also refine his tools in order to guarantee the harvest, organise the division and specialisation of labour in society, foster administrative organisation and finally the establishment of states; and use surplus production in outward-looking trading activity.

It was within these new relationships and social orders that the need and the search for a new material, a supreme means of expressing distinction, prestige and authority, became keener and asserted itself. By the 6th millennium BC in the Near East (Turkey, Syria and Iran), gold and copper had already been worked in their raw state by means of hammering. This technique was used to produce small objects and adornments (not tools, since shaping without alloy would have made them too malleable and soft in relation to the solidity of stone). It is interesting to note that, as soon as it was discovered, gold was immediately venerated for its brilliance and solar colour. This was probably because it was found by chance, in its raw state, on the surface of eroded areas and that its discovery seemed to be a gift from 'the nourishing earth'. Or was it because in its fascinating brilliance and chemical potential it could incarnate and give strength to the wearer? It does seem that all these propositions might be acceptable.[9]

Full exploitation of the potential of metallurgy through large-scale extraction and production of objects and jewellery, and job specialisation for miners, metallurgists, traders and peddlers, certainly dates from the 5th millennium BC. This happened in Northern Europe and the Balkans, a region which also had particularly favourable climatic conditions for economic development. The gold and copper mines of Bulgaria and the former Yugoslavia are, in fact, the oldest known to date. The working and exploitation of these two minerals was thus the subject of a genuine industry.

The discovery of Varna, a necropolis located in Bulgaria on the Black Sea coast, helped to give a better understanding of the role played by objects of adornment within such societies. The gold deposits were located in the south-west, centre and south-east of current Bulgarian territory. Many tombs with buried objects were thus found and studied.[10]

In particular, archeologists found circlets made of gold and copper (from 1.2cm to 3.7cm in size) and strips of metal that were round, half-round or quadrangular in section whose ends had been brought together or joined in order to make a more or less rounded shape. Traces of the pliers used to tighten or align the two ends are still visible on the edges of some of these primitive rings. Cylindrical forms in

gold, from 1.2cm to 3.5cm in size, were also made using the same technical principles, but from a hammered, rolled strip of metal.

These gold ornaments were worked only by hammering and beating metal in thick sheets; most of the copper objects were cast. This technique seems to have been characteristic of metallurgical practice in the Balkans: clay crucibles were in fact used for casting copper (melting point 1,083°C), which required considerable skills on the part of the craftsman. It was only after being shaped by casting that the objects were hardened by hammering. In any event, in comparison with the wide variety of types and designs of tools that existed at that time, it should be stressed that these gold and copper circlets were actually not very varied in form: they were always ring-shaped or cylindrical. (See Figs. 6 & 7).

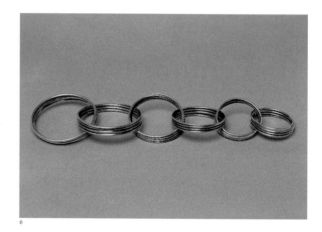

6

But what were these annular objects used for? Many of them were found with other ornaments in areas or places that were certainly linked to religious practice, as well as in many tombs. However, researchers have not yet been able to specify what part of the body these objects were supposed to adorn. Most of them have even been identified as pendant ear-rings (since the two ends have been brought together). Nevertheless, in view of the size or diameter of these small rings, they could have been slipped around a finger. Whatever the case may be, it is generally thought that the wealth of these necropolises and temples reflected the social and religious hierarchy. The structure of these communities was undoubtedly based on profound social differentiation: groups of chiefs, priests, warriors and their families, simple inhabitants and, finally, marginals. Their lives were punctuated, on the one hand, by religious ceremonies and, on the other, by funerary rituals (in which gold and copper objects and jewellery accompanied the deceased). As a whole, artistic activity was thus an integral part of social consciousness reflecting this highly spiritual community life.

Within this overall framework, the existence of ring-shaped adornments is quite feasible, conveying information about the aesthetic concepts and speculative thinking of these societies. In any event, specific analysis of the ornaments found during excavation of the Varna necropolis has been able to bring to life their particular significance in relation to notions of adornment and show; reconstructing some aspects of the religious and mythological system of the time could thus give us some insight into the spiritual life of these communities.

There was undoubtedly an entire mythology in which the image of the Mother Goddess occupied the highest position, while the figure of a male character (the chief) only appeared on the sidelines. This female/male alliance guaranteed the fertility of the land and women, but was also supposed to safeguard the coming harvest and ward off evil spirits. The demonological beliefs of this civilisation were based on the concept of the 'spirit of the dead', bringing misfortune, against which it was necessary to protect oneself. Jewellery worn next to the skin was also supposed to bring happiness to the wearer and allow them to possess it throughout their lives and beyond their deaths.

Gold, an unalterable (and therefore eternal) yellow metal, also played its part in this state of mind. It was considered to be the earthly manifestation of the sun. As to the motifs of the circle, ring, spiral and meander, they too were associated with and interpreted as a solar symbol. It is, moreover, accepted nowadays that this graphic element must be associated with the ornamental representation of the serpent. In the mythological thinking of the late Aeneolithic period, 'the serpent was the periodic rebirth of the plant forces of nature, "matching the trajectory of the sun and seasons". It is clear, therefore, that these motifs must be interpreted as the graphic symbol of the link between the Sun and the Serpent and, consequently, of the link between the Sun and the Earth's fertility'.[11]

The circlet – a simple coiled-up or curved gold and/or copper wire or strip, which may or may not have been joined at the ends – must therefore be interpreted as a motif and a possible ornamental representation of the figure and power of the beneficent sun. It must indeed be included, more widely, in a cult and a set of rites around Nature. It might be said that the manifestation within a society of a religious and mythological system based on the cult of the sun reflects a high degree of centralisation, hierarchical organisation and advanced level of development. However, the desire and need for keeping records and accounts that was then felt by that civilisation did not result in the invention of a genuine form of writing.

7 *British hair-rings, 2nd millennium BC modelled on 18th Dynasty Egyptian wig rings. Ashmolean Museum, Oxford.*

8 *Gold finger ring, 2600-2650 BC from the Royal cemetery at Ur (Southern Iraq). British Museum, London.*

The Sumerian seal ring

It was in the Near East, around the 4th millennium BC, where native gold and copper had already been used to manufacture objects and jewellery, that people began to take advantage of the particularly attractive resilience of an alloy of copper and tin. The discovery of bronze, which, once polished, can take on a beautiful golden colour, incontestably marked the beginning of a new era. These Mesopotamian civilisations, located between the Tigris and Euphrates, with their complex structure and hierarchical organisation, were also at the origins of the discovery of an early form of writing (pictographic and then cuneiform) and a numerical system. They also set up a means of payment using money rather than barter. It was in such a relatively flourishing context that Sumerian civilisation, which already had literature in the form of the Gilgamesh epic, performed brilliantly in the fields of art, jewellery-making and goldsmithing.

Two motifs are of particular interest in this context, one animal and the other ornamental. In the first case, rings were cut from soft materials ranging from serpentine to shells. The overall form was sculpted in the round and from a single block of material. The latter had to lend itself to the painstaking work of cutting and then finely engraving motifs or signs on the bezel. Chosen for their intrinsic quality, these various materials were also selected for the particular brilliance of their colour: rings were cut and crafted in serpentine, lapis lazuli, gypsum, alabaster, shells and other materials. The bezel might bear intaglio inscriptions, figurative representations or decorative motifs: whole or partial representations of wild animals such as lions and ibexes or domestic animals such as bulls. These are generally seen in profile and suggest slight movement. This iconography can be explained in the following ways.

For the Sumerians, a sculpted, engraved object had its own being. For the hunter, wearing a ring with an animal figure was a sign of possession and domination, seen by him as a token of protection. This animistic view of the world thus gave these rings a degree of freedom and made them the source of signs and meaning. By extension, they were supposed to speak in the name of their owner. This ability to extend one's influence, to impose and indicate presence when physically absent, may be likened to the beginnings of writing. These rings were in fact intended to be pressed on to wet clay or wax in order to leave their impression so that they could be used as seals of ownership. It is relevant to relate these seal rings to the cylindrical seals that were the characteristic motifs of the Sumerian era. However, the advantage of the seal or signet ring over the cylindrical seal was that it was easier to use anywhere without having to take it off the finger. An obvious sign of recognition, these rings were like signatures and accompanied their deceased owners to the grave.

The second important motif to note in this period is a type of ring made from metal and ornamental stones, with a more ornamental purpose. Fig. 11 is a gold hoop with slightly bulging extremities, and cloisonné work all around in gold filigree. This alternates quatrefoil, (four-leaved) shapes with elongated heart shapes, the latter being solitary, superposed or arranged at angles on the most prominent extremities). The ring is set with beautiful cornelian and lapis-lazuli inlays. The fact that no one view is particularly enhanced gives the whole ring perfect harmony in its clever, multi-coloured rhythm of rare, precious stones.

The main techniques for shaping metal were soon to be mastered and put into practice.[12] They were to enable the Sumerians to vary and give new life to their decorative motifs and to play on the many colours of stones, capturing the very essence of the goldsmith's art. This type of ring, which placed technical skill at the service of a harmonic alternation of forms and materials, was undoubtedly intended for display.

On leaving prehistory to cross the boundary into history, it is interesting to note that the idea of harmonious forms was a recurrent theme in ring design and production in all these civilisations and, moreover, constantly took on new life. This search for balance in shape, forms and colours, based on obvious aesthetic criteria in accordance with individual, social and tribal convention, can be likened to a quest for possible eurhythmy between body and object. The ring adorns the hand, joins in its movements and plays an active role in its owner's gestures. While assisting the latter in playing a social role, it secures power for him, helps him to draw attention and stimulates fascination.

9 Gold finger-ring with twisted wire, 2600-2650 BC from the Royal cemetery at Ur (Southern Iraq). British Museum, London.

10 Gold finger-ring with lapis inlay, 2600-2650 BC from the Royal cemetery at Ur (Southern Iraq). British Museum, London.

11 Gold, lapis lazuli and cornelian ring, Sumerian, c.2500 BC, Musée du Louvre, Paris.

12 *Painted and gilded cartonnage mummy mask of a high-born lady, wearing calcite ear studs, an elaborate broad collar, bracelets and armlets, a pectoral and real finger-rings, including one of cornelian, Thebes, c.1370-1250 BC. British Museum, London.*

The Egyptian prophylactic ring

Favoured by its geographical position, Egyptian civilisation developed along the Nile from 3500 BC. Structured in communities around the fertile river, it was under the authority of a single, divine and absolute monarch, unlike Sumerian civilisation. There was no rivalry between communities and therefore few wars. This very close-knit rural civilisation adored Ra, the Sun God, father of all gods, and believed in eternal life. The Egyptians' desire to leave material traces at all costs, as proof of their successful passage to the after-life, fostered the appearance and development of very elaborate graphic codes. With the aid of hieroglyphic writing, on the one hand, and aesthetic canons relevant to these beliefs on the other, they were able to anchor past and present in eternity.

These inscriptions and representations of scenes from daily and religious life meant that earthly pleasures could be indefinitely celebrated and prolonged in the next world. They ensured the immortality of the deceased. However, this immortality of the soul could only be achieved if the body of the deceased was preserved intact.

This divine right, reserved for the Pharaohs throughout the period of the Old Kingdom, was subsequently 'democratised' during the Middle Kingdom, becoming available to anyone who could afford a funeral with the appropriate rites.[13]

This specific relationship between body and spirit determined the whole attitude of the Egyptians towards art in all its forms. Names had acquired singular importance to them. God had brought human beings to life by giving them a name, outlaws had their

names destroyed or transformed into insulting phrases and those who reached the next world feared that they would not even remember their own names, which would be the equivalent of irrevocable death. By inscribing them on various media such as monuments, walls, and rings, Egyptians ensured their immortality through their names.

An inscribed name was valid for the individual for all eternity. Jewellery, including rings, also took part in this great voyage towards eternal life. Found mainly in tombs and always symbolic, these may be divided into three categories: the signet ring, the narrative ring and the ornamental ring.

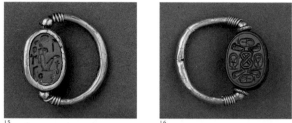

A signet ring in Fig. 17, in gold, is made up of two distinct pieces soldered together: a hoop and a bezel. The hoop, a three-quarter circle, round in section, is cast in metal from a single block. Some models had a more massive lower part, in which case-metal hooping worked in filigree hugged its finest extremities (Fig. 18). This original dissymmetry consolidated the whole and enabled the object to achieve harmonious balance. The gold hoop allows the ovoid bezel to be placed on its upper extremities. It has intaglio engraving that is perfectly readable. The inscriptions, which might also be found under the bezel (meaning that they were hidden), were always related to the different aspects of the owner's power. Names, important life events, invocations to the gods, fetish animals and so on were amongst the hieroglyphs and eloquent inscriptions and representations destined to glorify an uncommon nature in infinite time.

13 *Gold ring, swivelling bezel of cornelian cat on a plinth, c.1370 BC. British Museum, London.*

14 *Gold ring, swivelling bezel with granulation, surmounted by a frog in the round, c.1370 BC. British Museum, London.*

15 *Plain obsidian scarab ring, from Abydos, c.1820 BC. British Museum, London.*

16 *Green glazed composition scarab ring naming Hatshepsut, c.1470-1425 BC. British Museum, London.*

Signets made entirely of faience were also found made from one block. The siliceous paste was coloured with cuprous compounds. The use of non-precious materials (faience as well as coloured glass) was then very common. As substitutes for semi-precious stones, they allowed designers to play with other colours, materials, forms, motifs, decorations or compositions.

The narrative ring may be made up of a single hoop, like that of the signet ring, or of two or three smaller hoops, placed side by side and soldered at the top. However, in both cases, the hoop bears the bezel on which a scene or figurative symbol is fashioned in gold, semi-precious stone or glass. Figs. 13 & 14 show a cat carved from cornelian and a gold frog sitting on a granulated bezel. This portrayal of small animal scenes, powerful religious symbols and evocations is intended to focus our attention: a secular scene, a stage in the owner's life, a symbol of rebirth (scarab) or protective amulet (Udjat, the perfect eye). With regard to the specific development of the scarab ring, it should be noted that, initially, its bezel was perforated longitudinally as shown in Fig. 19. The hoop, gold in this case, was initially just a linen thread tied around the finger. This practice dates back far into antiquity, perhaps even to prehistory. However, amongst the Egyptians, this thread was gradually to thicken and become a circular metal reed, which was more solid and non-perishable, before reaching the stage of an object cast in one piece.

The ornamental rings gave the first Egyptian jewellers a real opportunity to practise their skill in the art of inlay. This demanding technique, combined with gold, required a lot of preparation and care: the turquoises, lapis lazuli and cornelians were to be placed alternately in the hollow cavities in the metal. The formal result had to be visually perfect.

The fingers and, more generally, the hand, had a very novel importance in Egyptian culture.[14] Its pictorial and sculptural representation and the way it was adorned corresponded to very strict, coded conventions as well as almost immutable aesthetic criteria. The unit of measure was derived from the arm, but in accordance with the width of the hand and fingers. The Egyptians had observed that the length of the foot was equivalent to three times the width of the hand. This ratio subsequently determined all the proportions of the human body in their drawings and pictorial representations. This faithful and regular use of aesthetic canons gave their art an incantatory dimension. It is not surprising, in this context, that ornaments for the hand also had a very prominent role in Egyptian society. These objects were made by artists and craftsmen – there was then no difference between the two – who were at the service of a master, and they had ultimate symbolic or prophylactic value. These rings could be worn on any bone of the finger or toe. Tutankhamun was found thus in his tomb, with his left hand covered with gold fingerstalls, the first joints of the fingers bearing two impressive rings.[15] The function of these objects was to accompany Egyptian man throughout his life, ensuring him of success when crossing over to the next world. Consecrating his earthly status and promising eternity, they were intended to evoke and invoke important events in life, death or the life-giving divine powers of Ra, the Sun God. The colour of the different materials used and the very nature of the metals reinforced the supernatural beliefs: faience, glass, turquoise, cornelian, lapis lazuli and jasper were lucky materials guaranteeing fertility, prosperity, wealth and immortality.

The main value of gold was not of a material nature. The yellow metal was venerated and considered to be the very substance of the sun: the 'flesh of the gods', dazzling and indestructible. Associated with eternity, gold contributed towards the magnificence of the Pharaoh, the divine representative. These conventions enabled rings to fulfil their ritual, religious, magical and indeed alchemic function. Egyptian civilisation remained faithfully inspired by the same vocabulary and the same symbols for 3,000 years. The endurance of this style was a token of the balance of the political and religious structure of the state, which guaranteed efficiency and social cohesion.

17 *Gold signet ring, Egypt, XVth dynasty, 1674–1567 BC, British Museum, London.*

18 *Massive solid cast shank with lapis lazuli cylinder as bezel, c.1370 BC. British Museum, London.*

19 *Green jasper scarab ring inscribed with good luck symbols, c.1470–1425 BC. British Museum, London.*

18

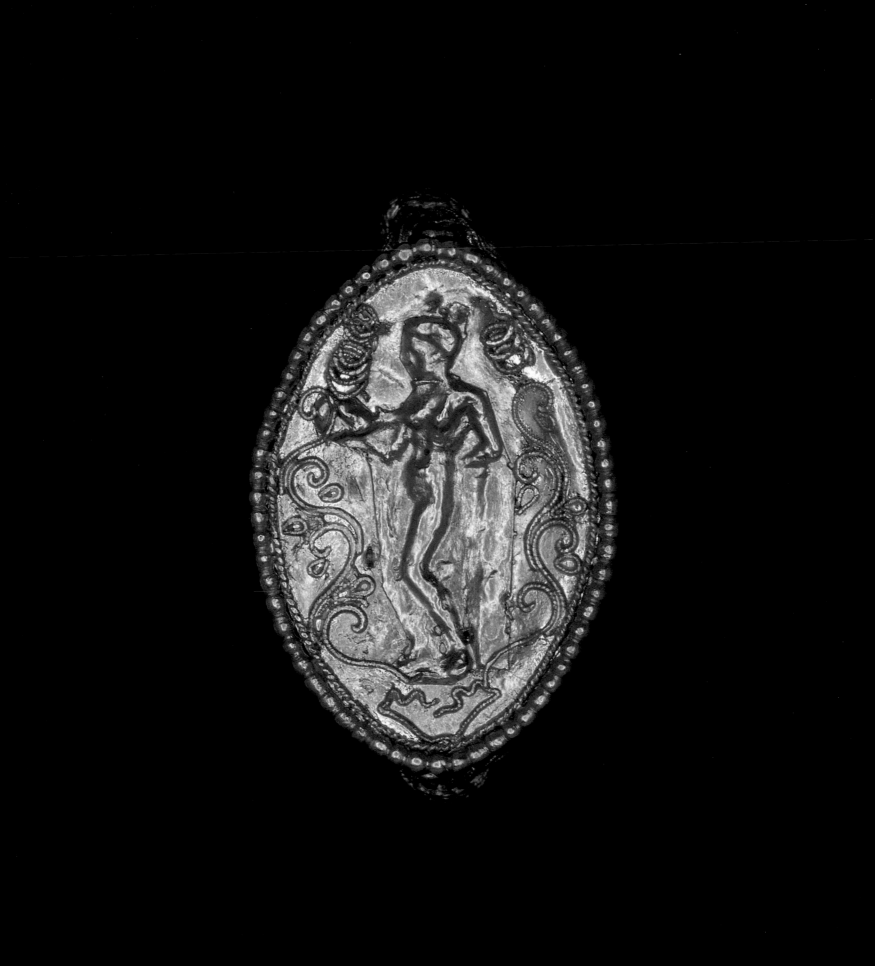

The Greek allegorical ring

Despite the Indo-European invasions and the strong influence from neighbouring civilisations (more particularly oriental ones), Greece was able to forge its own cultural and artistic identity. Its history developed through the Mycenaean (1500 to 800 BC), archaic (800 to 500 BC) and classical periods (500 to 338 BC) to the Hellenistic (338 to 30 BC) era. The whole of the Greek world was made up of several hundred small warrior states, more or less jealously guarding their independence. Each of these city states actually had its own political regime. However, while this mountainous, very scattered maritime country did not have any political unity, its inhabitants did develop a common national consciousness quite early on. Finally, political and commercial rivalry did not shake their feelings of kinship, and above all, their pride in being Greek. As relatively free citizens, they were thus united and linked by a common language, religion and worship. This is what is known as Pan-Hellenism or the union of all Greeks.

This shared religion and strong bond created a universal way of adoring and celebrating the gods, who were veritable incarnations of the forces of nature. There was no standard holy book: poets and artists had modelled religion by giving it a very familiar, almost humdrum character. Homer was the most illustrious of these artists. Many of the gods were endowed with entirely human personalities, feelings and reactions. They were worshipped by means of libations, offerings and animal sacrifices which were accomplished in accordance with common rituals; and they were questioned through the oracles and all its energy to the combatant. As of the 6th century BC, the coin, a small ingot made of precious material with a stamp guaranteeing the quantity of metal it contained, had greatly assisted trade and commerce. Each Greek city had its own currency.

Here, however, on the bezel of our ring, there is just one figure: Nike, the winged goddess, driving her quadriga towards Victory. The effect of rhythm and energy is a complete success. The symbolism of the chariot was common amongst the Greeks, since this is a theme also found in sculpture. The bronze chariot driver of Delphi is a famous illustration: the celestial chariot driven by the omnipotent Zeus conquers every obstacle. It can, therefore, represent all the cosmic and psychic forces to be driven, where the driver is none other than the ruling spirit. It is an image, moreover, that the philosopher Plato commented on and applied to the dual nature of man. A symbol of consciousness, the chariot and its figures are supposed to become one when seen from various conflicting spiritual angles.

24

25

25a

24 *Gold ring, 350-300 BC, British Museum, London.*

25 *Gold ring, 350-340 BC, British Museum, London.*

25a *Idem, view from beneath.*

The third ring of this period (Fig. 20) bears a flat, ovoid bezel, parallel to the axis of its hoop. A whole decorative pattern (interlace and ova of different sizes), using filigree and granulation techniques, focuses attention on the central figure: a standing female nude. The weight of the body is resting on the right leg, which is held closely against the slightly bent left leg. The outspread arms allow a glimpse of the nudity of the figure, but the head turned towards the right gives the whole an impression of both modesty and sensuality. There are some very beautiful examples of rings displaying the same concerns. Two are considered here (Figs. 24 & 25), for their remarkable technical and formal execution.

Nevertheless, the function of this type of ring remains enigmatic: they were made to be worn, to enhance the beauty and wealth of their owner. Tokens of love or friendship, they had a sentimental or possibly commemorative function and surely a religious and magical function also.[17] However, the motif of the female and male nude was also the major concern of Greek sculptors of the 4th century BC, who in portraying a perfect body were seeking above all ideal Beauty and transcendence of reality. It was also the starting point for the thinking of the philosophers of the time who, as friends of Wisdom, were attempting to discover and attain Truth.

At the end of the 4th century BC, Greece experienced a time of profound political, artistic and social change, witnessing the birth of codified architectural space in town planning and circular theatres; the use of new decorative motifs borrowed from nature such as acanthus leaves and foliage; and a search for the perfect balance between idealisation and naturalism, as in Polyclitus's canon. All these concerns came in response to new demands for embellishment and regularisation. They sought to capture the idea of rhythm and life in plastic expression.

At the end of the 4th century BC and throughout the following (Hellenistic) period, three other types of motifs appeared and were abundantly used in ring design: these were symbolic motifs such as the serpent, Hercules' knot and various ornamental motifs.

The serpent ring is formed from a single gold strand wound around in s spiral. At the two ends, one can see the head and tail of the animal. The ring is in the form of a coiled serpent. This motif has been found in abundance and was, moreover, frequently copied by

26

subsequent civilisations. The symbolism of the serpent is vast. It is true that, at this time, the circle symbolised the ideal of the perfect geometric form. In addition, the serpent is the emblem of Asclepius, God of Medicine, celebrated at Epidaurus, because he was endowed with the power to resuscitate the dead. (See Figs. 26 & 28).

27

The Heraclean or Hercules' knot, made of two gold loops, is also a motif commonly used in the jewellery of Hellenistic Greece. Calling on new techniques and repeating existing Persian, Etruscan or Scythian forms and motifs, the knot symbolised the power to heal wounds. The work and exploits of Hercules were, furthermore, very famous. This mythical Homeric hero was considered to be the idealised representative of combative force, the symbol of the difficult victory of the human soul over its own weaknesses. The association of these two symbols (the knot and Hercules) on a single ring was thus intended to reinforce the powers

28

of the object. Encircling the finger of the hand, this ornamental, talismanic ring was supposed not only to procure courage and energy for its owner, but also to guarantee power and victory in his personal life.

The last example from this period (Fig. 29), conversely, opens up another way of using gold and employing different precious stones that seem to match each other. As is the case here, the formal working of the hoop and bezel echo the treatment of the gold and the juxtaposition of the different-coloured stones. The hoop is a fairly broad, three-quarter circle. It is adorned at both ends by small, angular, geometric shapes, superimposed on each other in order to be glimpsed between the fingers and as their owner moved his or her hands. Small garnets complete the picture. The lower part of the hoop is a flat quarter circle, but the circular protuberance that can be seen on its exterior could possibly have served as a base enabling it to stand upright when taken off. The construction of the bezel has been designed in degrees in accordance with various geometric ratios and forms: ovals, circles, triangles and rectangles of various sizes are superimposed and set off to advantage the interplay of materials, lines and polychromy. The almost perfectly oval-shaped amethyst that tops the ring is set in a gold cabochon.

The development, spread and recurrence of these formal motifs have to be considered along with all the political, social and religious changes that could be seen in Greece at this time. Philip of Macedonia, who had contributed towards the unity of Greece at the expense of the independence of the city states, was pursuing his policy of conquering neighbouring territories. His son, Alexander the Great, who had become a key figure in this expansion of the Empire, encouraged cultural dissemination and the penetration of foreign cultures. This interlocking of West and East inspired the formal renewal of the art of Hellenistic Greece. During this period, which was to last more than three centuries, large urban centres involved in commerce and crafts (such as Antioch, Pergamum and Alexandria) also encouraged the transport of precious materials. In the hands of a new merchant class, gold ceased for a while to be the monopoly of kings and the nobility.

These objects no longer present the deification of the name, but reveal the appearance of concepts (serpent – victory, knot – power, geometry – absolute): representing an allegorical system which uncovered the 'world of ideas'.

29

27 *Gold Hercules' knot ring, end 5th century BC, Musée du Louvre, Paris.*

29 *Gold, garnet and amethyst ring, Hellenistic period, 1st century BC, British Museum, London.*

26 *Gold snake ring, 4th century BC, Musée du Louvre, Paris.*

28 *Snake ring, 4th century BC, Musée du Louvre, Paris.*

30 *Gold and chalcedony ring,*
1st century BC or AD,
Cabinet des Médailles,
Bibliothèque Nationale,
Paris.

The Roman ostentatious ring

At the beginning of the 8th century BC, the Italian peninsula was occupied by an Indo-European population. The Italiots had settled there since the Dorian invasions between 1300 and 1000 BC; the Greek colonisers had established themselves mainly on the southern coasts, whereas the Etruscans had made their home in Tuscany and the plain of the Po. But the latter also gradually began to conquer what is now Campania and seized Rome around 575 BC. The Romans stood up to them and successfully revolted against the invaders, setting up a government that in their eyes would guarantee peace both at home and abroad: the Republic. However, it took the foremost city of Latium almost two centuries to consolidate this republican organisation of Roman society: social tension could again have very easily upset the fragile political balance of this new Roman political empire.

The plebeians, who originally had no rights, had become an influential force and constituted a danger for the patricians who had come from leading families and were endowed with numerous privileges. Although despite the appearance of an egalitarian and popular government, the comitia, magistrates and senate continued to run the state and were responsible for policy and social cohesion.[18] Only the rich really had the right to vote and therefore take decisions. This development gave birth to a new social class, which was politically very influential: the nobilitas, rich patrician families, such as the Claudii and the Cornelii.

Having become very well-structured politically and increasingly determined in its aims of conquest, Rome

32 *Gold ring, Rome, 3rd century AD, Musée du Louvre, Paris.*

32a *Idem, view from beneath.*

32   32a

33 *Gold, garnet, sapphire and dark green chalcedony ring, Rome, 3rd or 4th century AD, British Museum, London.*

domestic cults.

The wearing of rings was thus gradually becoming democratised throughout the empire and a third example (Fig. 32) shows a ring with a relatively flat surface to its bezel, bearing a portrait in relief set within a circle, itself set within a larger diameter circle. It is a left-hand profile of a woman whose long hair has been dressed and arranged in a fairly loose bun, leaving some locks waving free. The smooth, finely cut face may evoke a certain softness. The two extremities of this female image (the neck and top of the head) are linked by a very finely-granulated circular line.

The second circle within which this first circle is entangled is purely ornamental. The proportions have been carefully calculated in relation to the respective areas of the two geometrical figures. On its surface, granules of varying sizes have been arranged in a circle; the whole being regularly punctuated with twelve bulkier gold granules. The impression given by the whole is one of gentleness, rendered by a degree of freedom in the treatment of the face of the female figure and her soft hairstyle, as well as by the wave effect engendered by the repetition and alternation of gold granulation of varying volume. When turned over, this ring reveals another mystery: in the central circle, we can now see the engraving of a whole horse, in profile and intaglio, executed in a realistic manner. The hoop is braided, jointed and made in the shape of a stirrup: it is a coin transformed into a ring whose reverse side remains invisible and secret.

The coin is from Carthage. The female image may be allegorical, embodying the more general idea of the motherland. At that time (3rd century AD), rings were very popular and worn by all Roman social classes. Taking over a foreign motif for oneself by changing its purpose is probably an illustration of the Roman desire to commemorate ancient battles (such as the famous Punic wars in which Rome was victorious over Carthage). It should be noted, however, that the material of which the coin is made surely had something to do with its transformation into an adornment for the hand. Gold coins were still a rarity and it was

more common to find silver or bronze coins in circulation. Reprocessing them into rings is also a sign of aesthetic development.

Fig. 33 shows a gold ring dating from the 4th century AD, made up of sixteen different settings holding five garnets, four sapphires and four dark green chalcedony, arranged alternately with no apparent rhyme or reason. Note that three stones are missing. This ring, with its coloured patterns designed for visual impact, demonstrates the Roman fondness for ornamental stones, which were even rarer at that time. Sapphires, for example, were not used anywhere in the Mediterranean basin before the Roman period. This ornamental ring indicates an obvious taste for polychromatic effect. Roman goldsmiths seem to have been trying to get away from convention, and the emotional, financial or legal value of their jewellery increasingly resulted in new forms of plastic and aesthetic expression.

It was also during this century that an entirely original technique was invented. This is known as opus interrasile and requires great skill. The Roman artist would take a piece of sheet gold on which he would trace the required design of the ring with a burin and then cut it out using a hammer and chisel. Cutting the metal in this way produced an almost three-dimensional appearance when the finished piece was placed on another sheet of metal. In one example, the gold open-work is just like lace in a ring shape, with sixteen rectangular panels each divided into three. This subdivision highlights the smooth, circular nature of the object. In each of these tiny rectangles, miniature geometric motifs seem to intertwine, giving a decorative effect to the whole piece. Yet there is a romantic message inserted into the leaf-like decoration and inscribed in the sixteen central rectangles of the ring. It reads 'Ptolemios's love charm'. This ring was there-

33

fore produced and worn for its power and intensity, a token and material evidence of love.

The Romans, for whom the letters of the alphabet already held a great fascination, and who delighted in writing them artistically, took full advantage of their stylistic potential. In addition, the opus interrasile technique allowed artists to apply their skills in geometric arrangement, and in axial and logical symmetry to the motif of the ring. There is a comparison to be made here with the coliseum, built in the 1st century AD.

The last example (see Fig. 34) shows a ring with a more massive and clumsy hoop bearing an engraved hardstone bezel. Here there is no filigree or granulation: the two little hands that can be made out on the flat surface of the bezel, which is in the shape of a truncated oval cone, are cut in intaglio in the stone inset with coloured glass paste. The artist has taken full advantage of the potential of his materials to give a decorative visual effect: the hands and ovoid periphery are of a darker hue. The massive gold hoop, bulkier and more angular on either side of the bezel, gives the setting a very solid appearance. Triangular, bevelled cuts or grooves flank these protuberances to set off the bezel perfectly.

This ring is also a sign of romantic commitment. It is true that Roman family life was very strictly regulated, from the cult of the ancestors through to marriage, with everything subject to omnipotent patriarchal control.[21] Founding a family and the initial importance of having a son were synonymous with pride and the certainty that the family cult could thereby continue.

The Roman aesthetic was accompanied by a desire for plastic simplicity, clarity and readability. The emphasis was on visual effects, the interplay of different materials and the aspects of colour, light and shade; it was always concerned with geometrical organisation; proportional balance was always very elaborate and included within a faithful representation of reality.

The art of the ring amongst the Romans was thus immediately opposed to what we have seen amongst the Greeks, who were more concerned with representations and allegories of divine cults. Its function was not the same either; the obvious attraction for the interplay of materials, light and shade that can be seen in their rings (effects which were, moreover, much favoured by the architects of the time in their new conception and definition of space) was accom-

panied by stylistic developments, speeded up by the social, economic and political context of the Republic. In addition, unlike the motifs used by the Greeks, developments were seen in the Roman ring not only in relation to its subject matter, but also its functional use. However, there were some recurrent themes: either the desire to glorify (focusing on the emperor or the empire), or to display one's difference, success or social allegiance, or to embody and celebrate one's commitment in love – although this emotion is not easy to represent as it is purely spiritual. Therefore, even if it is futile to try to determine a 'Roman style', it seems quite clear that during this period the ring became a means of glorification and display. Above all, the Roman ring had an ostentatious function.

34 *Engagement ring, 2nd–3rd century AD, Musée du Louvre, Paris.*

The symbolic ring

Between the 3rd and 4th centuries AD, the Roman Empire encountered serious challenges, both from within its own army and from successive Germanic attacks on its northern frontiers. The empire was to suffer the consequences of not having strict rules of succession for its emperors, or the necessary means to govern its huge expanse. Two emperors were to make their mark on the whole 4th century and bring about profound changes in the empire: Diocletian and Constantine were, in fact, to undertake many reforms destined to save the state. However, it was the latter who, as a perfect and absolute monarch, was to endow the eastern part of the empire with a second capital in order better to ensure its defence. His strategic choice was in fact the town of Byzantium, which took the name of Constantinople in 330 AD.

This important city was to become the empire's only capital at the expense of Rome. Faced with the formidable expansion of the Christian religion and in order to ensure the political and social cohesion of the empire, Constantine was to declare Christianity the official religion as of 313 AD and organise the provinces administratively in accordance with observance of this religion. The dogma decided at the Council of Nicaea determined beliefs and structured the entire empire into ecclesiastical districts, dioceses and monastic orders. The emperor himself officially encouraged expression in the plastic arts to glorify the new state religion. The art of the ring was not spared by these changes.

The ring in Fig. 36 dates from the 5th century: a simple hoop, round in section, bears a flat, circular,

36 *Gold ring, 5th–6th century AD, Victoria & Albert Museum, London.*

engraved bezel. A dove with unfurled wings hugs the extremities of the composition and seems both to protect and highlight an inscription in the central and upper part: the two letters 'X' and 'P'. Somewhat arcane on the first reading, the bezel is in fact made up of a symbol and literary metaphor. 'X' and 'P', the monogram 'Chi' and 'Rho', are the first two letters of the Greek word 'Christos', which were adopted to designate the name of Christ. The dove refers to the symbol of purity and simplicity in the image of His life, pure sublimation of instinct, leading to harmony and peace which, by extension, symbolises the Holy Spirit.

37 *Gold and onyx ring, early Christian period, 4th-5th century AD, British Museum, London.*

In order to understand the scope of this object, it is necessary to remember that Christianity is a monotheistic religion that developed in the Roman Empire as of the 1st century AD. Christians trusted in their omnipotent God, who was good and just towards the faithful, as well as in Jesus, his son, who came to earth to save His people and to teach faith in God, love of one's neighbour, forgiveness and sacrifice. The rapid progress of Christianity had been facilitated by that consoling, reassuring gentleness, a promise of eternal paradise, by the Pax Romana and by the missionary St Paul who, travelling throughout the length and breadth of the empire, was converting increasing numbers of pagans. It is true that the great conquests of the empire had to some extent altered and disrupted the traditional religion and the political and social ethics of the Romans, and that perhaps these first followers found, in the Gospel, the philosophical and theological certainties that the religious systems and cults of the time lacked. The violent persecution to which they were subjected in no way wiped out the dazzling progress of this Church and the community to which it was so faithfully bonded. It was under Constantine that public celebration of their cult was authorised, before it became the official religion. Under this emperor too, the conception of art was to change and to play a primary role in the life of every Christian.

In the light of these few historical and theological explanations, the meaning of the ring becomes rather more explicit: it illustrates a religious value and favours a symbolic rather than representative approach. It refers to the very first Christian symbols, manufactured and encouraged by the theologians of the 2nd century AD, who had a clear preference for a conception of God belonging to the world of ideas. The Holy Name and the Word had to manifest themselves through a series of coded symbols, promising Peace and Triumph over Death.

Fig. 37 has a circular gold and onyx bezel, on which a scene is engraved: two horses are drawing a chariot transporting a bearded man; an angel is hovering above them and seems to be showing them the road to follow. The whole is not very realistic and is treated without dynamism, with no suggestion of movement in the expression. The momentum of the characters seems to be frozen and the general impression that emerges is rather stiff. One might try to compare this ring dating from the early Christian period with one of the Greek rings we have previously studied, as they both illustrate the same scene.

It is clear that the one depicted by the Greek artist tends towards narration: the forms and characters are trying explicitly and almost genuinely to describe a movement, to tell a story. There is nothing like that here. The arrangement has been simplified and made heavier and stiffer by the representation and the positioning of the figures.

This example illustrates another plastic approach borrowed by the first Christian artists: in order to translate their idea of God, they took over themes and motifs that had already been present in Graeco-Roman antiquity, readapting them to the meaning and symbolism of their own religion. This representation of the chariot driven by winged Victory could easily be readapted for Christian iconography and simplified with no concern for realism, as its intention is, above all, didactic. The motif of the horse (here shown in its two opposite aspects, black and white), harnessed to a chariot and accompanied by an angel, refers to the solar, majestic allegory of Christ guiding men.

A further example is rather more elaborate: the two outer extremities of the gold hoop are sculpted and decorated with crouching hares, while a garnet has been set on the back; the conical bezel encloses an imperial gold coin that bears an engraving of a bust, only the obverse of which is visible. The arrangement is relatively simple and unrealistic. The features of the full-face portrait show only the rudiments of a rather stiff, fixed expression. The inscriptions that surround the representation seem to echo the shape of the coin and the mount encircling it like a halo. The proportions of the object are harmonious. The hollowed circle of the hoop mirrors the circular, horizontal plane of the bezel whose lower part tapers away; a movement accentuated by the bulging shoulders of the hoop. According to our knowledge of the coins and customs of the time, it is very likely that the face, which cannot be seen here, bears a representation of Christ as *rex regnantium*, whereas the other side shows an emperor as *servus Christi*. The reading of the object thereby becomes clearer.

Since the reign of Emperor Justinian (7th–8th century), who had inaugurated a theocratic system, political and religious power had been combined in the sole person of the emperor, representing God on earth. It was therefore common to find a figuration of the emperor 'in glory' on a coin and mounted in a ring. The purple colour of the garnet also reinforced this function of omnipotence, since the wearing of this colour was exclusively reserved for imperial use. The coin, as we have already observed, always stressed the sacred nature of the emperor, who could consequently manifest himself and impose his will on a wider public, with a view to asserting and justifying his divine status.

Fig. 38 shows a gold and niello[22] ring, dating from the 7th century. A very simple hoop bears a quatrefoil bezel, on the central part of which a scene with two figures is very soberly engraved, surrounded on either side by two little angels. The outlines are picked out and highlighted with niello.

This figurative scene is simply drawn. The line determining the form is quite basic: the haloed, face-less figure seen from the front is wearing a long-ridged robe and the child, at the centre of the composition, seems to be sitting on her knees. On the same horizontal line, two winged figures are symmetrically distributed in this purely descriptive scene, which shows Christ and the Virgin. The rhythms of the curved, fluid lines that flow and follow the representative forms give perfect unity to the whole.

The motif of the Virgin, the Mother of God, had taken on great importance in Christian thought since the 5th century and it was common to see her represented, without realism, but in conjunction with the figure of the Christ child, in the pictorial art of the time

(icons and mosaics). The strict codification or modelling of religious representation, which was then governed by orthodoxy, was supposed to offer and open the way of prayer to the faithful. All artistic expression was thus placed at the service of the greater glory of Christ and the state. The art of the ring had to fit in with this trend, at the service of ritual in order to teach the divine word. This was also an infallible means of imposing political power.

At the same time, profound changes were occurring in northern Europe: from the mid-4th century until the 5th century, the Angles, Saxons, Franks, Burgundians, Vandals, Visigoths, Ostrogoths and Huns were to surge into the Roman Empire and gradually settle there. These Germanic peoples with their oral culture and rather rural customs had common plastic references of Celtic origin, far removed from Greek, Roman or Byzantine motifs. Fig. 40 shows a Celtic ring from the 4th century, which has certain characteristics and properties that, as we shall see later, were subsequently integrated and assimilated. It has a gold hoop, made in one piece, which widens from the back to the front. There is no particular angle from which it

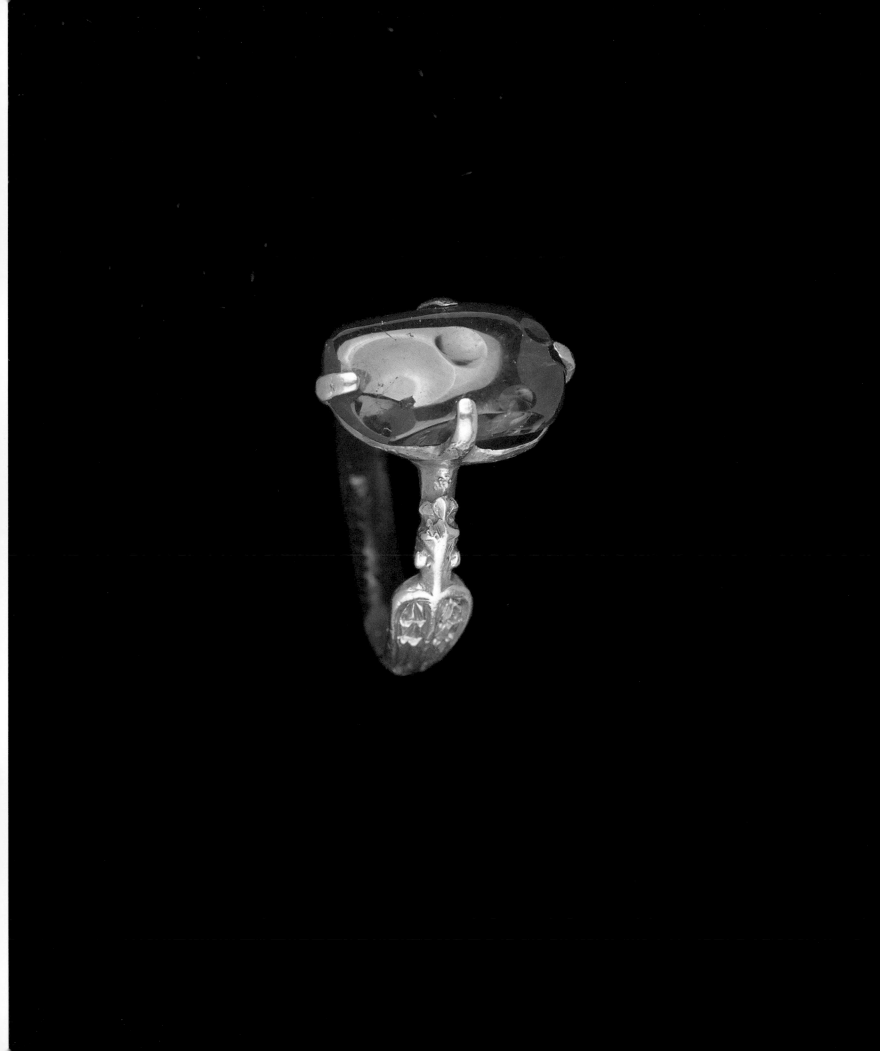

43 *Gold and sapphire ring from the tomb of Bishop Thierry de Verdun, d. 1165, Failly, Londesborough and Franks Collections, British Museum, London.*

The stirrup-shaped ring

A few rings exist from the Carolingian Empire in the 9th century, dominated by the imperial figure of Charlemagne established in Aix-La-Chapelle. It was, however, a vital and very homogeneous time in the history of western art as far as artistic patronage was concerned. This was centred mainly on the figure of the emperor, who reigned as master over his vast empire from Germania to Lombardy. On the death of Charlemagne, in 814, the much divided western political power was supported by the Pope, who was concerned, amongst other things, with codifying artistic production. While Capetian policy was gradually establishing a seignorial system, the people, gathered by order behind the walls, were busy with religious matters. In 845, the political split between the former eastern and western Roman Empires was compounded by a religious split.

The effect of this was the disintegration of artistic centres, and within this context, jewellery – almost always destined for members of the royal family and clerics – was usually produced by monks or goldsmiths.

This is demonstrated by a ring from the 12th century with a cabochon whose very elaborate gold mount clasps an impressive sapphire in its four claws (Fig. 43). Two meticulously-sculpted dragons hug the shape of the hoop on either side, widening at the two upper extremities and forming what look like two wings engraved in the metal on the outside. The two animal heads bear the heavy concave bezel topped with the blue stone. This impressive sapphire seems to be emerging or escaping from the mouths of the two

44 *Drawing in ink of rings from St Albans Abbey, England, 1257, British Library, London.*

dragons, a dynamic impression that places the parts of this object in close interdependence. This ring forms a harmonious, expressive whole, playing on polychromatic effect and its entirely figurative allusion.

Another type of ring of Anglo-Saxon origin (Fig. 45), also from the 12th century, is again made in one piece. The gold hoop, round in section, is bevelled in order that the upper part may widen conically to allow a sapphire to be set there. The stone, placed in a six-sided bezel, closely follows the outer line of the object and gives the whole a compact and very homogeneous appearance. A line cut into the metal runs vertically across the bezel whose solids and planes are arranged symmetrically on either side, giving the whole its density and perfect unity: the blue of the stone is shown off to the full to get the best possible refraction. The overall execution is extremely sober and the effect created is of manifest simplicity.

Although they are executed differently, these two rings are both examples of the so-called 'stirrup shape': each is in fact made up of an entirely circular gold hoop and a bezel set with a sapphire (although the gem in this period could have been an amethyst, diamond or garnet), the structure being conical in every case. This type of ring, which was very common in the 12th century, was usually reserved for bishops.

These two rings, which were the property of Bishop Thierry of Verdun (who died in 1165) and Bishop Hillary of Chichester (who died in 1169) respectively, were found buried in their tombs.

Since the break-up of the Carolingian Empire in the 10th century and the first stage in feudal history in the mid-11th century, political, economic, social and religious changes had established a very influential Christian society that was increasingly keen on conquest. This was the beginning of the Crusades launched against Jerusalem and the pilgrimages to Santiago de Compostela. The Church was all-powerful and the figure of the bishop occupied a strategic social position. Artistic activity in western Europe was based at the service of the omnipotent Church and its bishops. Some magnificent religious pieces, commissioned and executed in precious materials, have come down from this period: ciboriums, chalices, crosses, etc. Made in gold and precious stones, these pieces were intended to fit in with and fulfil a well-defined role within the Roman and new Gothic architecture of churches.

Rings were part of this powerful and somewhat ostentatious Christianising movement: it was very common to bury bishops with their rings, whether pontifical or given on their consecration. Esoteric symbolism was more widespread than ever at this time around metals and the virtues of precious stones. The latter had always, it is true, played a role in catalysing feelings or superstition: amethysts, turquoises, rubies, emeralds, garnets and topaz had had specific functions in each civilisation.[23] Wearing a ring of gold and sapphire in the 12th century was of two-fold significance: this blue stone, celestial above all else, was supposed to lead the soul towards meditation. Rémy de Gourmont has, moreover, reported the thoughts of the Bishop of Marbode (11th century) on this subject in his work *Le latin mystique, les poètes de l'antiphonaire et la symbolique au moyen âge*. His description of the sapphire is as follows: '[it] has beauty similar to that of the celestial throne; it designates the heart of the simple people, of those moved by a certain hope, those whose lives stand out through their morals and virtue.'[24] This stone of hope – a prophylactic against the evil eye, a symbol of purity and luminous strength in the image of the kingdom of God – could symbolise and more generally exalt the solar light emanating from Jesus. In this period particularly, light was the essential concern of Suger (1081–1151), Abbot of St Denis, who studied it as much from a spiritual as from an architectural or decorative point of view.

Religious furniture and rings inlaid with precious multi-coloured stones worn on the right-ring finger and on the glove during high mass were supposed to reflect divine light and transmute 'what is material into what is immaterial' and, by analogy, go 'from the lower to the higher world'. The ritual (dating from the 6th century) for the consecration of a bishop already stipulated that Episcopal dignity and authority must be symbolised by a ring worn on the right hand; a ring

which even became canonical in the 12th century, meaning that it had always to be in gold, decorated with an unengraved precious stone. It seems that the papal ring, the 'Fisherman's Ring', did not appear until the 13th century. However, despite aspirations to this philosophy, the function of these objects still remains ambivalent. Because they are an ostentatious materialisation, these treasures – precious, personal objects – seem to line up on the side of the perversion of matter and the impure exaltation of real desires. De Clairveaux, who headed the Cistercian order as of 1094, denounced and fought against this attachment to luxury, which, according to him, was a profane debauchery, moving the spirit away from meditation and thus from God. In art, he advocated the greatest possible sobriety.

It should perhaps be noted here that the example shown in Fig. 43 is much more elaborate than the one in Fig. 45 and that, in this, it may recall the Byzantine oriental rings of the early Middle Ages or those of Celtic origin, with their skilful ornamentation. What is more, it is figurative, featuring two opposed dragons – animals that relate to the bestiary traditionally used in contemporary Roman art, which was then supported by the order of Cluny under the leadership of St Denis. It is thus a double symbol here, both ambivalent and celestial, where the two fantastical beasts that confront each other (a theme which is also found in European and Muslim alchemy) may, in fact, be one and the same symbol: the spiritual impulse and power of life spitting out the egg of the world, the image of the creative Word.

On the other hand, the extreme sobriety of the ring in Fig. 45 comes closer to Cistercian aesthetics in its desire to revive purity and simplicity.

Whatever the case may be, these two examples of stirrup-shaped rings provide an illustration of the two religious reform movements (Cluniac and Cistercian), which came into being in the 12th century and subsequently extended to the whole of militant Christendom and which had many artistic resonances. (See also the drawings of rings in Figs. 44).

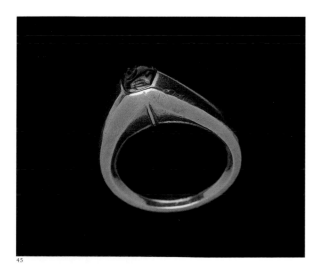

45

45 *Gold and sapphire ring, England c.1200, British Museum, London.*

46 *Gold ring with sapphire intaglio, France, late 13th–early 14th century, Victoria & Albert Museum, London.*

The emblematic ring in the 13th century

The medieval apogee of the Kingdom of France – headed by the Capetian dynasty since the 10th century – arrived in the 13th century with Louis IX (1225–1270). The great Gothic cathedrals, the pride of the Church, flourished in commercial cities that were more and more active. A new social class made up of rich townspeople was making its presence increasingly felt, gradually freeing itself from religious and political powers. This had inevitable artistic consequences.

The gold and sapphire ring in Fig. 47 fits in with an explicit formal logic. Although dating from the 13th century, it reveals the full influence of the previous century. A gold ovoid hoop, triangular in section, bears a high ovoid bezel, set with a sapphire held by four claws. There are some characteristic details. The hoop is a three-quarter circle on the outside of which fine engravings have been nielloed; the whole of the following inscription is in Lombardic letters: *Ave gratia plena DM* ('Hail [Mary] full of grace'). Two animal heads with open mouths grasp the bezel at the two extremities where it is elongated horizontally. The open-work surround of the base bears an animal motif, as birds with unfurled wings support the blue stone held prisoner by the four prominent gold claws.

Probably made for a clergyman, this original and very elaborate ring illustrates a tendency and a theme that were common in the 13th century. The Church was in fact triumphal and imposing itself through its architectural achievements, its councils and its decisions, which wove a net of both ritual and spiritual constraints. Supported in addition by the superabundant charity of the faithful, it was becoming ever richer and thus more influential and present in the urban social environment. The great Gothic edifices erected to its glory were as much civil as religious. Like many works of art from this period, they celebrated and dedicated themselves, above all, to the Virgin Mary.

More clearly on this object are two eagles with unfurled wings who seem to be lifting the set stone, which is thereby shown off to the full. In mythology and, by extension, Christian symbolism, the eagle with wings unfurled could be synonymous with omens and messages from the heavens, although these were already linked to the figure of St John the Evangelist. As of the 6th century, the four apostles might appear, either in their human features, or through attributes, referring to the four regions of the world to be evangelised. St John, the preferred apostle of Christ and represented by the eagle, embodies the Holy Spirit flying above the Church. The 13th was the last century of crusades launched towards Jerusalem. The Latin inscription, placed on the outer edges of the hoop, would clasp the whole finger of its owner; the first words of the prayer dedicated to the Virgin Mary are juxtaposed here, no doubt to express or evoke the eternal celestial Kingdom, the pure female figure of the Virgin and the transcendence of the miracle of creation. Venerated throughout Christendom since the 4th century, she came to occupy a position almost equal to that of Christ in 13th-century religious devotion.

Another gold ring (Fig. 46), semi-round in section, bears a flat, oval bezel, around which a Lombardic inscription is engraved ('*Tecta Lege Lecta Tege*' – 'Read what is hidden, hide what is read'), in the centre of which motto a hooded female profile, in the classical style, is engraved on a sapphire.

The search for regularity and quality in execution shows clearly in these two delicate, refined rings. One can feel that the technique, design skills and intentions of goldsmiths were becoming more refined and clearer. While borrowing classical motifs and forms, goldsmiths were now interested above all in reinterpreting them. They applied all their know-how to this end. The motif of a gold ring and precious stone with a delicately engraved motto either on the bezel or on the hoop was very common at the time. These Latin inscriptions were included in the more general practices of clerics since the 10th century and Latin was the foremost scholarly written language. It is not surprising, therefore, that such inscriptions should be found on bishops' rings; this practice or fashion was encompassed in the more general attraction and taste for Latin writing and its intellectual esotericism. Fortified by these written mottoes and thanks to the precious stones that went with them, these rings were supplemented with virtues and magical powers.

Because of this judicious juxtaposition of a motto, stone and symbolic figure, they were emblematic in every sense of the term.

47 *Gold and sapphire ring, 13th century, British Museum, London.*

48 *Graeco-Venetian gold, ruby and pearl ring, c.1400, British Museum, London.*

International Gothic and the metaphorical ring in the Renaissance

The international scope of the Church thus enabled the Gothic style to spread through Europe: the cathedrals at Chartres, Paris, Reims, Amiens and Beauvais in France, as well as Assisi (St Francis), Burgos, Ulm and Lincoln, had been the most beautiful accomplishments of the 13th century, while the increasing number of openings in their walls had allowed the art of stained glass to blossom. More specifically in France, the art of miniatures had also begun to be practised in secular workshops. When, in the 14th century, food shortages, the ravages and looting of the Hundred Years' War and successive epidemics of the plague were weakening and ruining the population, the Pope – installed in Avignon since 1309 – was scandalising the whole of Europe. In England, the King was fiercely claiming his hereditary right. At this time power gradually ceased to be contained within the sole and unique royal person and the leading European families became even more influential. In this general atmosphere of political struggle and circulation of wealth, where religious devotion was tending to become increasingly individual, artists had begun to work under the orders of lay persons and well-off patrons of the arts.

The French example in Fig. 49 has an engraved sapphire representing a figure standing, three-quarters view, bearing a sceptre in its left hand and an orb in its right; two initials, 'S' and 'L', can be made out. The blue stone is itself embedded in a triangular, semi-spherical gold bezel. The outer surface of the gold hoop is enamelled with a series of very neatly executed fleur-de-lis. On the inside, the following

49 *Gold ring with engraved sapphire, 14th century, Musée du Louvre, Paris.*

49

nielloed Lombardic inscription can be read: '*C'EST LE SINET DU ROI SANT LOUIS*' ('This is the signet of King St Louis'). The inner inscription, as well as the more general decoration of the ring, are meticulously done and probably date from the second half of the 14th century. The intaglio of the sapphire itself seems to be from an earlier date, and it is possible that the stone in this object belonged to Louis IX himself.

This ring is a variety of the so-called stirrup shape that we saw in the 12th and 13th centuries, but nevertheless shows an obvious concern with detail and an attempt at a more regular and more mechanical execution, as much in the design as in the technique of enamelling.

The Anglo-Saxon ring in Fig. 50 adopts a substantially different formal and plastic solution: here the gold hoop and sapphire form a very compact whole. The beautiful blue, octagonal, precious stone is set in a mount with six claws. These are joined together by a motif in a three-quarter circle engraved in the massive, polished metal. The very elaborate, symmetrically cut hoop is made up of neatly executed, interlacing leaves and flowers. On the inside, the following Gothic letters may be seen: '*Willms Wytlesey*'.

Both examples share a high degree of precision and an obvious taste for detail, with perfectly mastered, indeed almost mechanical, execution. They were ordered by two important personalities, one royal and the other religious. Louis IX had in fact been canonised a few years after his death in 1297 under the name of St Louis. Profoundly Christian, he had been keen to ensure that his kingdom should always be well governed and sought thereby to put an end to the quarrels between Capetians and Plantagenets. Since he became and remained the most loved king in the history of France, many kings from 1610 to 1824 bore his name in commemoration. His memory was cele-

brated every 25 August. This ring, in his effigy, glorifies his proud memory. It is accompanied by the emblem of the kings of France – the symbol of the blood (the fleur-de-lis); while the royal figure holds in one of his hands the political symbol of his authority, the supreme royal power (the sceptre), and in the other, the symbol of his totalitarian domination of the world in geographical and legal terms (the orb). We have already seen this practice amongst the Romans, commemorating their peace-maker Augustus. It should be noted however, that Louis IX also had dictatorial tendencies and instigated persecution against the Jews.

The owner of Fig. 50, William Wytlesey (who died in 1374) had been the Archbishop of Canterbury. The Christian Church was then in the midst of a crisis: European Christendom was irrevocably divided between two popes, one in Rome (an Italian) and another in Avignon (a Frenchman). Faced with the Great Western Schism, the King of England and his Church had taken the side of the Pope in Rome. This ring came into being in the midst of these quarrels. Intended for the Archbishop of Canterbury, it adopted the stirrup shape of bishops' rings from the 12th century. A wave of protest was, however, already sweeping England, denouncing these abuses and the profusion of material signs, which proved obvious wealth. John Wycliffe (1320-84), a lecturer at Oxford, challenged the religious life of this Church, which in his opinion was too concerned with luxurious possessions. Having undertaken an English translation of the Holy Book, he considered that the biblical source should be the only spiritual reference and possession for the faithful, who should read and interpret it personally and freely. However, almost two

50 *Gold and sapphire ring, 14th century, Dame Joan Evans Collection, Victoria & Albert Museum, London.*

50

centuries went by before such denunciations were really heeded.

We can see here a synthesis of imperial, royal and Episcopal traditions, although technical, aesthetic and political concerns were already establishing the powerful metaphors of the late Middle Ages.

The ring in Fig. 48 dates from the very end of the 14th century and illustrates the changes that were gradually taking place. On either side of the broad, flat, gold hoop, two rubies and one pearl are set in small collets, which are themselves decorated with fine gold granulation of different sizes. On the back of the hoop, a ruby is set, again in a granulated décor, but one that is simpler and more regular. The prominent bezel is made up of a semi-circle placed on a rounded base of slightly larger size. Fine gold interlacing, both filigree and inverted, punctuates this domed shape crowned with an irregular pearl. The rather majestic whole bears witness to an aesthetic sense that is both Celtic and orientalist, through the techniques employed (granulation and filigree), the classic effects linked to architectural forms (domes) and the linear cadences (interlacing).

The ring of Anglo-Saxon origin and this latter ring of Venetian origin fit firmly within the so-called 'International Gothic' style, which reached its peak around 1400 and resulted from the assimilation of two traditions. This courtly art – created by artists working for the major ruling families of Europe – was characterised by the elegance of its lines, delicacy and interplay in the use of colours and meticulous overall implementation, echoing the art of the Psalters or miniatures of that time.

Those who commissioned works of art had been the most influential men in society, but they no longer had that privilege in the 14th century. Society was structured like a pyramid into three social orders – those who governed, those who prayed and those who worked the land – with wealth and power concentrated in the hands of an élite whose assets were increasing, either through religious association, or through flourishing trade.

At the end of the 14th and beginning of the 15th centuries, International Gothic style was at its peak and achieving perfect synthesis of earlier formal and plastic motifs and iconographical themes. The courtly art of artists and goldsmiths was slipping away from purely symbolic or emblematic art towards representations of nature. This involved using many decorative natural elements, designed and executed with ever greater technical precision. Daring formal innovations can also be seen in these artistic objects. Motifs borrowed from nature or architecture were, in fact, exalting the tentative beginnings of a new attitude towards spiritual matters. The 14th-century ring quotes reality and is, in this respect, metaphorical. The reality to which it refers is the basis of life as being the mirror of the divine essence, which is everywhere and in everything (this is the basis of Aristotle's thinking). Observation of nature therefore became the basis that artists worked from.

51 *Silver ring (detail), 15th century, Franks collection, British Museum, London.*

Identity and the power of the Name in the 15th century

From the 14th to the middle of the 15th centuries, with the ever greater expansion of towns and the appearance of rich merchants, works of art celebrating and glorifying divine nature had made International Gothic the last style common to the various states of Europe. This was the period in which Gothic art was in its so-called flamboyant phase and when form seemed to take precedence over the overall structure. However, at the threshold of the 15th century and more particularly in Italy, 'enlarged humanism' was gradually establishing itself, valuing Measure, Rule and Man in his Beauty and his relationship with Time and Space above all. The arts and literature had ceased for all time to be the sole privilege of royalty or any religious authority. In Italy, followed by France and the whole of northern Europe, the advent of intellectual and philosophical humanism was to bring in new concepts and new systems of individual and civic values.

A ring of Italian origin (Fig. 52) has a fairly broad gold hoop, semi-round in section and polished on the inside. However, all around the outside we can still read a nielloed inscription in Gothic letters, accompanied on either side and at the top (on each shoulder) by a pattern of foliage standing out against a nielloed background. These leaves and flowers together with the inscription – which may be translated as *'I sleep with caution, I watch in safety, I spare the vanquished, I flee no-one'* – are very skilfully done. This device echoes the gold bezel itself: chased, nielloed, polished and ovoid in shape, it tops the hoop and clasps an onyx of varying hues from black to white. Cut in relief,

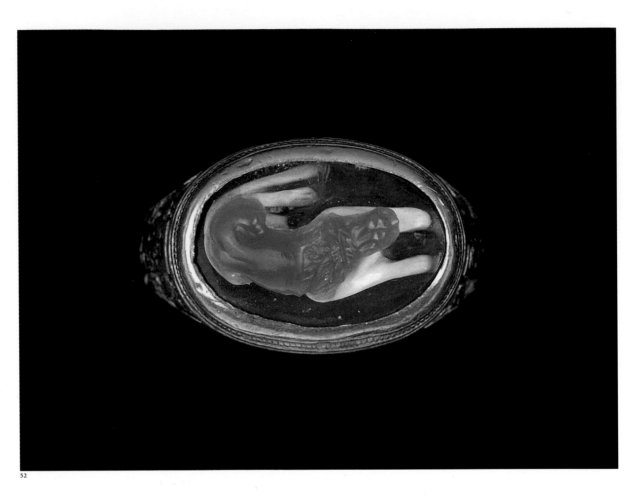

52

it represents a dog lying down. It is a cameo, but while it is easy to feel the harmony of the piece, its significance and function are not so explicit. To what did the image of the dog and the inscription refer?

The symbol of the dog, representing faithfulness, provides only partial clarification. In fact, in all cultures, it was a symbol which also had antagonistic aspects. Even though it was associated in Western civilisation with the faces of night and day, it was more specifically associated with the noble, war-like world of International Gothic. The dog was a sort of hero, trained for guard duty and hunting, and this comparison or metaphor was extremely flattering. The formal point of view is more relevant. The cameo ring was not discovered in the 15th century, but dates from the Roman era. This type of ring must, in fact, be placed within the more general context of the artistic practices of the time, when the forms of antiquity were 'rediscovered'. However, far from being totally forgotten during the previous periods, this form of plastic expression certainly enjoyed a resurgence in the 15th century, but in a new light. It was the manner in which it was interpreted that was new. Far from making do with purely formal interpretation, the goldsmiths of the time adopted the form and adapted it to their concerns with order and measure, creating a new conception of space.

The signet ring was always cut in intaglio. The particular feature of the cameo ring is, conversely, that it is executed in relief. In this example more particularly, it can be seen that the small figurative sculpture on the top of the object seems to detach itself and become independent of the bezel on which it appears to rest. This practice can possibly be connected directly with what was happening at the same time in Italian monumental sculpture, as it sought to break free of the architectural framework (the Gothic niche) for which it had been intended in the previous century.

It is interesting to note also that a very acute shortage of precious materials had pushed a large number of goldsmiths to take up careers as painters or sculptors. According to historians and economists, the 15th century had found it quite difficult to get over the violent crises of the previous century. Painting was no longer done in gold or lapis lazuli, but in watercolours or oils. Sculpture, for its part, was only produced to order and thus at lower cost to the artist, who had a guarantee that he could pay for his raw material: Ghirlandaio (1449–95), Botticelli (1444–1510), Verrochio (1435–88), Dürer (1471–1528) and even Cellini (1500–71) were goldsmiths by training.

The anonymous Italian goldsmith who worked on this small sculpture of an onyx dog, has not only attempted to play on the ambivalence of the animal symbolism, being both black (night) and white (day), but has also followed his own interpretation of past forms and more contemporary aesthetic concerns. Unfortunately, few precious objects remain from this period – most having been destroyed during the Sack of Rome in 1529.

The Anglo-Saxon ring in Fig. 53 seems to be attached to the forms and functions of the previous century: made entirely of gold, this object dating from the middle of the 15th century has been made all in one piece and is of the signet type. The flat, circular bezel is edged with fine gold beading, encircling an engraved inscription. On the broad hoop, where the name of *'Henry Smale'*, also engraved, may be read, the letters are Gothic and the last one ends in a very indented leaf motif. At each extremity and on the shoulders of the hoop, a stylised crown topped with a fleur-de-lis can be made out. The name engraved on the hoop probably refers to a rich English merchant of the time, whose complex personal seal may be identified on the bezel. The important personality of the owner must also have had a strong influence on the design of this significant little object.

54 *Silver ring, 15th century, Franks collection, British Museum, London.*

The signet ring, picking up the older motif of the seal ring, a sign of power and authority, was like a signature and therefore continued therefore to be of fundamental importance to influential merchants in the 15th century. Signing one's name always had been an overriding concern for the oldest civilisations: 'I am who I am', was God's answer to Moses who asked him his name, hence the name of Yahweh, an archaic form of the verb 'to be' in Hebrew, and ontological proof of his existence. The Holy Name was also to be applied to the manifestation of God in the world, and designates Christ as the Word of God incarnate. Easy to use, ready to be printed on wax to certify and authenticate important documents, these merchants' marks, placed alone on the bezel and/or the hoop, might be joined from the 14th century onwards by a more personal device or official emblem. The owner usually wore such rings on the right index-finger.

A magnificent ring in gilt bronze (Fig. 55) bears an amethyst mounted on a gold leaf. It is a papal ring. It forms a very compact whole and on the outside of the broad hoop we can see the four symbols of the Evangelists, a tiara, crossed keys, arms and the name of Pope Pius, who ruled from 1458 to 1464. This ring, also known as a 'Fisherman's Ring', could only be worn by the pope for whom it was made. It was destroyed after his death, during a complex ceremony whose purpose was to invest the new pope by means of a new ring. This object was used to stamp or seal the pontifical documents. We are able to see from this to what extent knowledge and power were combined on the basis of a more individualised name.

Another example (Figs. 51 & 54) is made entirely of silver: it is a hoop whose upper part, which would correspond to the position of the bezel, is in three parts. In each longitudinally divided section, a holy figure has been engraved and only the respective attributes allow for a degree of identification and personalisation. The piece was probably nielloed in

53 *Gold ring, England, mid-15th century, Octavius Morgan Collection, British Museum, London.*

55 *Gilt bronze and amethyst papal ring, Pope Pius II (1458-64), Italy, 15th century, Schmuckmuseum, Pforzheim.*

order to highlight all the engravings, which show St Barbara (a virgin martyr from the 3rd century), St John the Baptist and St John the Evangelist.

Representations of the lives of the saints in western art go back to the beginning of the 11th century. One of the first saints to be represented on an illuminated manuscript was probably St Benedict in 1066, followed by the figure of St Augustine in the 12th century and then local saints, such as St Omer. This practice is also related to the iconographic and narrative work which began between the 12th and 13th centuries. This ring takes over the tradition: here, the series of representations consists of several small pictures of saints, placed alongside each other, with the whole telling a perfectly logical story. These small individual sequences are within everyone's reach, thus increasing their hold over the public. The assembly is supplemented by an ornamental register. This is a plural and narrative representation or image, whose keystone is external. The interpretation is given elsewhere, as this ring seeks implicitly to refer to Christ; He is therefore outside the representation. The figures of intellectual saints and martyrs are reminders of pain as present in the life of Christ; the suffering of the spirit that must learn to disengage its immortal soul from its mortal body in order to attain the divine through contemplation and meditation.

This repetitive iconography, representing series of saints who all seem to look alike, is didactic. Its conceptual aspect is related to a desire to simplify the representation. Such teaching through images also makes use of natural references. The artist-goldsmith has endeavoured to make the least detail significant. This ring from the 15th century takes on this tradition from previous centuries, while introducing a more contemporary concern. Here the representation of a figure of authority – in this case St John the Evangelist – follows a canonical model and affirms, through the Name, the will of the person who commissioned it.

This iconographic intention is present in the gold ring shown in Fig. 56. In what corresponds to the bezel of this heavy, broad object, an engraving represents Christ leaving the tomb. The engraving occupies the whole of the lower space, but Christ is represented without any particular concern for perspective. Behind Him, the instruments of the Passion – the cross and nails – can be identified.

While the Church did refer to the body of Christ until the Roman era, he had to remain either invisible, or idealised and thus not incarnate. Only the Church building, erected for the meeting of the faithful, embodied and made this mystery visible. Western spirituality was thus gradually to reverse the terms of the debate and move on from the mystical body, that of the Church, to the visible, stigmatised body of Christ. In all arts, Christ Crucified – the suffering Christ – appears with His body pierced, open and bleeding.

On the right side of the bezel, the following inscription is found in Latin: *'The Five Wounds, the Cross and the Passion of Christ are my help'*. Accompanied by the names of the three Magi, the inscription clarifies the significance of the five elliptical forms shaded and engraved on the outside of the bezel: they symbolise the wounds of the martyr, embodying Pity, Mercy, Comfort, Grace and Eternal Life.

The Platonic Academy of Florence was the mainstay of contemporary philosophical and theological

56 *Gold ring, England, 15th century, British Museum, London.*

renewal, in which man, the 'microcosm', was connected with the Divine. Pico della Mirandola and Marcel Ficin made reference to Plato, Plotinus or Pseudo-Dionysius, the latter having already written a theological treatise on divine names, which were supposed to have magical force in themselves. Marcel Ficin had translated and summarised the thinking of Plato and Christian theology. It is therefore within this tradition and belief surrounding the Name (including both the essence of the person and magical power) that we must see the practice of wearing these signet rings and, more generally, of inscribing enigmatic devices. These small, easy-to-use objects were, above all, aids to meditation, but also reflected the search for a new Identity.

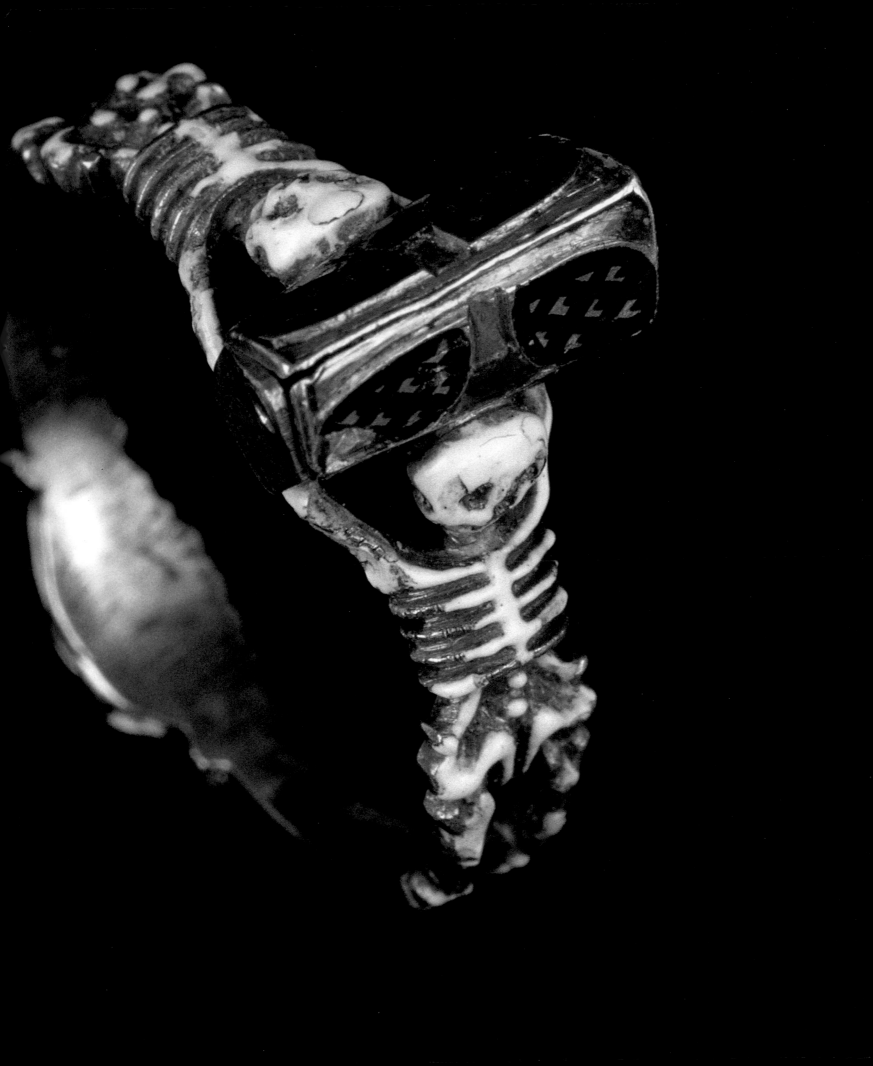

57 *Gold and enamel ring, England (?), 16th century, British Museum, London.*

Science, faith, love and death in the 16th century

Sixteenth-century Europe had deliberately set out to conquer the world, in search of the gold, precious stones and spices it lacked. World views of geography and the entire market economy were consequently turned upside down. The Spanish Empire anchored its power solidly in Mexico, while the French and English were settling in North America. Europe was becoming richer: leading merchants shared out all the wealth from abroad; gold remained the main means of exchange and domination, while the invention of printing provided a means of circulating ideas. The abuses of the Church were, moreover, provoking increasing indignation, while the authority of the papacy, which had already been weakened by the Great Schism, was also increasingly under challenge. The German, Martin Luther, a professor of theology, and the Frenchman, Jean Calvin, in protesting against the religious authorities, gave rise to the Reformation; they called the Church into question, advocating a return to a simpler, more human and also a more just religion. Western Christian Europe was then divided between countries following the Reformed and Catholic Churches respectively and, while the Counter-Reformation was being organised by Rome, religious wars were raging. Developments in ring design must be seen against this background of disruption.

The German signet ring in Fig. 58 dates from around 1530. It keeps the shape that we have seen previously. The solid gold hoop is half round in section, plentifully decorated and very finely chased on the outside with a pattern of foliage. The very cleverly reproduced acanthus leaves seem to wrap themselves all around

58 *Gold, rock crystal and coloured foil ring, Germany, 16th century, Imperial Treasure, Kunsthistorisches Museum, Vienna.*

the circumference of the hoop, finally fetching up on either side of the circular bezel. The impression of movement and fluidity that emerges from it is in opposition to the considerably simpler inner surface. This shows various inscriptions, spaced out and separated by horizontal and diagonal engraved lines crossing each other and intertwining, which may refer to indications for a sundial. The flat, completely circular bezel holds a rock crystal engraved in the centre and all around the perimeter. It bears the arms of an archduke, having possibly belonged to Ferdinand I who became King of Bohemia in 1526.

While this signet takes over an entire formal and symbolic tradition that was already extremely well known, it does speak to us in its own way of the whole spirit of its time. The antique and medieval motif of the acanthus leaf, abundantly used in architecture for decorating Corinthian columns, was also reserved either for funerary decoration – a symbol of the trials of life and death, embodied by the plant's own prickles – or for the decoration of the clothing of great men who had themselves triumphed over the difficulty of their functions.[25] It is also a motif that we very often find reproduced in 16th-century Germanic Protestant art; particularly in the work of Hans Holbein (1497–1543). It can, in fact, be found in the idealised background to his portraits of famous personalities who were his contemporaries: Erasmus, Jacob Meyer or Henry VIII, on whose court he depended and where he, as official artist, had also to design jewellery and gold work. It is therefore very likely that a goodly number of these drawings were in wide circulation and influenced artists and goldsmiths in their own productions. In addition, his successive places of residence, Basle and London, the foremost sites of Humanism and Protestantism, were also major centres for printing and distributing books, plates and engravings.

A symbol here of trials overcome and transformed into glory, this ring, with its coat of arms and acanthus leaves is intended to symbolise triumph over the biblical curse as ensured by Faith and the Grace of God and advocated by the Protestant religion. However, as it could also, more discreetly, act as a sundial, it also illustrates a concern for astronomy, the movement of the planets and, more generally, science.

The ring in Fig. 57 is made up of a relatively fine hoop, semi-round in section, as well as a bezel with rectangular volumes. On the decorated shoulders and hugging the circular shape of the gold hoop, there are two curved skeletons, seen from the back, the bones sticking out and jagged, holding each other by the hand and grasping what actually corresponds to the bezel itself in the shape of a coffin. The cover of enamel and gold may be gently lifted, revealing a fragile skeleton lying on its back.

This type of ring, known as a *memento mori*, was not uncommon during this period: representations of death, whether explicit or implicit, had existed since the medieval era.

The population had begun to rise again, but bloody religious wars had broken out from 1562 to 1598. The threat of death hung more than ever over everyone's head during the second half of the 16th century; a century that was probably amongst the most troubled in European history. The Humanists, the real scholars and learned people of the century, were struggling politically to enable Man to find his own balance, realise his full potential and blossom in wisdom.

Whether directly or indirectly involved in events, the French writers, moralists and poets of the century, such as Rabelais (1494–1553), Ronsard (1524–85) and Montaigne (1533–90), believed above all in Man, in his own feelings, his capacity for self-analysis and pursuing an art of living in order better to learn how to

59

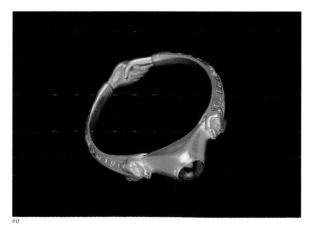

60

die. Death remained very present, and was at the centre of daily life, signified by the cemetery constructed in the heart of the village – it was a constant concern for everyone. Associated with the human body, it remained the great mystery; it was the last major sacrament in the life of a Christian. It is true that the Church encouraged fatalism about the hour of death, which could strike at any age of life. Wearing a *memento mori* ring both recalled and exorcised that death inherent in the human condition: it was the magical, marvellous means of warding off evil fortune, trying specifically to establish contact and direct dialogue with the world beyond.[26]

Another type of ring (Fig. 59) that was very common in the 16th century has a bezel in the form of two joined hands, firmly clasped together and placed one on top of the other. The hoop is almost flat and simply decorated on its upper extremities with two types of small ferrules. Everything is designed to focus the gaze on the symbolic bezel, which at once evokes the materialisation of a contract. This *fede* ring, celebrating an engagement or marriage, was not a 16th-century invention, being more symbolic than formally innovative, since this type of ring was already found in the 12th century. The motif of the two joined hands is said to date back to the Roman era.

Another example (Fig. 60) dates from the 13th century. It picks up the so-called stirrup shape more precisely, but has two clasped hands on the back of its hoop. At the upper extremities, two small dragons seem to be holding in their mouths the high gold bezel set with a sapphire, while the following inscription in Latin can be found on its outer face: '*I am a token of love, do not throw me away*'.

There are many other examples of similar *fede* rings, which proves that this particular form of ring is recurrent. It fits into a significant ritual in social and artistic history that is specific to this motif. As early as the Roman era, the compulsory engagement of the betrothed – following the agreement of the two families – preceded marriage. This was celebrated in accordance with a well-established rite, symbolised by the exchange of a ring. This symbolic object in solid gold, or a simple iron circlet surrounded with gold, would be purchased from a goldsmith and then placed on the left ring-finger (according to Egyptian belief, a very fine vein ran directly from this finger to the heart).[27] This very symbolic tradition is, moreover, still pursued today and proves the full solemnity and depth of this mutual commitment, symbolised by the wedding ring.

59 *Gold ring, France or Germany, mid 16th century, Reubell bequest, 1933, Musée des Arts Décoratifs, Paris.*

60 *Gold and sapphire ring, England; provenance: Hatfield Forest, Essex, British Museum, London.*

Marriage was the most important ceremony and rite of passage in the social and emotional life of each individual. Mixed up with obligations and mutual prohibitions, it was consecrated by the Church as of the 16th century. Amongst the peasants, this ceremony was organised in a curious manner with a symbolic struggle in which the future husband tried to place the ring on the finger of his betrothed, the latter making every attempt to make it fall to the ground.[28] Its value was reasserted by the Council of Trent (1545–63), when the Catholic Church strove to redefine dogma by restoring discipline in the face of the rise of Protestantism, the gold thread of marriage was not to be broken except by death. Royalty, for its part, also stressed the sacred nature of the ceremony.

By then, marriage had ceased to be a private affair and become caught up in social and cultural relations, in which: 'the King and the Church were the key players in an exercise in moralising and supervising a population deemed to be both lacking in discipline and superstitions. The idea was to try to control Christians from the cradle to the grave, as shown by the parish registers where the sacraments of baptism, marriage and extreme unction are recorded'.[29] The civil state had been created by Francis I and by the Decree of Villers-Cotterêts in 1539. The 16th-century ring frames the life and death of a faith obliged to come to an accommodation with science.

The extent of the link between love and death is also demonstrated by these two symbols of rites of

61 *Gold and ruby ring, Ashmolean Museum, Oxford.*

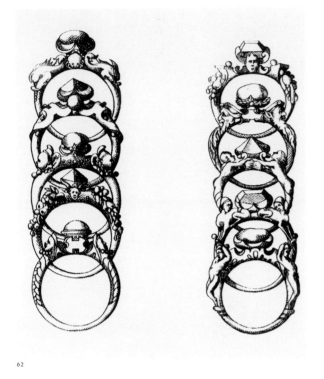

62

passage: the *fede* ring with its two clasped hands and its diffuse device, a symbol of mutual commitment; and the *memento mori* ring, with a skeleton or death's head and its personal device, a symbol of a funerary and magical pact. In both cases, it seems that the owners are 'trying above all to free themselves from the anguish of death by integrating it within the normal run of things, in the habitual (ritual) cycle of existence'.[30]

The next engagement or wedding ring in Fig. 61 gives further weight to the argument. At first sight, it is a simple gold hoop whose shoulders are highlighted with two small set rubies and a more prominent, square bezel. Also in solid gold, the latter is chased and enamelled on the lower part and worked entirely in quadrilobed intaglio on the upper part; this separation gives it an impression of lightness, as four rectangular rubies sit imposingly in its gold mount. However, when the object is not being worn, the ring is made up of two equal parts: two gold hoops (with inscriptions), each bearing a bezel with two rubies, which fit closely and exactly together to form a single ring. This same type of ring, known as a gimmel ring, was also found with garnets and chrysoprase, and with two or three hoops, sometimes even bearing – hidden in their cavities – a skeleton or new-born baby, inseparable symbols of death, life and love.

Yet the great innovation of the 16th century lies in the design of rings: the discovery of printing and new engraving processes on wood and copper allowed plates and models specially intended for goldsmiths and jewellers to circulate to good effect. All the thought that had gone into the divine proportions – ideas developed in the previous century by the great architects of the time such as Alberti and Brunelleschi – found marvellous application in the cutting of gemstones. We still have some very beautiful examples of these precious collections of designs, whether anonymous or not, including those of the Frenchmen René Boyvin, Pierre Woeiriot and Daniel Migno, or the German Peter Flötner, which were the starting point for the styles and trends to come. As of the beginning of the 16th century, replacing simple cabochons, precious stones were cut in multiple facets: 'point', 'hogback', 'table', 'step' and 'cushion' cuts. This more analytical attitude on the part of goldsmiths opened up the field of their study. It found substance for their theories in their creations.

René Boyvin, for example, offers a variety of rings following a relatively simple set of themes: only the shoulders of these rings are decorated and ornamented, either with a plant motif used alone or in combination – fruit, foliage or acanthus leaves, or a figurative, human motif – women, children and other simple portraits. The slightly elevated bezel is set on each occasion with a cut stone – cut as a cabochon, point or table, for example. All the models display compositions that are well balanced and symmetrical. (See Fig. 62).

Pierre Woeiriot seems to have striven to be more descriptive in his designs: skeletons clasping a skull or watch, which, for him, are invitations to enjoy life to the full. He tends to be more figurative as well, as on the shoulders of his rings the human figure is always deployed in different forms such as women or satyrs, for example, while showing off a bezel that is always heavily laden and decorated in the manner of a capital that the stone overhangs. In each of these models (Fig. 63), the designer refers to the human body and matches it with an aspect of architecture or, more generally, of nature.

The two pages of the last two anonymous collections of designs (Figs. 64 & 65) also offer a variety of these trends: human bodies shown full-length, as busts or portraits, and death's heads, mixed alternately with leaves and flowers and worked in relief on the hoop, which is crowned with a cabochon or cut stone. In all these ring designs, there is a sense of aesthetics based on a stock of common motifs, skills

64 *Anonymous designs of gem-set rings with enamelled hoops, 16th century, Victoria & Albert Museum, London.*

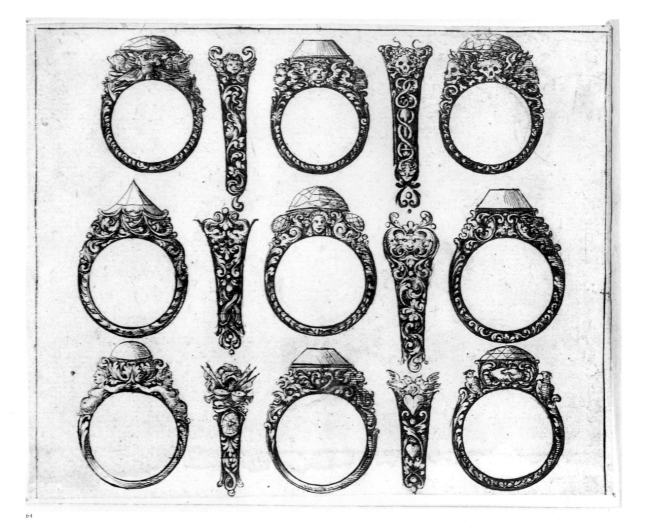

64

65 *Anonymous ring design (pen, black ink and colour wash on vellum), Germany, c.1580, British Museum, London.*

and obvious virtuosity that serve to show off a stone and produce a personal overall effect that is refined and indeed almost mannered.

More generally and probably echoing the architects of the Italian Renaissance, as well as in relation to the theories of musical harmony (there was a belief in the existence of a universal musical harmony according to which the whole universe was governed by musical relationships), these 16th-century goldsmiths and jewellers were probably seeking to achieve resonance between man and the world, through their plastic references and the very size of the gems in their jewels. The symbolism of numbers was not a discovery of the 16th century: it was gradually grasped in different ways through its algebraic and geometric properties. In this way, geometric figures were consequently the starting point for these artists. Without forgetting the underlying spiritual intention, a specific cut enabled them to show off to the full the brilliance of a stone from any viewpoint and with every movement of the hand.

On the basis of these simple volumes and their division, goldsmiths attempted to form a balanced whole. Through their research into forms and volumes, they were undoubtedly attempting to place the human body in close correspondence with musical theories and the properties of the number of gold, which was divine (according to the Franciscan monk Lucas Paccioli in 1509) since it was unique like God, a symbol of harmony, governing the proportions of the

65

human body (microcosm) and the universe (macrocosm). The diamond, for example, cut in the shape of a pyramid or point cut, had been adopted from the end of the 15th century by the Italian royal families (mainly the Medici), then the French royal families (Henry II), and finally by the nobility, as an emblem of their powers and ideals. The diamond ring took its place in coronation ceremonies, enhancing the ambition to govern with sovereign power.

Developments in Christian spiritual thought and this application of geometric principles to divine creation could not take place without developments in the status of the goldsmith and jeweller. The craftsman/artist, who in the Middle Ages worked on the basis of an outline or plan using casting and moulding, was perhaps less meticulous; he dealt with the broad lines and then rectified as he went along. Gradually, he began to pay greater attention to conception. In his *Livre d'anneaux d'orfèfrerie* ('Book of rings of goldsmiths' work', 1561), Pierre Woeiriot stressed the fact that designing and producing rings requires technical precision as well as the taste of both painters and sculptors; and that each element must be arranged to ensure the harmony of the whole.

Benvenuto Cellini[31] in his *Treatise on the Work of the Goldsmith*, in 1568, examined the technique of setting transparent stones on a foil; a technique that allowed the internal flaws of a stone to be disguised in order to achieve the greatest possible sparkle and best possible refraction. He acquired a perfect mastery of this technique.

Such technical and conceptual issues show the concern and desire of goldsmiths to elevate an independent, free art into work in which theoretical research was increasingly essential. The goldsmith was becoming a theorist and Cellini is perhaps the greatest example, being as famous for his sculptures and work as a goldsmith as for his writings. This interdisciplinary approach which had already been observed in the 15th century, was becoming widespread. This allowed openness, inter-relationships and balance for the benefit of all. The art of the goldsmith fitted in with the aesthetic and philosophical enquiry of the time, the search for ideal Beauty, which was so dear to Renaissance artists, in a newly conceived world based on neo-Platonic thought.[32] The new lines of questioning thus came to be taken on in the most intimate manner.

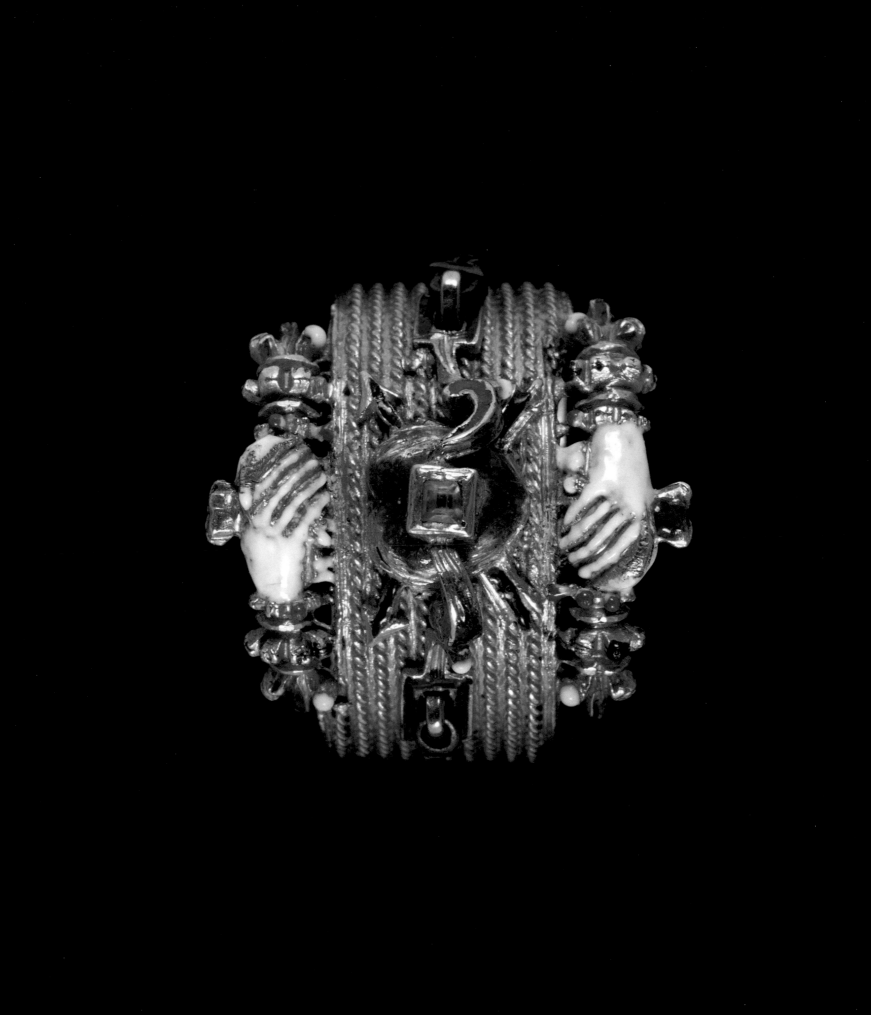

66 *Gold and enamel ring, Flanders, early 17th century, Waddesdon Bequest, British Museum, London.*

Between baroque and classicism in the 17th century

During the first half of the 17th century, the Habsburg family of Spain and Austria possessed an immense empire. In order to extend its influence, it had undertaken to dominate the whole of Europe including France, which it encircled by means of its strategic possessions. Following the bloody religious wars of the previous century, a new political and religious balance seemed, however, gradually to be taking shape. The Christians, already separated into Catholic and Orthodox factions since 1054, remained divided, with Catholics faithful to the Pope such as in Spain, France, Poland and the Italian States on the one hand, and Protestants, who no longer recognised the authority of Rome, such as Anglicans in England, Lutherans in northern and central Europe and Calvinists in Geneva on the other. This situation continued to give rise to many long conflicts, especially from 1618 to 1648, during the so-called Thirty Years' War. Holland and six other provinces of the Netherlands (the United Provinces), which had been in revolt against Spanish authority, became one of the richest independent countries in Europe. In Rome, in reaction to the Protestant reform, the Pope was endeavouring to restore his credit and artistic influence. Meanwhile, France was installing a ferocious absolutism under the reigns of Louis XIII and then Louis XIV. The art of the ring during this period swings back and forth between baroque exaggeration and classical balance.

A gold and enamel ring from the early 17th century (Fig. 66) comes from Flanders. The broad hoop is rimmed with very fine threads of gold, which are twisted in closely packed rows, looking as if they have been woven or rolled around the overall structure generously punctuated with black and blue enamels. At each of the extremities, two inverted white enamel hands stretch their long, clenched fingers towards the inside, thus highlighting the central motif, which is also very elaborate. We can easily recognise the motif of the *fede* ring, but it has been rendered here with complex, indeed exuberant care. We can see that the design is based on very keen knowledge and observation. Using an already existing type of ring, the designer has endeavoured to discover and create another form of overall harmony, colour and light, risking a bold and unexpected innovation, deliberately playing on the unusual.

67

67 *Gold and enamel ring, Venice or Southern Germany, 16th and 17th centuries, Schmuckmuseum, Pforzheim.*

68 *Gold and enamel ring, Venice, 16th century, Victoria & Albert Museum, London.*

68

The 16th-century Jewish rings from Venice and southern Germany in Figs. 67 & 68 are different, but all belong to the category of wedding rings. They take other plastic options: rather oriental in style, they too are made of gold and enamels, but they have simple gold hoops bearing a high, rectangular bezel (produced using the casting technique), or a simple, broader hoop without a bezel, but decorated all around with filigree, domed and open-work enamel shapes, or a hoop decorated with blue enamel, bearing a bezel made up of superposed geometric shapes. These rings are possible references to and reductions of architectural motifs. These objects, which display great technical prowess, were used as symbols in the Jewish marriage ceremony; they were slipped onto the right index-finger of the bride and then kept by the family.

These miniature architectural creations, following the spiritual conventions of the Jewish religion and making the most of the technical and aesthetic qualities of the precious metal, also fit in with a singular Venetian taste for gentle, golden light. (At the time, Venice was one of the richest cities in Europe with its own unique style in the plastic arts and painting.) However, these portable motifs, heavily symbolic and ostentatious, are miniature gates open towards heaven. In this way, they re-express a reciprocal commitment, a very strong union, mutual trust and man's faith in God. Like the Ark of the Covenant of the first Hebrews, this type of ring was a token of divine protection, a mobile sanctuary, guaranteeing the covenant between God and His people.

These wedding rings express the common features and characteristics of the 17th century, representing a search for exuberance in an organised environment. This attraction for prolixity, which had to express or arouse emotion, was born in Italy (more particularly in Rome), before it spread and reached the whole of Europe. This Baroque inclination consequently affected all the arts.

The word, of Italian and Portuguese origin ('barocco' designating the formal aspiration of the Middle Ages towards complexity and diversity, and 'barroco' meaning an irregular pearl), was initially pejorative. The use of this term in the 17th century designated a structure with more fluid, rough forms than those observed in the previous centuries. In architecture, for example, we might find bold planes with elliptical shapes, church facades in a lively style made up of curves, counter-curves and theatrical

volutes as in the work of Della Porta and Borromini. Painters like Rubens, Caravaggio, Poussin, Lorrain, Velasquez and Rembrandt had developed dramatic narration, chiaroscuro and trompe-l'oeil. Sculptors like Bernini had opted for new postures and flowing drapery.

Everything had to work towards moving and dazzling people in a troubled environment. This art played on all feelings, in order to demonstrate the omnipotence of the Church and State and subdue all beneath its power. Rings, like the sumptuous court clothing of the time, were part of this demonstration.

The ring in Fig. 69 is of Spanish origin and made of gold. It has a bezel bearing several table-cut precious (emerald, amethyst and rock crystal) and non-precious stones, arranged in the form of a cross. This was known as the 'cluster' style, which was very popular at the Spanish Court (as can be seen from the many portraits from the time). It would be worn on the right index-finger, sometimes attached to the wrist with a small black ribbon. However, despite the simplicity of its structure, made up of additions and simple juxtapositions of different stones, in a polychrome mosaic, this object shows a concern to achieve visual effect. During this period, people still believed in the prophylactic and indeed curative power of precious stones. Knowledge of the laws of refraction was increasing, making it possible to perfect and refine faceting (especially for diamonds) and setting techniques which made increasingly fine work possible. Very beautiful compositions based on stones of different origins, precious or otherwise, such as enamels or pearls, were thus made, guaranteeing successful visual effects.

Furthermore, as in the previous century, many collections of designs were circulating in most parts of Europe. In France, then reeling under the monarchist authority of Louis XIV, the designs of Gilles Légaré (Fig. 73) are perhaps amongst the most characteristic: writhen hoops, twisted to the extreme, bearing skulls, cruciform bones, skeletons or multiple small funerary objects – all references to death decorated with faceted stones.

A group of three rings bearing death's heads (Figs. 70–72) illustrates the *memento mori* motif, which had already been abundantly used in the preceding centuries, but here it has been reworked and its effect redefined. In a very realistic, naturalistic style, these models were inspired by the recent taste for botany, scientific observation of nature and thus science and

69 *Gold, rock crystal, emerald, amethyst and coloured false stone ring, Andalusia, 17th century, given by Dr. Hildburgh, Victoria & Albert Museum, London.*

71

70

life, as if better to prepare the Christian for his forthcoming death. The same attraction and tendency can be seen in Dutch pictorial art of the time (in the still-life paintings or vanities of Kalf or de Ruysch). During the century, *memento mori* rings became heavily personalised: they bore the name of their owner, in the form of initials, dates, or coats of arms. However, this type of ring no longer merely encouraged individuals to live a virtuous life, but came gradually to embody the actual memory of a loved one and become commemorative or a reliquary.

Between 1648 and 1714, France, the United Provinces and England were vying for ascendancy in Europe and on the high seas. France had the necessary resources to make war on her neighbours, enlarge her kingdom and assuage her desire for military and economic domination. French power was then at its peak and Louis XIV was annexing territories adjacent to his borders such as Strasbourg in 1681. This policy of annexation, which provoked all the European states to enter into a coalition against him in 1686, marked his decline to the advantage of English power.

The vigour of Louis XIV, a monarch thirsty for authority, pride and power, continued to leave a deep impression on the second half of the century. In order

to enhance his glory, he sought to protect scholars and artists like Lulli, Molière, La Fontaine, Boileau and Labruyère, and he had built the most luxurious showcase possible, Versailles. This sumptuous environment was the site of lavish festivals, where the king could strategically contain his court and the nobility. As an absolute monarch ruling by divine right, he governed alone and – remembering the Fronde – had stripped the nobility of their powers of administration over the provinces. Everything was thus regulated according to etiquette. Versailles had become the

72

heart of the kingdom, the residence of the king and his court, the showcase of power and the pivot of his hold over his entire people.

The château was erected between 1660 and 1680 by Le Vau, J. Hardoin-Mansard and Le Nôtre, who was responsible for the gardens. It is in the classical style, namely with a noble façade, made up of elements from classical antiquity (such as the Ionic columns bearing an entablature), seeking ideal Beauty in the balance and harmony of its proportions. Yet it seems to echo the baroque spirit in the gigantism of its dimensions, as well as calling on numerous decorative motifs and themes. This 'monument' was to influence the following artistic generations and the 17th-century

ring swung between these intellectual games and effervescence. These small, precious objects were more than ever the privilege of the powerful and rich, although collections of extremely individualised designs had been circulating for close on two centuries by this time, without it yet being possible to speak of popularisation. Their artistic forms and search for visual effect were used above all for the sake of appearance, becoming perhaps also more sensual than intellectual.

From one excess to the next, classicism and exuberance vied for influence throughout the century, bringing into contact different stylistic movements and trends.

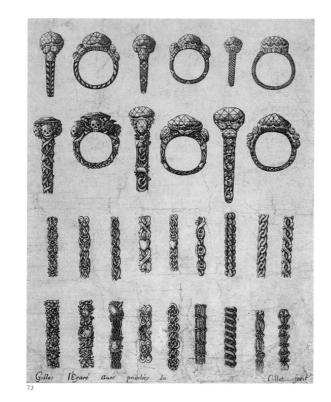

73 Gilles Légaré, ring drawings from 1663, 'Ornament Prints', vol. 6, British Museum, London.

73

74 *Gold ring set with ivory under glass, France, given by Meyer, 1914, Musée des Arts Décoratifs, Paris.*

From rococo to neo-classicism in the 18th century

From the early 18th century, Europe was, more than ever, dominant in the world and had a decisive advantage over other centres of civilisation. it had deliberately destroyed the civilisation of pre-Columbian America and set out to transform the New World. Having failed in its endeavour to evangelise the Far East (India, China and Japan), it did, however, carry out intense trading activities there.

The Age of the Enlightenment was a century made up of contrasts, upheavals and innovations of a technical, political and social nature, yet in it the ring motif would continue to play both an artistic and aesthetic role. The ring in Fig. 77 has a gold hoop with shoulders which are decorated and ribbed with a leaf motif, bearing a bezel made up of small diamonds each set in its own open-work gold collet. It is possible to discern, in what we might call the lower part, two horizontal, parallel gold pieces streaked with small oblique intaglios, which are also parallel to each other. This structure of precious metal holds four rose-cut diamonds and forms a basket motif. Placed just above is a standard flower figure in the style of a marguerite, made up of a rose-cut diamond, edged with smaller diamonds making up the petals. A dozen diamonds forming small flowers with long, fine golden stalks seem to burst out on either side of this central motif, as in a firework.

The overall effect, which is relatively successful, seems to be inspired by the keen taste of the previous century for the classic juxtaposition of precious stones – as in cluster rings – and the softer, baroque-style forms. However, it takes on an entirely different scope

and meaning here. These giardinetti or 'flower garden' rings, which were very common in the early 18th century, had many possible variants: with a gold structure handled with considerably more naturalism, with gems of different colours, accentuating the overall effect. The basic idea, rendered here in a much finer, scrolled structure with alternately symmetrical and asymmetrical voids and solids, was made possible by the progress achieved in the faceting of precious stones, as well as foiling.

These light, brightly-coloured rings – drawing on and imitating nature with a great deal of realism – fitted in more generally with the artistic tendency we know as rococo. This term, like many other terms in the aesthetic and critical vocabulary, was initially used in a pejorative way. The word 'rococo' did, in fact, cover formal preference for incongruous assemblies and was even accused of echoing the corrupt customs and tastes of the society of the time.

Nevertheless, this style very quickly established itself with its innovative intentions. Without really having any theory to back it up, this rococo art suggested new plastic solutions (based on spontaneity, nuances in formal or polychrome juxtapositions, and more rhythmic composition) and sought to go beyond the very strict rules inherited from classicism or baroque – which was art with political and religious aims. It is true that the latter, of Italian origin, had triumphed throughout 17th-century Europe and was characterised by its exuberance and rough, indeed tortured forms, which the French had been able to subdue with a dose of classicism.

Baroque continued therefore, despite everything, to dominate throughout 18th-century Europe and particularly in Dresden and Vienna. However, in France especially, the baroque offensive was to be waged under a new guise, worked over with decorative exaggeration. Rococo, the final phase in baroque

aesthetics, had also been described, in 1734, as rocaille style, by comparison and analogy with the ancient terms of 'rocaille work' and 'shell work'. It is true that this term recalled the appearance of the interior of grottoes, favoured motifs in the art of formal gardens, and also evoked the use of decorative forms of shells. This style, which influenced all arts, was characterised by many formal complications or the breaking up of forms, and a preference for asymmetry, flora, exoticism and shaded colours.

Consider two engagement rings in the light of this changing scene. One has two enamel turtle-doves with ruby eyes, one bird apparently turning towards the other. The other has a butterfly set with different gems – diamond, ruby, garnet and chrysoberyl – on a wavy gold ring, giving a good illustration of rococo characteristics. Engagement rings were also found in the form of pierced hearts, doves or trophies; sometimes accompanied by inscriptions, generally engraved in French (as French was then considered to be the language of love and good taste). All these rings, symbols of conjugal fidelity or personifications of the soul, were exchanged as tokens of love and faithfulness. The motif of the *fede* ring had not disappeared and another simplified example proves it: the gold hoop, with its shoulders representing two hands stretched towards each other, seems to have been made to offer the fortunate beloved a heart of ruby (Fig. 75). All these rings drew inspiration from published pages of jewellery designs: they were well adapted to the taste of the day, whose watchwords were elegance and lightness. Tokens of love as much as of fidelity, these small objects were also worn in order to show off in the salons and worldly receptions, still lit with the golden glow of candles. (See Fig. 76.)

Putting the final touches to female as well as male attire, these rings also echoed an increasingly strict code of elegance. Customs and standards of social behaviour had, in fact, continued to change since the 16th century and the noble courtesans were the first to understand the importance of civility, refinement and good manners. Changing their own vision of the world little by little, they thus had nothing in common with the relatively free gentlemen of the Middle Ages and 16th century: absolutism, as we have seen, had considerably reduced their power and sphere of personal action. They were obliged to obey royal power, since it was divine, as well as to observe increasingly narrow social and ethical commands – taking great care over deeds, gestures and language.

77

This process of 'civilisation' of social customs had gradually established itself, relying in particular on the treatises on civility, famous since the 17th century, which were signs of entirely new sensitivity, morals and education. This was the work of the Counter-Reformation in its devaluation of the body, a Christian concept of contempt for the flesh. Costume and adornment highlighted rituals governing appearance and whiteness of the skin – considered important for men as much as women, but exclusive to the upper social classes. Powdered wigs, jabots, lace, ribbons, make-up and jewellery were all strategies to improve appearance and served both to adorn and 'hide the dirt' which might be vermin or syphilis; hygiene and collective use of water being deemed to be dangerous sources of skin diseases. They showed off the clothed body, because it was good form to leave not a scrap of skin uncovered. The social élites followed these restrictive collective rites, which protected them from animality.

Fashionable men and women wore make-up and powder, adorned and perfumed themselves: 'They had to make themselves into fashion models, hiding their individuality under the mask of appearances; really play a role, dramatising their gestures in public, on pain of not being admitted into smart society; as the important thing was to "be seen"... This tyranny of keeping up appearances, with the body trained, adorned and kept as far away as possible from its

78

79

80

78 *Ring set with ivory under glass, France, late 18th century, given by Meyer, 1914, Musée des Arts Décoratifs, Paris.*

79 *Gold ring with porcelain imitation jasper, France, 18th century, Reubell bequest, 1933, Musée des Arts Décoratifs, Paris.*

80 *Gold ring set with carved ivory and mother-of-pearl under glass, France, late 18th century, Reubell bequest, 1933, Musée des Arts Décoratifs, Paris.*

animal nature, no doubt enabled them better to bear the fear of their demise…, but at the price of intense repression' of their emotions.[33] In this world of men and courtesans, women had no other option than to go out adorned with their most beautiful finery but also hidden behind these masks, the marks or weapons of beauty. The gap between the élite and the people who were seen as a great peasant mass with no other right than to work – was, moreover, growing wider than ever before. The breakdown of the sacred aura surrounding the *ancien régime*, headed by the completely unsuitable and weakened royal figure of Louis XVI, was inexorably under way.

Although Europe seemed to be getting richer because of new mechanised modes of production and transport in the beginnings of the railway, a genuine revolution had already started in people's minds from an intellectual point of view. French theorists and philosophers played a decisive role in Europe at this time. Montesquieu, Voltaire, Diderot and d'Alembert, not to mention Rousseau, had begun to criticise and increasingly to challenge absolute monarchy, the society of order and religion in the very name of Reason and Liberty.

Despite the heavy hand of the censor, these ideas had spread beyond the frontiers through books and newspapers, giving rise to public opinion in a real sense. Even some European sovereigns, 'enlightened despots' such as Frederick II, King of Prussia, were subsequently to try to take over these new ideas. The commercial bourgeoisie was taking advantage of relative economic prosperity, seeking position and recognition in a still very hierarchical society, in which power was concentrated in the hands of a minority. These rich town-dwellers were now the ones who ordered and wore rings and jewellery. Adornment had ceased forever to be the privilege of the ruling class. The new industrial techniques and growing popularity of (glass) paste, discovered by J. Strasser, used for its optical qualities and as a substitute for precious stones, were able from now on to suit all purses.

The pen drawings in Fig. 82 – in black ink touched up with watercolour – illustrate this new fashion as observed at the end of the 18th century. Jean Raps, who produced these designs between 1781 and 1785, offers variations on a theme: rings with enamelled, ovoid, rectangular or triangular bezels, whose perimeters are always punctuated with very small stones. This ring, which favours a particular viewpoint, has a flat, rectangular, enamelled bezel, whose rim is edged

and set with small marcasites, used instead of diamonds. Standing out to good effect on a uniform blue background, the central floral motif, outlined and highlighted by fine engraving, is made up of the same small stones. This model was intended to be produced in pearls and rose-cut diamonds, but still set on blue enamel. The rococo spirit, far from being a French privilege, had spread throughout Europe.

The ring in Fig. 81 has a gold hoop and a bezel that is also ovoid, but its motif, standing out on a blue background, has been executed in white porcelain. The scene represented moves away from the previously observed floral motifs. It is a figurative scene with two characters: the male figure, seen in profile and half crouching, with a bent right leg and holding a toga on his back, is looking at a young woman dressed in the ancient style, who is standing on his left. The female figure's balance rests on the left leg and her head is turned towards the man. This style of composition is familiar from Greek classical art.

The last quarter of the 18th century saw a return to nature, as well as a rediscovery of classical antiquity through the recent discoveries and the analyses conducted on site by the archaeologist and historian Winkelmann. The latter had, in his *History of Art in*

81

81 *Gold ring with porcelain imitation jasper, England, late 18th century, Victoria & Albert Museum, London. Photographer: D.P.P. Naish.*

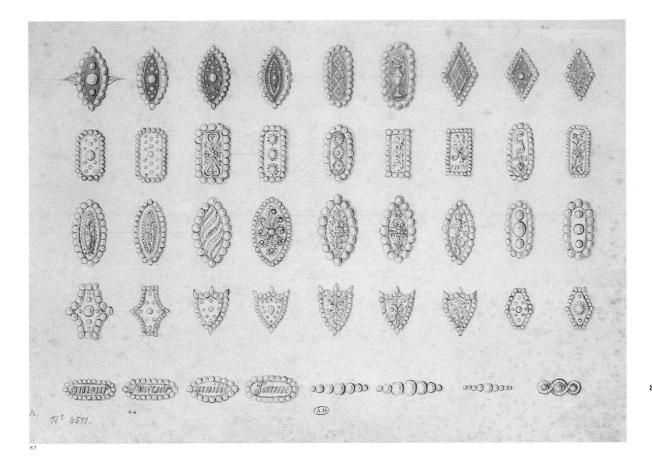

82 *Jean Raps, drawing in pen and black ink with watercolour embellishment, late 18th century, Musée des Arts Décoratifs, Paris.*

Antiquity, redefined the way in which these classical works of art had previously been seen and valued. Rejecting the rococo style, this neo-classical aesthetic, which was not imitative since it was purely intellectual, preferred geometrical sobriety. It was to affect all the arts of Europe and find concrete expression in a craze for figurative scenes in ruins and nature.

The ring illustrated in Fig. 79, produced in the much copied style of Wedgewood and Bentley's Etruria factory in Staffordshire, also helps us to understand the process of mechanisation – indeed industrialisation – that was then developing in England, where it reached a much more advanced stage than anywhere else. This neo-classical style actually lent itself very well to mass production: the white porcelain objects and rings made by workmen attached to the factory, copying well-determined models, no longer bore the personal mark of the artist/craftsman. This mechanical execution and the differentiation between designer and producer were gradually to become decisive in the art of jewellery.

Two French examples (Figs. 78 & 80), in gold, with bezels sculpted on ivory, represent standing female figures, dressed in the ancient manner, shown with a tree or broken column. They bear an inscription in French and were offered as a token of friendship.

All these rings show that noble feelings did not have to be matched by the intrinsic value of the materials: it was even very common in this period to find this style of 'non-precious', but commemorative, rings, enclosing the hair of the loved one in their bezels. Clothing was beginning to follow the trend: more flowing draperies were preferred to the cumbersome crinolines or hoops.

A final trend could be observed in England and then in France after the revolutionary events. It is illustrated by the renewed interest in portraits, with the subject usually wearing period costume. The gold ring in Fig. 74, bearing a circular bezel, illustrates this practice which is found in the pictorial and sculptural art of the same period. These rings, which fit into the more general category of keepsake rings, with obvious moral, historical and political value, serve to proclaim and defend policy or party, but also ideas or ideology.

The 18th-century ring thus brought in many different innovations – aesthetic marvels made possible by technical progress and the use of substitute stones, and an increased clientele in search of social recognition. These developments reveal the extent to which adornment and costume are linked.

83 *François-Désiré Froment Meurice, gold and oxidised silver ring, 1844, Londesborough and Franks collections, British Museum, London.*

Neo-classicism, eclecticism and industrialisation in the 19th century

In the late 18th and early 19th centuries, the foundations were laid of what is now known as 'modern life'. The English beginnings of the industrial revolution, which were based on the manufacture of consumer goods, were spreading a new conception and specialisation of work throughout Europe. Leading bourgeoisie and industrialists were profiting from the new system of wealth creation, based on production and productivity. They were asserting their authority more than ever and extending their markets to the colonial empires. The rest of the population, often uprooted from their native countryside, were seeking an acceptable social and financial position. The living conditions of this dissatisfied urban proletariat provided thinkers such as Marx and Nietzsche with an opportunity to denounce this production system as 'alienating' for people. These philosophical – as well as scientific and technical – changes profoundly altered the concept of the artistic object and the status of artists and the people to whom their work was addressed.

The scarab ring in Fig. 85, although produced between 1850 and 1860, is still strongly influenced by antiquity. The reference may be explained by the unchanging stylistic preferences of Napoleon throughout the Empire, in the traces and memories of his oriental conquests. He had reorganised France, which was very divided internally, and encouraged a modern economy. However, he had retained from his Egyptian and Italian conquests a taste for neo-classicism and a degree of exoticism. Using an Egyptian symbol again was a way of reasserting power and domination, as in

84 *Gold and glass mosaic ring,*
Italy, Rome c.1820, given
by Meyer, Musée des Arts
Décoratifs, Paris.

this ring, which is also a good example of the classical preference sometimes known as 'Empire style', which affected all arts.

From the early 19th century, there was a preference for the styles and motifs of antiquity. Empire style, ordered and founded on discipline, symmetry and classical references, was intended to establish a firm parallel between the Roman Empire and that of Napoleon I. The latter sought above all to magnify his reign through literature and the arts and took upon himself the right to intervene in artistic production.

Increased centralisation of educational and aesthetic codes supported this authoritarian intervention. While the appearance of the first academies of art dates back to the 16th century in Italy, their numbers had increased in the 18th century, spreading throughout Europe. Strictly respecting codified rules, these official institutions continued to inculcate in their pupils the outlines of art and imitation, as well as perfect technical mastery. Far from being an artistic movement, academicism produced standard works and objects. It certainly received the support of the authorities and the favour of the public, but reflected more the talent of well-trained craftsmen than a genuine creative inspiration. A good number of artists, goldsmiths and makers of fine and costume jewellery were thus trained. In France, for example, under the First Empire, jewellers continued to work for the court, since Napoleon Bonaparte had re-established the 'etiquette' of the *ancien régime* and had even, in 1805, inaugurated the Rome Prize for engravers on fine stones and promulgated the so-called Brumaire Law regulating and controlling the trade in precious metals.

An Italian ring from 1820 illustrates this well (Fig. 84). Its flat, rectangular bezel has bevelled corners. The motif represented – two turtledoves, the one above pecking the other below – is not new in the history of the ring, as it had already been seen in the previous century. Here, however, the inverted shapes match each other and stand out in a space with a much darker background. The treatment of the whole, although not very innovative, remains harmonious. It has been executed entirely in mosaic, proving that the attraction for the motifs of antiquity remained alive and fashionable. This style was to extend throughout Europe, beyond the military defeat of Napoleon in 1815 and during the Restoration.

Another ring, in gold and enamel, made between 1830 and 1840, illustrates another trend of the time

85

86

(Fig. 86). Its flat, open-work metal hoop allows one to glimpse an interlacing of sinuous lines, plant shapes coiling and uncoiling in the same movement. An asymmetric structure, still showing natural influence, stands on the rectangular bezel with its black background. While this spatial arrangement had also been used previously (in the *memento mori* rings of the 18th century), the social function of this object seems to be quite new. The 'vinaigrette' mounted as a bezel was actually used to ward off faintness during overheated receptions (candles were still used for lighting). The owner of the object could thus breathe in, through the open-work enamel, the vapours of essences with which the sponge inserted at the bottom of the bezel was saturated. Apart from its practical and medicinal function, we can see how this ring has taken over an existing form and emptied it of its religious or commemorative content to make it into a costume accessory. This phenomenon of the loss of spirituality in jewellery in general and rings in particular could be explained through the emergence of industrialisation in fashion.[34]

One example from 1844 is a ring designed by François-Désiré Froment-Meurice (1802–55), a well known and respected jeweller of the time. The shoulders of the hoop are sculpted in the round and seem to show off two little figures. This arrangement might also recall the *memento mori* rings of the 16th century. Nicknamed the modern 'Benvenuto Cellini', this artist alone embodies the development in the craft of the goldsmith/jeweller that was then taking place. More autonomous since the suppression of the guild system in France, these new artists, who were both creators and manufacturers, were no longer restricted to community training and could combine artistic sensitivity and knowledge with industrial techniques and processes.[35]

On the basis of the last two models, it is clear to what extent the design and conception of these rings remain under the influence of the forms of the ancient, Gothic and Renaissance periods; the models were certainly reappropriated and reinvented, but rendered increasingly stereotypical by mechanisation. In addition, 'imitation' materials were making their debut: since 1830, the use of iron and steel and gems such as aquamarine, quartz and lead crystal (strass) was becoming widespread. Although gold was still around, more refined casting techniques and the mechanical stamping procedure, enabling large numbers to be made, led the manufacture of jewellery to become democratised. The wearing of this 'new form of adornment' was also becoming codified: there was now jewellery for the day and the evening, precious and 'junk' jewellery, jewellery attached to a specific moral, social, geographical and national code.[36] All these trends and fashions were set by the major production centres: in Paris especially, but also in Pforzheim, Birmingham, Gablonz in Bohemia and Providence in the United States.

For example, Fig. 87, of Breton origin, is made entirely of silver: the inside and shoulders of the flat hoop are engraved or incised and, on either side of the bezel, two hands are holding a central rounded heart, which seems to be topped with a crown. We have seen to what extent these 'pledge' or 'faith' rings had taken over, with very little innovation, a formal, stylistic and functional tradition (*fede* rings). This type of engagement ring still sealed, in this particular region of France, the commitment of two people and embodied a token of love, charged with supernatural beliefs or powers.[37] (See also Fig. 88.)

However, in these post-imperial years, the issue of

85 *Scarab ring, Paris 1850-60, Victoria & Albert Museum, London. Photographer: D.P.P. Naish.*

86 *Gold and enamel ring with 'vinaigrette' bezel, France (?) 1830-40, given by Meyer, Musée des Arts Décoratifs, Paris.*

style in jewellery remained unsolved. With regard to rings, regionalism, influence and the reference to known historical forms, initially known as the 'romantic' style, provided a possible response. This is what we have seen through our examples. This democratisation and increase in the number of consumers of art and 'luxury goods', brilliantly embodied by the wearing of jewellery mainly by women, justified this imitation of past works.

87 *Silver engagement or fede ring, Brittany, 19th century, Musée des Arts et Traditions Populaires, Paris.*

88 *Silver engagement or fede ring, Brittany, 19th century, Musée des Arts et Traditions Populaires, Paris.*

87   88

As of the second half of the century and in circumstances favourable to industrial expansion, eclecticism allowed the range of past models to be extended to new objects in contemporary materials, which were now available in the leading stores.[38] Men who, until the 17th and 18th centuries, had worn fine rings, were gradually delegating to their wives the social display of their own wealth. In fact, masculine fashion from England was becoming increasingly austere, with the wearing of jewellery and rings tending to become exclusive to women. As the iconographic and literary sources of the time confirm, it was expected that these bourgeois women would wear only a few rings, respecting the new codes dictated by etiquette. Furthermore, the wearing of jewellery was no longer hindered by sumptuary laws, but was now codified by a kind of asceticism and rigidity in social behaviour, which were typical of the bourgeoisie.[39]

However, throughout the Second Empire, attempts were being made to open up an aesthetic space between the classical standards established at all levels of society and the commercial thrust of industrialisation. Alongside the fierce competition between makers of mass-produced jewellery, designer jewellery took its first major steps, proposing and adapting its own redefinition of jewellery and rings.

Strongly encouraged by the universal exhibitions held in France since 1855 and influenced by the purchase of the Marquis de Campana's collection by the Fine Arts Administration in Paris in 1861, designer jewellery was able to respond to the need for luxury and the reactionary taste of the two main classes that were then dominant – the bourgeoisie and aristocracy.

In these favourable economic circumstances, the great jewellery houses like Cartier and Boucheron in Paris, Garrard in London and Tiffany in New York were able to take advantage of the new demand. In 1847, Louis-François Cartier took over the jewellery workshop of his master, Picard, in the Rue Montorgueil: the Maison Cartier was born and opened its doors in 1853 to private, affluent clients. Unfortunately, very few rings from this period remain. Only order books with lists of shapes allow us to analyse the main influences after 1870. Most of these rings are eclectic in style.

In 1858, Frédéric Boucheron had opened his first shop in the Palais Royal, before becoming established in the Place Vendôme in 1893. Apart from producing jewellery with motifs based on nature, he was the leading specialist in rings bearing coats of arms with pierced engraved diamonds. These examples of rings engraved in 1900 by the lapidary Bordinckx – the first Western craftsman to mechanise this work – show how mounting and setting and the introduction of platinum were used to show off precious stones and materials.

These items of designer jewellery, with their mainly traditional forms and motifs, tended above all to show off the purity and sparkle of rare stones, observing very strict criteria in terms of quality, lightness of setting, and execution, and thus increasing their value. In contrast to mass-produced objects, this 'new luxury' deliberately set itself up in a bourgeois sphere, who were the main clientele of these famous houses. The rich bankers and major industrialists who were now at the forefront of the social and economic scene sought to distinguish themselves by means of new codes and new jewels, such as rubies, topaz and turquoise for brunettes; amethysts, emeralds, garnets, pearls and coral for blondes.[40]

The history of the ring shows that, far from being a superficial 'luxury',[41] its form had been constantly adapted to reflect the society and the age it belonged to. In the Middle Ages rings had fitted into an uncontroversial, royal and religious luxury, a mark of transcendence to be respected in a kind of dazzled fear. During the Renaissance, with the phenomenon of princely courts, the rise of monarchical power, the hold of market capitalism and the assertion of the state, rings had been gradually transformed, becoming perhaps more 'sensual' in expressing the frenzy of possessing the world. The rings of the baroque and classical eras, increasingly centred around the royal personage, had been given a more specifically political and individual role, amplified by the theatrical nature of the court on perpetual display. In the 18th century, in a world where the power of money was gradually taking over from inborn privileges, rings had become more and more individual, secular and materialistic. In the 19th century, using earlier forms and styles as models, mechanically-produced rings, as well as fine jewellery rings, were created in an attempt to imitate or legitimise the position or social rank of their owners. In both cases, the results were artistically inadequate and poorly crafted.

However, as of 1861, giving pride of place to artistic references and the trade of the artist-craftsman, the English Arts and Crafts movement had reacted against social and commercial opportunism, as well as against the impact of mass production on art and creativity. William Morris and John Ruskin had attempted to reinterpret and redefine what could be considered a work of art. Subsequently, numerous English artist-jewellers had gone further in their thinking about the status of jewellery and rings in four different ways: independently; by working anonymously for Liberty (a company set up in 1875); in a traditional technical manner as in the jewellers' guilds, or working under the guidance of the architect-decorator Charles Rennie Mackintosh. The great artistic unity of the rings resulting from this research lies in the successful fusion of stones, materials and natural, primitive or indeed Celtic figures and motifs. Unfortunately, this deliberately non-conformist approach, which put individual creativity to the fore, attracted only a limited clientele of enlightened art lovers, who had themselves broken with the very strict social codes of the time.

It was not, therefore, until the turn of the century that a different conception of jewellery and women took shape, altering the very concept of rings and their wearers still more profoundly, and consequently laid the foundations of 20th-century jewellery production in Europe and the United States.

Art Nouveau as a break from the past: 1895-1914

Despite a period of peace and prosperity, signs of a crisis of confidence were already emerging in Europe at the turn of the century. While the values of progress and reason continued to spread until the start of the war in 1914, the intellectual and artistic élite was beginning to develop a new sensitivity, in effect challenging the optimism and certainties of positivism, liberalism and blind faith in industry and the future.

At a time when everything was being called into question, when there was a desire for change and people were taking refuge in nationalistic popular passion, a degree of cultural unity was, nonetheless, manifesting itself in almost all European countries. This common artistic language, Art Nouveau, representing both continuity and discontinuity, was directly influenced by English Arts and Crafts research and by the breakthrough of Japanese art on Western soil. More a general artistic frame of mind than a style as such, Art Nouveau set itself up as a reaction to, or perhaps a rejection of, everything that had gone before. It sought to impose itself as 'total art', as a holistic concept of life and art belonging henceforth to one and the same aesthetic.

Fig. 92 (& Fig. 89), dating from between 1899 and 1901, features a pair of dancers in gold. The two naked figures, sculpted in the round down to their knees, are closely entwined. The man, seen from the back, seems to be whirling his partner around while she arches her back in his arms and throws her head back, tossing her hair, giving an impression of movement and rhythm. Their two finely-chiselled faces give a glimpse of the intoxication of their impulsion, while their lower

90 *René Lalique, green gold, enamel and diamond ring, France, c.1900, given by Arconati Visconti, 1906, Musée des Arts Décoratifs, Paris.*

91 *René Lalique, gold, enamel and amethyst ring, France, c.1900, given by Dreyfus, Musée des Arts Décoratifs, Paris.*

90

91

92 *René Lalique, gold ring with baroque pearl, France c.1900, given by Oppenheim, Musée des Arts Décoratifs, Paris.*

92

Figs. 90 & 91 show two rings in gold, enamel, diamond and amethyst – both of them the work of this artist-jeweller – illustrating his preference for plant motifs and flowing interplay demonstrating a perfect mastery of technique (in this case twisted gold threads, the use of green enamel and a stone clasped in claws). The unchallenged leader in French Art Nouveau, Lalique quickly made his artistic mark: he brought noble and less noble materials together in a new and artistic way, assembling plant, flower, animal and feminine motifs chiselled into curves, inverted curves and offsets. Through his almost sculptural compositions, which no longer 'operate' from just one preferred point of view, he succeeded in moving away from the eclecticism or historicism of the 19th century and was able to give new expression to the feminine form.

Although Lalique was also very famous and acknowledged at the time, he was not the only one to have imagined and created a new type of jewellery. Georges Fouquet, the brothers Vever, Lucien Gaillard and Eugène Feuillâtre were also able to overturn the conventional hierarchy, associating the traditional raw materials of jewellery-making in new ways. They revitalised the art by means of a new approach to the historical and artistic past (especially the Renaissance period), through their recent discovery of Japanese art and by co-operating with artists from other spheres.[42]

Although all these great jewellers regularly exhibited their work at salons and universal exhibitions, they

limbs, in an intimate embrace, merge and fade into the hoop. This then flares out again into a plant shape, or wave, which itself bears an impressive baroque pearl at its crest.

The impression of dancing and of a shared reciprocal abandonment is cleverly induced by the fluidity of the curves and roundness of the figures, echoing the very irregularity of the pearl. The oval shape of the latter appears like a crown atop this beautiful composition by René Lalique.

also produced, alongside their spectacular, artistic pieces, less ambitious jewellery that was accessible to a wider audience.

Fig. 93, a German ring from 1900 made all in one piece, is a gold hoop, semi-round in section, flaring out in the upper part to form a figurative motif. The profile of the young girl, seen from the left and executed in slight relief, almost disappears under a shock of curly locks transforming itself into a leafy and ornamental decoration. Obvious romanticism and a dreamlike atmosphere emanate from this object made by Theodor Fahrner in Pforzheim.

Pforzheim was then the hub of the German jewellery industry and this factory was undoubtedly one of the most important between 1900 and 1930. Working in co-operation with leading painters and architects of the time, Fahrner thus manufactured rings in very different styles, reaching and adapting to a wide market.

A ring from 1906 in gold, rubies and diamonds, probably made for Rupp & Company by the artist Georg Kleemann, gives us another German example in Fig. 94. The entirely original hoop, rectangular in section here, is in the form of a heart and its extremities, joined together like two lovers' arms, clasp a beautiful diamond. The flat elongated bezel has a smaller diamond in the centre and, in the upper part, a geometrical figure dominated by three triangular rubies.

This object is of an entirely innovative geometric design, indeed avant-garde for the time. To illustrate this, another example in Fig. 95, of a more baroque style, dates from 1907. Here the bezel is laden with spiral motifs and sinuous lines of gold thread that seem to be holding or imprisoning a sapphire, emerald and ruby in their meanders. Made for the House of Karl Rothmüller in Munich, this ring is formally attached to the Art Nouveau tradition.

In contrast to British Arts and Crafts, German Art Nouveau or *Jugenstil* is characterised by a desire to associate art and industry, to initiate and raise the awareness of a larger number of people, through this new form of aesthetics. Furthermore, the Deutsche Werkbund ('Artists' Centre'), set up in Darmstadt in 1907 by Peter Behrens and Joseph Hoffman, also applied this theory and thereby contributed towards the (re)construction of the country's economic and cultural identity. This group of artists, was supported politically by Prince Ernst Ludwig de Hesse, who was

93 *Theodor Fahrner, 18-carat solid gold ring, Germany, Schmuckmuseum, Pforzheim.*

94 *Georg Kleemann (?) for Rupp & Co. Gold, ruby and diamond ring, 1906. Schmuckmuseum, Pforzheim.*

keen to see industrial development in his own duchy. He invited young European designers to live and work there and design jewellery and *objets d'art* to be mass-produced by the company. Its influence was clearly felt until the 1930s.[43]

What was happening in Germany at this time with regard to jewellery should probably be seen in relation to the various avant-garde artistic and pictorial movements of the same period. For example, Schmidt-Rottluff (1873–1948) made some magnificent rings that bear witness to this general artistic froth. These jewels are clearly marked by his own aesthetic research focusing on the subjective expression of psychological feelings, which had been directly influenced by Van Gogh and Munch. With their formal, colourful language and deliberately expressive technique, these rather impressive items of adornment are stamped with a degree of primitivism.

A fine gold open-work motif of vines and leaves runs along the cylindrical hoop of an Austrian ring from 1914 (Fig. 97). A magnificent ovoid opal of the same length sits on a flat gold mount. The interplay of solids and voids, accentuated by the very transparency of the stone, gives this very beautiful object made by Josef Wimmer tremendous lightness and fragility, characteristic of the Wiener Werkstätte ('Viennese workshops').

Another example in Fig. 96 (1917) by Dagobert Peche, which is also very light and airy, is made up of very fine gold threads. They form a floral and plant motif that seems to uncoil and coil in space.

This artist could also work with more solid and material volumes: a beautiful chrysoprase set in a beaded gold mount, with alternately solid and open-work rectangular compartments and a trefoil motif.

These two Viennese rings illustrate the Austrian Art Nouveau tendency. The *Sezession,* founded in 1897 by Josef Hoffman, who taught in Vienna, had already sought to revive and extend the concept of the work of art to the most everyday objects. The Viennese workshops were created in 1903 by Hoffman, Olbrich, Klimt and Koloman Moser. Very close in their approach to the English Guilds and Arts and Crafts movements, as well as French Art Nouveau, the Viennese workshops were radically opposed to mass production of jewellery and objects. They based their thinking and research on creation and the personal creativity of each individual. Their pieces with alternately flowing and geometrical forms and motifs were all made by hand. Many talented artist-craftsmen, such as Dagobert Peche or Carl Otto Czechka, approved of this aesthetic idea and joined the Wiener Werkstätte in designing jewellery and everyday objects.

95 *House of Karl Rothmüller, gold, sapphire, ruby and emerald ring, Germany, 1907, Schmuckmuseum, Pforzheim.*

96 *Dagobert Peche, gold ring, Austria, 1917, Osterreichisches Museum für Kunst, Vienna.*

In Denmark, the artist-jeweller Georg Jensen produced jewellery of a bare, purified design, trying to remain faithful both to craft techniques in harmony with his Scandinavian culture and commercial requirements. His rings, which are always in silver and semi-precious stones in his characteristic style, are still sold today.[44]

Several decades later, at the instigation of Louis Confort Tiffany, Tiffany & Company was also making accommodations to fashion and adopting an Art Nouveau style for its designs of glass costume jewellery and various other objects. At the turn of the century, this internationally renowned jewellery house was able to combine the Tiffany family's craft-working skills with new commercial demands.

Helped by speedier means of distribution, Art Nouveau extended its influence widely and came in a variety of forms, depending on the culture of each country. In this way, with the flowing, sinuous lines of its design, the change of focus in motifs in favour of natural and anthropomorphic references, using and combining resolutely modern materials and processes, Art Nouveau jewellery freed itself from past styles. Its artistic and aesthetic value was more important than its intrinsic value. The ring, which was often a one-off at a relatively affordable price, came in a formal and ornamental variety turning to good account either manual skills, as in England or France, or advanced industrial techniques, as in Germany. Consequently, it could fit in with the principles of aestheticism, and take part in the desire for 'total, social art', which was quite in keeping with the time. Using the theme of women and flowers, this vast movement introduced a new ideal of jewellery. Far from detractors who were then denouncing the ornamental or superfluous use of the female body in such jewels,[45] these artist-jewellers seemed to want to make this their creative signature and a mark of their individuality, perhaps predicting the changes in the female body image that were to take place at the turn of the century.

In fact, by accentuating sexual dimorphism more than ever, the bourgeois morals of the 19th century had definitely ended the wearing of jewellery and other accessories by men and delegated to women the task of portraying fortune and social position. In a society that was moving, despite everything, towards uniformity, woman, imprisoned in a costume inappropriate to her daily life, had become more than ever a kind of statutory ensign of men.[46] It is true that, through its iconography of the 'woman-flower',[47] the

Art Nouveau ring still fitted in with a symbolistic mythology of woman – a figure at once legendary, literary, pictorial and musical, emblematic and thoroughly characteristic of the end of the last century. Relying on these solid artistic and spiritual bases – symbolism on a European scale or the Nabis movement, or, alternately, the motif of the arabesque, sometimes bent almost out of shape for the purposes of decoration – Art Nouveau jewellery stuck closely to the structural and emotional power of lines. The rings studied here show this quite clearly.

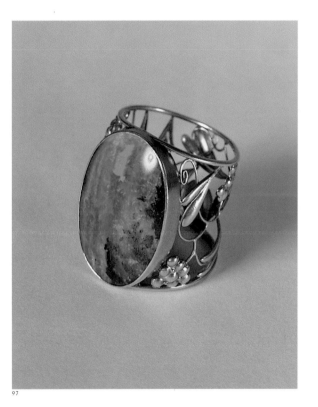

97

97 Josef Wimmer, gold and opal ring, Osterreichisches Museum für Kunst, Vienna.

Far from being a redundant or tautological art from the formal or iconographical point of view, Art Nouveau jewellery definitely enlarged the concept of adornment, seeking to decorate parts of the female body differently and perhaps now to be more in resonance with it. Just as women at the end of the 19th century seemed to want to free themselves from the status of decorative object, thanks to 'the aesthetics of Art Nouveau, the value of the jewel was no longer determined by the preciousness of its materials, but by its artistic design, a harmonious marriage of matter, perfect form'[48] and tailoring to the wearer. 'The jewel as a precious object had been demystified and other more democratic stylistic codes were being determinedly laid down, giving rise to aesthetic canons that are still valid nowadays'.[49]

i

ii

iii

iv

98

98 *Rings made in the trenches by soldiers of the first world war: (i) zinc, (ii) brass, (iii) brass and copper, (iv) brass.*

Art Deco and the 'reckless' years: 1915-39

Four rounds of aluminium cut out of a shell casing, melted in a steel cap and then cast in a limestone mould, roughly polished and bearing engravings or inscriptions – this is a description of some of the rings produced on the war-front itself by soldiers improvising as ring-makers (Fig. 98). They provide poignant evidence of the horror of the bloody war from 1914 to 1918. This demonstrates to what extent and in what extreme circumstances and events life, love and death are still symbolically and very strongly embodied in rings.

During the next twenty years after this comprehensive disaster – which had wiped out artistic production for more than four years – valiant attempts were made in all fields to 'get back to normal'. While the political revolutions and counter-revolutions that progressively gained ground in war-weakened Europe and the Soviet Union were gradually leading to relative international stability, they certainly brought about a degree of renewed material prosperity.

The world of fine jewellery, deeply shaken by this long period of uncertainty, was thus reinforcing its concept of jewellery as an investment by creating rings with generous, simplified forms, bearing very beautiful precious stones.

Under the dynamic leadership of Louis Cartier (1875–1942), the House of Cartier made some sumptuous pieces at this time. They were often made of platinum with geometric shapes, enhanced with coloured, sometimes engraved gems, such as emeralds, sapphires and rubies, as well as coral or black onyx, with diamonds on the shoulders. At the request

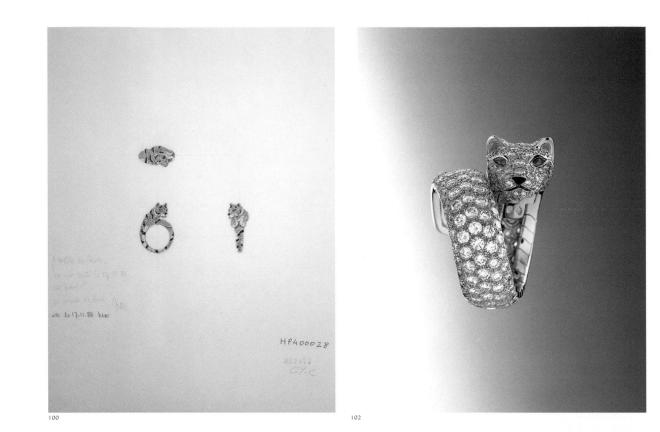

99

99 *Cartier, 'Trinity ring' in white, yellow and red gold, made since 1918.*

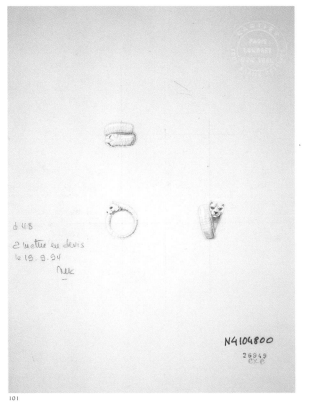

103

100, 101 *Cartier, 'Panther' ring designs.*

102 *Cartier, yellow gold 'Panther' ring set with brilliants, emeralds and onyx.*

103 *Van Cleef & Arpels, platinum ring set with navette brilliants, c.1919, House collection.*

of the poet Jean Cocteau, Louis created the very famous 'Trinity Ring' in 1918 (Fig. 99), an intermingling of three hoops, semi-round in section, in yellow, white and red gold. This idea was related to the rings of Saturn,[50] but probably more so to the oriental theosophical theories that had been very fashionable since the beginning of the century. According to these the meeting of three circles symbolised the mystical union of the male, female and spirit, itself derived from the holy union of the Father, Son and Holy Spirit and the earth-heaven-humanity triad.[51] This ring, given by Cocteau to the author Raymond Radiguet, to some extent recalling the symbol and form of the gimmel ring of the 16th century, still commands that symbolic fascination. (See also Figs. 105–108.)

Then, in 1925, Jeanne Toussaint, Cartier's mastermind, took over the management of the fine jewellery section, a post she held until the end of 1950. Nicknamed 'Jeanne the panther' because of the commotion she created, she became the guiding hand behind more animalistic and naturalistic pieces. The panther motif, which also came in various forms on rings (see Figs. 100–102), is also still available today.

From 1906, the firm of Van Cleef & Arpels (with premises in the Place Vendôme) also imposed its style. Rings produced from 1919 onwards were inspired in turn by the East and nature (the firm has always remained faithful to this flower motif). In 1933, long research led to the perfection of the 'invisible setting', an exclusive and patented process, whose secret lies in the preparation of a hidden gold netting in which the precious stones fit together in a dense mosaic, sliding along grooves. Fig. 114 shows a ring from 1940 with invisible-set rubies, rimmed with baguette diamonds, with a rounded structure and uniform red flat tint. Held up to the light but from the back, its intense vermilion colour resembles a stained-glass window. (See also Fig. 115.)

The apparent simplicity of this paving of precious stones, in which no trace of a claw can be glimpsed, should not obscure the fact that its delicate structure requires long months of work to perfect. In fact, each stone cut in a particular way has allowed additional facets to be obtained. Here, the rubies are of the same size, inserted and juxtaposed on the domed structure: depending on whether one looks at or wears it, this gives the impression of a continuous undulating, sparkling wave. The invisible-setting process revolutionised traditional jewellery-making techniques. It was taken over by other jewellers and lapidaries, but it is still today the keystone of the fame of the House of Van Cleef & Arpels. (See Figs. 103, 109, 110 & 113.)

Cartier, Van Cleef & Arpels, as well as Boucheron, Mauboussin and Chaumet, were also opening branches in Monte Carlo, Cannes, Deauville, London and New York, keen to satisfy the desires of rich and ever more demanding clients. (See Fig. 104.)

Haute couture too was enjoying a boom. The 19th century had already seen the appearance of the fashion phenomenon and the possibility of freer creation, in contrast to the *ancien régime*, which had placed great store on costume using the sumptuary laws to dictate what people could wear to indicate their position in the social hierarchy and guarantee its survival. Although women's clothing had only changed very slowly over the century, it was the 'asymmetry of appearances that had led women into new forms of behaviour and given their outfits new functions.'[52] These centuries-old practices held sway until the 1850s, when a trade and a genuine 'craft' of luxury clothing sprang up around the Rue Saint-Honoré in Paris, just next to the fine jewellery houses. Louis Hyppolite Le Roy, followed by Frédéric Worth, who was the first to put his name and label on clothing, had gradually acquired fame and a reputation for good taste that could not be ignored.

From the early 20th century, the very strong personality of Paul Poiret began to assert itself. He too created, under his own name and in addition to his very luxurious fashion collections, a range of perfumes (ten years before Coco Chanel) and a shop selling decorations and accessories (fifteen years before Lanvin). *Haute couture* thus entered its golden age, which lasted until the 1930s. Like designer jewellery, *haute couture* as produced by designers such as Chanel and Patou, was aimed at both French and foreign female customers, who were refined, well-off and increasingly 'emancipated'. This new aesthetic in clothing endeavoured to adapt itself to women with increasingly androgynous shapes who, since the war, had been making strides in independence.

Alongside these very prestigious garments, destined

104

104 *Boucheron, platinum ring with carved jade cabochon, two blue enamel baguettes on gold on either side, in a motif of round diamonds, millegrain edging, 1926.*

105 *Cartier, Art Deco style ring, set with central jade cabochon surrounded by cabochon rubies, buttressed with two baguette-cut diamonds, Paris, 1934.*

106 *Cartier, Art Deco style ring, cabochon emerald on black enamel base with two pyramidal consoles made up of three cabochon rubies on yellow gold mount, Paris, 1935.*

107 *Cartier, ring with oval cabochon emerald set lengthwise in a cartridge with onyx sides, brilliants on either side, brilliant-paved half-moon motifs on the flanks and with calibré-cut coral edging.*

108 *Cartier, ring with engraved emerald on black enamel base, sapphire, ruby and diamond consoles, platinum mount, Paris, 1927.*

105   106

107   108

VAN CLEEF & ARPELS
JOAILLIERS
22, Place Vendôme, PARIS
Créateurs des
BIJOUX "TOUCH WOOD"

Tous nos Bijoux Bois
sont montés avec des pierres précieuses sur platine et or.

109 *Van Cleef & Arpels,*
advertisement, c.1920.

for a privileged minority, the production of clothing had already become industrialised as of the mid-19th century, dynamised by technical progress that brought down the cost of manufacture and made prices more affordable. The market for ready-made clothing was flourishing, in the image of the large stores in which the garments were now sold.

From 1910, Poiret (not to mention Max Ernst, Picasso, Braque, Miró or Sonia Delaunay) was making a whole series of stage jewellery for Serge Diaghilev's *Ballet Russe*, whose *Scheherazade* by Rimsky-Korsakov was all the rage in Paris.

He had begun to co-operate in 1913 with the firm of Gripoix and jewellers such as René Boivin or Paul Iribe in making some of his jewellery. He was thus the

instigator of the new 'costume' jewellery, worn as an accessory to clothing and subsequently known as 'fashion' jewellery. Closely followed by Elsa Schiaparelli and Gabrielle Chanel, Poiret is, however, considered to have been the first couturier to create a limited series of jewels that were no longer merely imitations of real jewels, but genuine creations, perfectly matching the outfit, worn and presented by models during the first fashion parades.

Plastic allowed for cheap manufacture as of the 1920s. The technique of producing these unhallmarked jewels by moulding and dyeing had been mastered perfectly. In 1914, Chanel created the concept of 'fancy' or 'paste' jewellery: she saw it as a genuine accessory, a symbol of independence

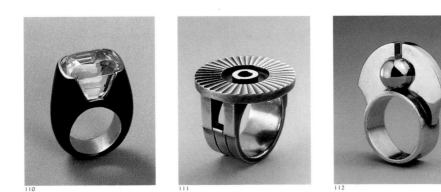

110 *Van Cleef & Arpels, ring in black enamel with yellow sapphire, c.1920.*

111 *Jean Desprès, gilt silver ring, 1932-34, France, Musée des Arts Décoratifs, Paris.*

112 *Jean Desprès, silver ring, 1930-36, France, Musée des Arts Décoratifs, Paris.*

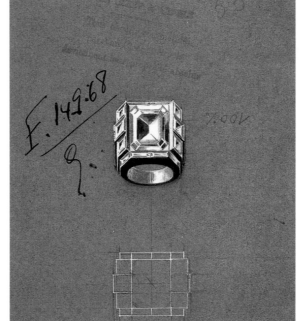

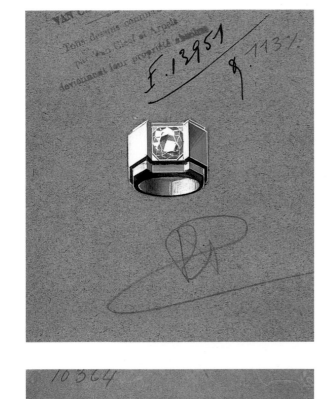

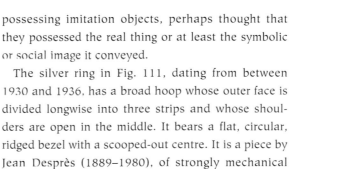

113 Van Cleef & Arpels, signet
   ring designs in platinum or
   gold, baguette-cut diamonds
   and cabochon emeralds,
   1930s.

designed for the new woman, with her ever-shorter hair and unrestricting clothes suited to her day and evening life.

The beginnings of these phenomena of fashion and diversification should no doubt be placed within the broad unifying movement that was occurring in the field of luxury goods. As copies became commonplace, thanks to progress in chemistry and technique, luxury or the appearance of luxury was beginning to become accessible to larger numbers of people who, in

possessing imitation objects, perhaps thought that they possessed the real thing or at least the symbolic or social image it conveyed.

The silver ring in Fig. 111, dating from between 1930 and 1936, has a broad hoop whose outer face is divided longwise into three strips and whose shoulders are open in the middle. It bears a flat, circular, ridged bezel with a scooped-out centre. It is a piece by Jean Desprès (1889–1980), of strongly mechanical inspiration, recalling the great interest of this jeweller in aeronautics. The bezel here is a symbolic echo of a moving aeroplane propeller. All his jewellery creations were strongly influenced by his work and experience as an industrial designer in an aeronautical construction factory during the war.[53]

This is illustrated by another Desprès ring (Fig. 112), in gilt silver, made up of a circular hoop, crowned with a small sphere, held prisoner between two vertical planes, concave at the extremities for the comfort of the fingers.

In contrast, the soft, rounded platinum structure of a very beautiful piece by Jean Fouquet (1899–1984) (Fig. 116) bears a succession of diamonds, amethysts and opals, arranged in vertical parallel lines, whose contrasts give geometrical rhythm to the upper face. The volumes in this piece play on polychromy and the effects of the cut and setting of the stones (pavé-set diamonds and opals unusually cut into semi-cylindrical baguettes), create a balance that is at once soft, flowing and rectilinear.

The jewels of Jean Fouquet, characterised by their simple, pure shapes, reveal an explicit attraction for broad surfaces or planes of simplified composition; very often using the interplay and reflections of many colours. As of 1930, he had been a founder member of the Union Des Artistes Modernes (UAM), with the architects Mallet Stevens, Chareau, Le Corbusier, Perriand, etc. and artist-jewellers such as Gérard Sandoz (1902-89) and Raymond Templier (1891-1968). This association contributed towards 'the development and creation of a non-élitist modern art, intended for a mass audience, of which jewellery was an integral part'.[54] All these artists, who were friends of Braque, Miró and Aragon, amongst others, regularly exhibited at the autumn salons and universal exhibitions.

This linear aesthetic – whether 'mechanistic', geometric or Art Deco, highly-stylised and making daring use of colour – in fact, has its origins before the war, although it had no official status until 1925 when the *Exposition Des Arts Décoratifs et Industriels Modernes* was held in Paris. Its interplay of lines, curves, circles and contrasts of forms and light, this rhetoric, in reaction to the fluid aesthetics and explicitly figurative references of Art Nouveau, takes its inspiration from the avant-garde movements of the beginning of the century. From Cubism the inspiration came from its arrangement of planes, its deconstructions of forms in space, its decompositions of reality and use of non-traditional materials, as in the work of

Braque and Picasso. Futurism, as applied by Marinetti, Boccioni, Balla and Severini, supplied its mechanical references and allusions, its dynamic vision, rhythms and attraction for the beauty of speed and celebration of 'modernity'. It was also non-figurative in its lack of reference to reality and the creation of another world – as in the work of Kandinsky and Malevitch; its dream-like, theosophical and Orphic enquiry into light – as expressed by Robert and Sonia Delaunay and Kupka, following the writings of Apollinaire; its formal and mechanical contrasts – as in the work of Fernand Léger; and its endeavours to ensure the unitary balance of plastic elements, as demonstrated by Mondrian.

114

In this way, whether fine designer-jewellery, fashion accessory or the work of artists or ordinary jewellers, Art Deco jewellery was geometric in form, with modern (mechanical and aeronautical) references and strong polychromatic tendencies or preferences. No stone was particularly favoured, but chosen and assembled in accordance with the overall effect; as produced by the interplay and contrasts of light. Keeping their heavy symbolic and social connotations, rings too were able to adopt this formal and absolutely modern language. All these artistic themes informed the aesthetics of Art Deco jewellery, constructed, elaborated and dictated by intellectual, economic and social imperatives and peremptory fashion trends.

However, Art Deco was also, very subtly, on the fringes of the more general style known as the 'inter-

114 *Van Cleef & Arpels, ring with invisible set rubies edged with baguette-cut diamonds, c.1940.*

national style'. The latter, which preferred simplified composition of volumes rather than complex ornamentation, was then affecting architecture and objects. In addition, this style was closely linked to the Dutch De Stijl movement and the modern aesthetics of the Bauhaus. Although different, these two schools were based on the theoretical concept that art and creation contributed towards the development of society. They had faith in the machine and mechanical progress and tended in the direction of simplicity, lack of ornamentation and functionalism of shapes.

Thus swinging back and forth between aestheticism ('pure' forms) and exuberance (daring contrasts of forms and colours), Art Deco jewellery stands as an aesthetic response to the strong post-war social and consumer demand. These were the reckless years. We know that, subsequently, the Great Depression, which struck America in 1929, was to drive down sales and purchases of jewellery in the following decade, leading to the appearance of protectionism.

Thanks to the nihilistic, iconoclastic spirit of Dada from 1916, followed by the militant revolutionary spirit of Surrealism from 1924 – which were the only artistic movements opposed to the overall 'return to order' – and the surrounding functional and economic rigour, an opening began to appear. These artists were gradually to help jewellers to break out conclusively from traditional artistic categories. Furthermore, Max Ernst, Dali and Arp were to make an attempt at the art of jewellery.

Paris still entirely dominated the artistic scene: England's Mappin & Webb, Germany's Theodor Fahrner, Denmark's Georg Jensen and America's Marsh & Co and Harry Winston were producing French-inspired Art Deco jewellery.[55]

The Art Deco exhibition was held at the Grand Palais in Paris in 1925, (though it had been planned for 1915) it gave its name to and characterised the whole period. Delayed due to the war, it retained its initial aim of showing off the industrialisation of arts and crafts and thereby excluding copies of ancient styles. The 500 square metres devoted to jewellery attracted more than 400 exhibitors; jewellers who favoured artistic content at the expense of market value. In their leanings towards 'autonomous' creation, they were opening up the way to modernity. 1925 was also the date of the very first Surrealist exhibition in Paris, at the Pierre Gallery, which again presaged the coming decade.

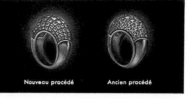

Regardez bien ces merveilleux bijoux et vous verrez rapidement en quoi consiste leur surprenante nouveauté. La gemme est mystérieusement et impeccablement retenue par la base : pas de ces griffes qui souvent déchirent les étoffes délicates, pas de serti dont les bandes métalliques surplombent et recouvrent en partie la pierre. Ainsi rien ne vient interrompre l'harmonieuse continuité de la matière précieuse dans les assemblages de rubis flamboyants, de saphirs veloutés... le bel effet obtenu est aussi inattendu que féerique. La supériorité du nouveau procédé est nettement illustrée par la comparaison des deux bagues d'émeraudes reproduites ci-dessus. Cette heureuse innovation, due à Van Cleef et Arpels qui en possèdent l'exclusivité, cause une véritable révolution dans l'art du joaillier, et présage d'un changement important dans la mode de la joaillerie.

VAN CLEEF ET ARPELS
21, *Place Vendôme, Paris*

CE PROCÉDÉ APPELÉ " LE SERTI MYSTÉRIEUX " EST PROTÉGÉ PAR DES BREVETS TANT EN FRANCE (Brevet n° 764.966) QUE DANS LES PAYS SUIVANTS : ANGLETERRE (Brevet n° 432.074), ALLEMAGNE (Brevet n° 1.317.609), ÉTATS-UNIS (Brevet n° 68.518).

VOGUE

115

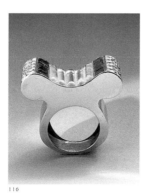

115 *Van Cleef & Arpels, advertisement for Vogue, c.1936.*

116 *Jean Fouquet, platinum ring, set with diamonds, amethysts and opals. c.1930, France, Musée des Arts Décoratifs, Paris.*

116

51 Métique Bague 6º doigt

Choese

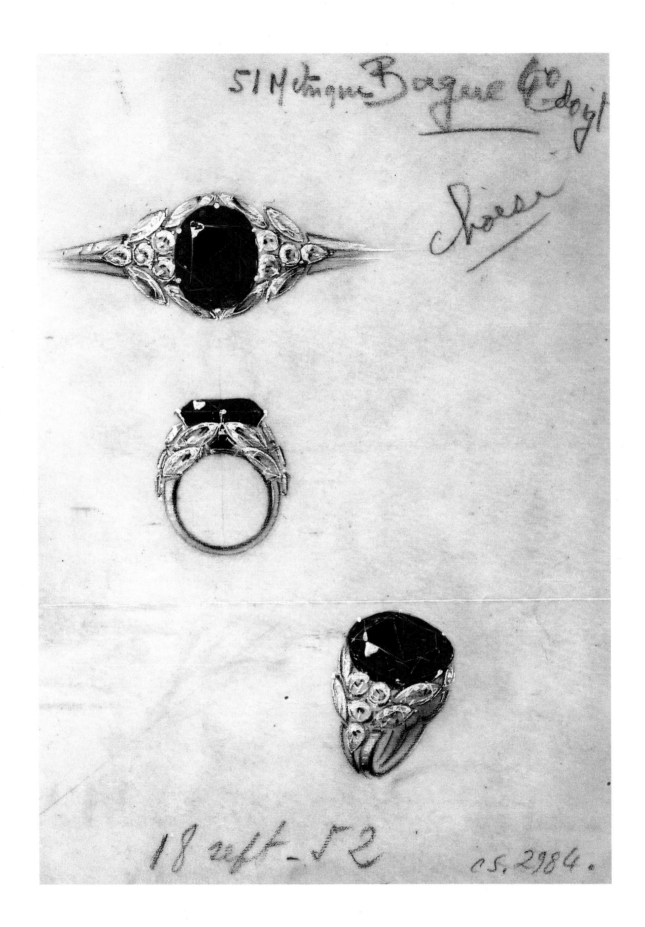

18 zept — 52   c5. 2984.

117 Van Cleef & Arpels,
gouache drawing for a
25.63 carat oval ruby
belonging to the Maharani
of Baroda, 1952.

Rings in the 1950s: tradition and creativity

Hitler's ambition, coupled with the inability of the democracies and Russia to come to an understanding, provoked another war: six years that witnessed the collapse of Europe and then its carving up by the two major political and economic powers (the United States and the former Soviet Union). The artistic scene then moved away from Paris to set up in America, in New York.

During this decade, the world of luxury goods, including jewellery, made light of the paradoxes: the violent destruction and massive restrictions only partially halted the production and sale of rings or adornments. The albums and archives of the fine jewellery trade prove that there was some production, albeit on a reduced scale. Precious stones and metals have even been hoarded. Trading in jewellery during the war no doubt offered clients more than ever a fall-back in the form of easily transportable capital.

Already foreshadowed at the 1937 *Exposition Internationale Des Arts et Techniques dans la Vie Moderne* and in contrast to the previous period, the forms of these jewels, often made hollow or from thin plates of gold and platinum and few stones, tended to become rounder and softer. The production of rings in the immediate post-war period further accentuated this tendency: gold was again preferred, but used solid, working all the surfaces/planes so dear to the 1920s but this time in volume. Curves, scrolls, flowing lines and motifs close to a naturalistic vocabulary appeared, but used rhetoric and symbolism unlike that of Art Nouveau. Melissa Garbardi used colourful terms to describe and define these objects with their sculptural gold structures, created in France by Van Cleef, Cartier, Boucheron, Mauboussin or Mellerio: These included the 'bridge' ring, when the two symmetrical shoulders of the hoop were joined by a stone or paving; the 'open book' ring, in which the shoulders made up two sloping planes; the 'Turk' ring, evoking an oriental flavour; the 'turban' ring, in which the spiralling volume specifically looked like an oriental head covering; and finally the 'ribbon bow' ring, in which this motif was reproduced more or less explicitly.[56] (See Figs 117–126).

118

118 *Van Cleef & Arpels, polished gadrooned gold ring set with two blue and yellow Ceylonese sapphires, 1944. House collection.*

119 *Van Cleef & Arpels, design c.1940 signed by Pierre Arpels.*

119

All the international exhibitions, annual salons, prizes and competitions at international level gave a further boost to the creation and distribution of new models and sought to encourage the purchase of these jewels.[57]

The great Italian houses, established in all the historical cities of the country, each had their creative singularity and lines. The houses of Bulgari, Masenza and Petochi in Rome, Faraone, Cusi and Calderoni in Milan, Missiaglia in Venice, Settepassi in Florence and Fassano in Turin all had in common the extremely high quality of the stones used in their jewellery.

While the high tax on English jewellery after the war somewhat curtailed the production of new pieces, the houses of Mappin & Webb, Asprey, Drayson, Collingwood and Garrard, all based in London, remained attached to their long tradition of classical prestige.

While retaining political neutrality, the Swiss fine jewellery trade, established in the main towns, including the houses of Patek Philippe and Baszanger in Geneva, and Bücherer and Meister in Zurich, also felt the effects of the war. Unlike these traditionalist jewellers, Gübelin in Lucerne, which was especially

120 *Cartier, 18-carat yellow gold ring set with a coral cabochon surrounded by gold leaves with square-cut emeralds and diamonds, gadroon pattern body, Paris, 1947, belonging to the Duchess of Windsor.*

interested in art, had the idea of co-operating with young designers using perhaps less conventional references.

Spain also had some famous fine jewellers, remaining faithful to classical and traditional benchmarks, such as Masriera i Carreras and Bagués, both houses having been founded in Barcelona at the beginning of the century. There were also five perhaps less conformist individuals – much influenced by artistic activity – who became real models for the country: Jaume Mercade i Queralt, Ramon Sunya i Clarà, Oriol Sunyer, Manuel Capdevila and Alfonso Serrahima i Bofill.

Germany, which had been a dynamic country, completely au fait with artistic creation and jewellery, was deeply affected by the war. Totally destroyed, Hanau and Pforzheim in particular – with its profusion of designer and mass-production jewellery houses such as Hermann Hottinger, Babler, Henkel und Grosse, Fr. Kohlrausch, Fahrner and Knoll – took more than ten years to get over this major political and economic disaster.

However, it was in the Scandinavian countries that the fine jewellery trade, which was also heir to a long tradition, was the most enterprising. It called on artists known for their avant-gardism. In Copenhagen, the houses of Just Anderson, Dragsted and Michelsen all worked for the royal court. Especially after 1954, however, the firm of Jensen was working with Nana Ditzel and Thorun Bülow-Hübe; two highly talented

120

female artist-jewellers. In Oslo, the house of Tostrup had been founded in 1832 by Jacop Tostrup, while the house of David Andersen had been founded in 1876. In Stockholm, there was Bolin, supplier to the imperial court. Scandinavian rings and jewels, with their round volumes, refined lines and smooth or polished surfaces were almost always made of silver. There was certainly some avant-gardism too, since many Jensen rings are still made today.

In New York, Arthur King, David Webb, Harry Winston and Tiffany were very successfully competing with the French jewellery houses. The French designer Jean Schlumberger actually worked for Tiffany throughout the decade, imposing his style and personality. He even became chairman in 1956.[58]

Along with the *haute couture* of the time, fine jewellery had, more than ever, a strongly prestigious image; they were both the fierce guardians of tradition, indeed of a degree of classicism. Rings and other jewels, developed and produced to order in the designers' studios, continued to be made using handcrafted techniques.

The clientele of all these leading houses was made up only of rich, privileged personalities. Given postwar economic change and social behaviour, these clients were not, however, bringing in sufficient revenue.

In parallel with the opening of branches in almost all the major cities of the world, the fine jewellery trade then engaged in a policy of diversification. The creation of less costly lines of jewellery, as well as various accessories, were gradually to produce a not inconsiderable turnover and thus enable these leading firms to get through a much less wealthy period. Yet it was not until 1946 or 1947, especially in France, that the reduction by the Blum government of the tax on luxury goods (from 33.33% to 13%) brought about a substantial revival in the fine jewellery market.

The same phenomenon affected clothing. Quite separate from Parisian *haute couture*, which had dictated fashion to the entire world before the war, 'ready-to-wear that everyone can afford' had been launched in Europe in the 1950s. This was to prove very popular with fashion magazines. Even though couturiers also created ready-to-wear collections, the number of haute couture houses went down from thirty-nine to seventeen between 1966 and 1967;[59] bearing witness to genuine social change.

These very varied 'new clothes' – issuing from garment industries with methods of production and

...Il est des "Signatures" auxquelles on tient

VAN CLEEF & ARPELS
Joailliers
22, PLACE ∎ VENDÔME
PARIS   LONDON
NEW-YORK

121 *Van Cleef & Arpels,*
advertisement by
Pierre Simon, 1946.

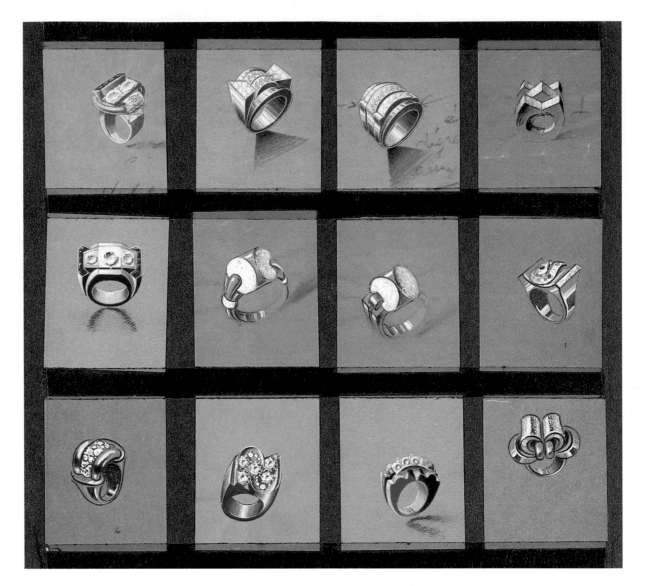

122 *Van Cleef & Arpels, plate of 1940s designs.*

distribution copied from the American ready-to-wear market – encountered very great success and certain interest. In fact, they enabled fashion to become more and more democratic and steadfastly opened the way for the stylists and designers of the 1960s who, using new forms and materials, would make a total break with the past.[60]

Mention has been made of objects made by artists – jewellery by Calder, Picasso or Max Ernst – and this concept of the artist-jeweller proved to be an aesthetic phenomenon illustrative of the whole decade, broadly encouraged and welcomed with orders from galleries and public expectations. Painters and sculptors, such as Sonia Delaunay, De Chirico, Tanguy, Chagall, Léger, Derain, Arp, César, Arman and Giacometti, designed jewellery and rings and usually entrusted someone in the trade or an industrialist with the task of making them up from their models. An examination

of the subtleties of design and implementation follows in the next section.

While items of adornment, for most of these artists, remained subordinate to their more monumental personal and artistic concerns, we can feel, nevertheless, that the form of these 'artists' jewels' interprets adornment in a different way. These artists attempted to go far beyond the conceptual limits that had so far been dominant in the field of jewellery. Rings from Penalba and Takis, both famous sculptors, show this magnificently.

Although these pieces did, in the final analysis, conform to an artistic policy with strong commercial connotations, they did at least launch jewellery towards formal and aesthetic limits that were still under exploited, in particular in taking account of the wearer. As far as rings are concerned, while it is true that the circular form had always been almost inevitable, these artists were to go on to use this initial formal constraint as a springboard, by developing a much freer overall shape.

Now the artist's jewel is also to be seen against the more general phenomenon of democratisation of art, also known as 'aestheticising' the humdrum, which was to greatly develop later. The American idea of the 1930s (and that of Bauhaus), of designing and producing objects that were both beautiful and functional, enabled Europe to reconstruct itself after the war: it became a decisive factor and selling point in a market that was by now globalised and increasingly competitive.

The political, economic and social dynamics of the 1950s thus swung back and forth between taking refuge in tradition and creative vigour, gradually leading to jewellery being considered as a genuine form of artistic expression. More generally, this state of affairs also drove painters and sculptors to challenge the aesthetic and representative boundaries of their art. Following events as destructive and unimaginable as the Jewish genocide or Hiroshima, it was essential to rethink representation, to formulate other solutions, and to find other formal and plastic rationales. Like the abstract movement at the beginning of the century – but now free of all spiritual or theosophical references or justifications – Abstract Expressionism tried to construct a world without representation. It was to be a world abstract from visible reality, with universal themes and focused on the means or techniques of production. This 'New

York school', distinguishing itself for the first time from European trends, brought together a variety of styles and artists such as Gorky, Pollock or De Kooning, as well as Rothko, Newman or AdReinhardt, coming together around the same desire for commitment and physical combat with the canvas.

Activity in the plastic arts over those years, which was more objective and pragmatic than post-war sculpture and reacting to the values of the society with its increasing production and consumption, also began to demand the physical commitment of the artist. Modern sculpture carried forward and put the finishing touches to certain earlier styles: as in the expressive figuration of Germaine Richier, or the biomorphic figuration of Moore, Hepworth and Arp, technology, science and Constructivism, the beginnings of Pop Art and the New Realists. Active and therefore eclectic, modern sculpture also remained preoccupied with the desire to place the gestures and the raw energy of the sculptor in the forefront as in the work of David Smith.

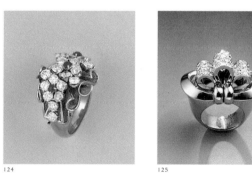

124

125

126

123

It is true that America and Europe then definitively lost their 'innocence', idealism and faith in man and his future. The second world war marks a historic and cultural turning point: in the face of so much hostility, the involvement of matter, objects and the body itself now became an integral part of the work of art. With regard to the more specific field of rings and jewellery, the attitude of artists was gradually to become more radical, more critical and more analytical. In addition, this thinking and application in the field of adornment was to be backed up by much more specific training of artist-jewellers, with greater openness and potential for cultural exchanges on a world scale. These were the decisive details that were to allow the concept of jewellery to be challenged.

124 Van Cleef and Arpels, gold tulle ring decorated with Hawaiian flowers in brilliants, faceted ruby centre, c.1939, House collection.

125 Van Cleef and Arpels, 'ribbon-bow' ring, three shells in brilliants on platinum, tied and surrounded with polished gold, 1946, C. & S. Lemarié collection.

126 Cartier, ring with central diamond surrounded by diamonds, onyx body, gold and platinum mount, Paris, 1949.

123 Van Cleef & Arpels, black pearl on brilliant-paved background, baguette-cut diamonds mounted on platinum hoop. This ring was amongst the jewellery worn by Princess Grace of Monaco at her wedding (18th April 1956).

Conclusion and overall perspective

The history of the ring shows that it cannot fail to be part of a wider picture. This is also the case in the fields of architecture, painting, sculpture or jewellery of every type, in which a similar overall view has always been taken, representing a given society as a whole. Despite its relatively small size and predetermined circular shape – a constraint that it has, moreover, been magnificently turned to its advantage over the centuries – the ring has succeeded in expressing fundamental human concepts: magic, identity, protection, allegory, ostentation, religion, symbolism, signature, metaphor, love, commemoration, ornamentation and investment. Its basic meanings, functions, systems or values have thus come together to give it its full richness in every important period of its history.

In considering the ring as a historical and artistic document, the fundamental concern has thus been to look at the broader context whenever a new typology appeared. By relating these developments to other artistic, sociological and political events, specific designs may be linked to a given period. This absolute continuity rather than hierarchy between the various forms of the art also shows that rings, like art over the centuries, are far from having a merely ornamental or aesthetic purpose. While aesthetic value certainly does seem to be a recurrent theme throughout the history of rings, it is relative and depends on the period of reference. This raises questions about the concept of the work of art and the boundaries of its definition.

Notes

1. Yvette Taborin, *La parure en coquillage au paléolithique*, XXIX supplement to Gallia Préhistoire, CNRS, 1993 and 'La parure au paléolithique', in *Archéologia*, typological records Nos. 311–316.

2. Yvette Taborin, op. cit.

3. Ibid.

4. Ibid.

5. Ibid.

6. Claude Lévi-Strauss, 'Lebensspender Schmuck', in *Ornementa 1, Internationale Schmuckkunst*, exhibition catalogue of the Pforzheim Schmuckmuseum, 30 September to 19 November 1989, Prestel-Verlag, Munich, 1989.

7. Leroi-Gourhan, *Le Geste et la Parole. Technique et Langage*, Albin Michel, Paris, 1964.

8. 'La main dans la préhistoire', in *Les Dossiers d'Archéologie*, No. 178, January 1993.

9. Mircea Eliade, *Forgerons et Alchimistes*, Champs Flammarion, Paris, 1977.

10. *Le Premier Or de l'Humanité en Bulgarie, 5e Millénaire*, catalogue, Musée des Antiquités Nationales de Saint-Germain-en-Laye, 17 January to 30 April 1989

11. Vassil Nikolov, 'L'art et la mythologie des agriculteurs du Chalcolithique final sur les terres bulgares', in *Le Premier Or de l'Humanité en Bulgarie, 5ème Millénaire*, catalogue, Musée des Antiquités Nationales de Saint-German-en-Laye Exhibition, 17 January to 30 April 1989.

12. Christiane Eluère, *Chercheurs d'Or et Orfèvres des Temps Anciens*, RMN, Paris, 1990.

13. *Ramses le Grand*, exhibition catalogue, Galeries Nationales du Grand Palais, Paris, 1976.

14. Claude Sourdine, *Le Main dans l'Egypte Pharaonique*, Peter Lang, Berne, 1984.

15. Christiane Desroches-Noblecourt, *Vie et Mort d'un Pharaon: Toutankhamon*, Hachette, Paris, 1963.

16. Semini Karouzou, *National Museum*, Ekdotike Athnon SA, Athens, 1992.

17. William Dyfri and Jack Ogden, *Greek Gold. Jewellery of the Classical World*, The Trustees of the British Museum, London, 1994.

18. The Comitia, popular assemblies that met in the forum, voted on laws and elected the magistrates. The latter, who always came from the leading families and were elected for the comitia for one year, pursued their careers (the career of honours) before becoming consuls or censors. The senate was the real master of domestic, foreign and military policy; there were about 300 senators and the voting list was established by the censors. Unlike the magistrates whose functions were short term, it embodied real, permanent authority, always fully informed of public affairs.

19. Hélène Guiraud, 'Bagues et anneaux à l'époque romaine', in *Gallia*, Vol. 46, CNRS, 1989.

20. Hélène Guiraud, op. cit.

21. Jérome Carcopino, *La Vie Quotidienne à Rome à l'Epoque de l'Empire*, Hachette, Paris, 1939.

22. Black enamel or silver sulphide used for inlay. To niello a metal surface (or simply the contours as in the example here), recesses must first be hollowed out before the niello is applied and then heated

23. Claude Lévi-Strauss, op. cit.

24. Jean Chevalier and Alain Gheerbrant, op. cit.

25. Jean Chevalier and Alain Gheerbrant, op. cit.

26. Robert Muchembled, *Société, Cultures et Mentalités dans la France Moderne, XVI–XVIII ème Siècle*, Armand Colin, Paris, 1990.

27. Jérôme Carcopino, op. cit.

28. Robert Muchembled, op. cit.

29. Ibid.

30. Ibid.

31. Henri Focillon, Benvenuto Cellini, Agora, Presses Pocket, Paris, 1992.

32. Dominique Puaud, 'Les Tthéories des Proportions de l'Architecture à la Renaissance', Master's dissertation, Université de Haute Bretagne, Rennes, 1989.

33. Robert Muchembled, op. cit.

34. Phillipe Perrot, *Les Dessus et les Dessous de la Bourgeoisie*, Fayard, Paris, 1981.

35. Véronique Alemany-Dessaint, *Orfèvrerie Française*, Les Editions de l'Illustration Baschet & Cie, Paris, 1988.

36. Claudette Joannis, *Bijoux des Régions de France*, Flammarion, Paris, 1992.

37. Ibid.

38. Phillipe Perrot, op. cit., and Gérard Monnier, *L'Art et ses Institutions en France, de la Révolution à Nos Jours*, Gallimard, Paris, 1995.

39. Ibid.

40. Phillipe Perrot, op. cit.

41. The concept of luxury appeared in the 17th century, as a synonym for superficiality, elegance and refinement and then, in the 18th century, for scarcity and excessive ostentatious sumptuousness. See Phillipe Perrot, *Le Luxe, une Richesse entre Faste et Confort, XVIII–XIX ème Siècle*, Seuil, Paris, 1995.

42. Evelyne Possémé, 'La bijouterie Art Nouveau et Art Déco', in *Métiers d'Art*, Société d'Encouragement aux Métiers d'Art, No. 22–23, Paris, September 1983, pp.46–53.

43. Caroline Fullée, *Bijoux du XX ème siècle*, Céliv, London, 1990.

44. Barbara Cartlidge, *Les Bijoux au XX ème Siècle*, Payot, Paris, 1986.

45. Evelyne Possémé, op. cit.

46. Philippe Perrot, *Le Travail des Apparences. Le Corps Féminin XVIII–XIX ème Siècles*, Seuil, Paris, 1984.

47. Ibid.

48. Gerda Buxbaum, 'Splendeurs du non-précieux', in *L'art du Bijou*, Flammarion, Paris, 1992, pp.49–110.

49. Ibid.

50. Barbara Cartlidge, 'Les bagues du XX ème siècle', in *La Bague de l'Antiquité Jusqu'à Nos Jours*, Office du Livre, Bibliothèque des Arts, Fribourg, Switzerland, 1981, p.156.

51. *Petite Bibliothèque des Symboles*, Editions du Chêne, Paris, 1994, p.4.

52. Ibid.

53. Melissa Garbardi, *Les Bijoux de l'Art Déco aux Années 40*, Editions de l'Amateur, Paris, 1986.

54. Ibid.

55. Patricia Bayer, 'Art Deco 1920–1939', in *Joaillerie*, pp.129–145.

56. Melissa Garbardi, op. cit., pp.248 256.

57. Sylvie Raulet, *Bijoux Des Années 1940–1950*, Editions du Regard, Paris, 1987.

58. Ibid., pp.97–217

59. Didier Grumbach, 'Worth, Poiret, Chanel, et les autres', in *Jardin des Modes*, October 1994, pp.76–79.

60. Yvonne Deslandres and Florence Müller, *Histoire de la Mode au XX ème Siècle*, Somogy, Paris, 1986, pp.231–232.

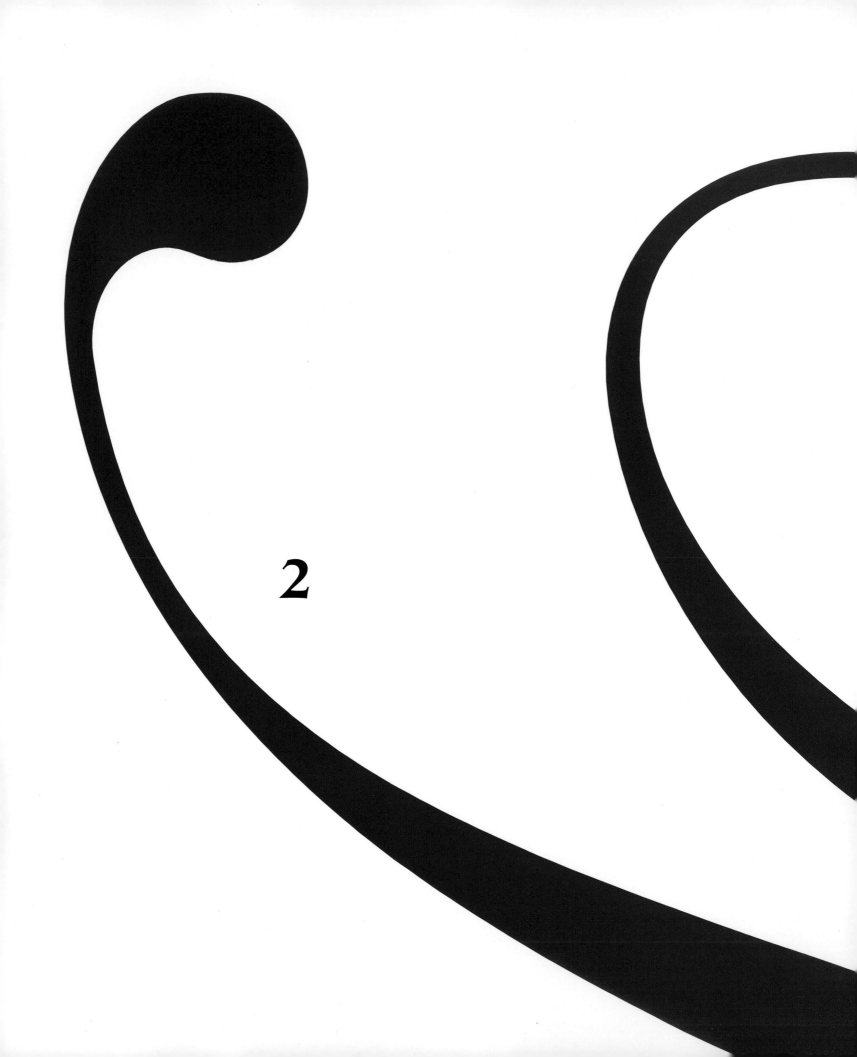

2

Fine jewellery and mass production

A comprehensive study of the last few important
decades in ring design must include both fine and
mass-produced contemporary jewellery, for differing forms
of manufacture have influenced the purpose and design
of this small item of adornment.[1]

Designer and mass-produced rings

Examples of contemporary designer rings include, from Cartier, the 'tiger ring' (Fig. 127) in diamonds and gold, depicting this wild beast with remarkable anatomical precision. It seems as if an attempt is being made to render the tiger's muscular tension and suppleness. Fig. 128 shows a signet-type ring – the bulky mass of the object, with its pavé-set gems or baguettes, as well as the elegant setting (four metal claws fetching up on the table-cut diamond), shows off the fiery magnificence of the stone. Fig. 135 shows a piece of fine contemporary jewellery that isolates its deep blue sapphire as far as possible from its metal

129

129 VAN CLEEF & ARPELS
*'Galliéra' ring, invisible-set
rubies on gold, navette
diamond mounted on
platinum, 1992.
This piece was amongst the
jewellery specially designed
for the 1992 Exhibition at
the Musée de la Mode et du
Costume, Palais Galliéra.*

128 CARTIER *Signet ring,
diamonds.*

128

130 CARTIER *'Panther' ring design, yellow and grey gold.*

131 CARTIER *'Elephant' ring design, yellow and grey gold.*

132 CARTIER *Ring design, brilliants, oval Zambian emerald.*

133 CARTIER *Cross-over ring design, gold, brilliants, cushion-cut blue sapphire and oval faceted Burmese ruby.*

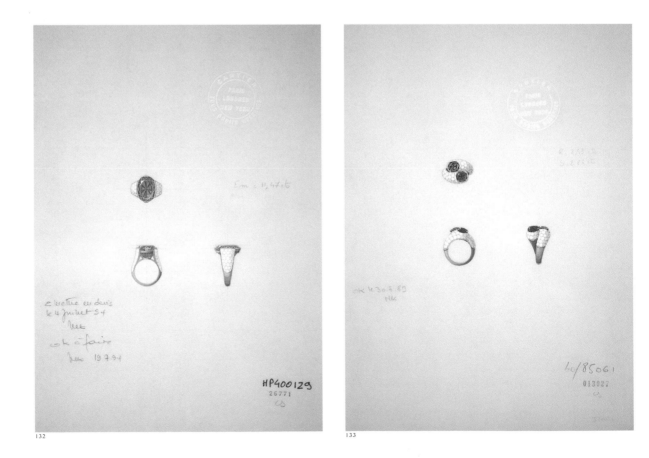

134

135

136

135 CARTIER *Contemporary fine jewellery ring, sapphire and diamonds.*

134 VAN CLEEF & ARPELS *'Double ball' ring, invisible-set sapphires, mounted on gold and brilliants mounted on platinum, 1961.*

136 VAN CLEEF & ARPELS *'Hopscotch' ring, polished gold, brilliants, 15-carat oval cabochon sapphire, drop-shaped sapphires, 1994.*

structure. The animal theme, the signet ring, the *pavé-set* gems and Cartier's designer rings thus continue to represent the favoured creative focus of this leading firm. (See also Figs. 130–133).

Fig. 136 is a 1994 'hopscotch' ring by Van Cleef & Arpels which has a magnificent oval cabochon sapphire, shown off by a generous polished gold mounting, with smoothly alternating brilliants and sapphire drops. Figs. 134 & 129 – the 'double ball' (1961) and 'Galliéra' (1992) – display the pioneering technique of this great jewellery house: the invisible or 'mysterious' setting. Discovered in 1933, this also allows stones to be set very closely on a mounting of hidden precious metal which may be gold and/or platinum. The rings use sapphires and brilliants, or rubies with a magnificent 'navette' diamond in the centre.

As previously discussed, the major Parisian jewellers deserted the Palais Royal as of the 19th century to set up shop around the Place Vendôme and Rue de la Paix in Paris. In addition, their style –

138 CARTIER *Cross-over ring, ruby, sapphire and diamonds.*

139 O.J. PERRIN *'Bamboo' rings, gold, diamonds and semi-precious stones.*

137 POIRAY *Two-claw rubellite pear ring, gold and rubellite.*

tending towards an ever lighter and more ethereal arrangement or mounting of stones – became one steadfastly attached to relatively classical and traditional standards. Despite this conservative choice, some of them have now become major classics, making a definitive mark on the 20th century with their house styles. The fruits of their long and patient search for quality are demonstrated in the 'Trinity ring' (made since 1924) in white, yellow and red gold, Cartier's 'cross-over' ring in Fig. 138 (made since 1936); Van Cleef & Arpels' 'mysterious setting', Boucheron's 'gold gadrooning' (used since 1988); Maboussin's 'Nadia' (made since 1983) and 'Olympus' lines (made since 1989);[2] and Chaumet's domed gold ring. With the advent of the invisible setting, it could be commented that 'since the mounting has almost completely disappeared' and 'there is no more than a tiny thread of metal on the outline of the piece, [with] only the stones appearing in all their radiance', ...'jewellery has now reached its ultimate stage of development?'[3]

137

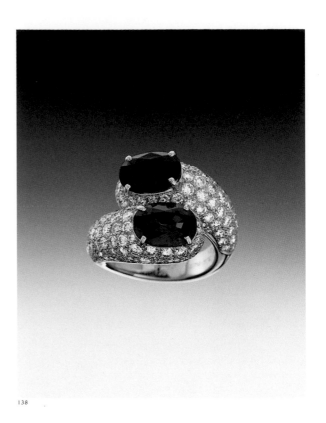

138

However, industrialisation enabled mass-production of rings, gradually and irrevocably depriving them of that privileged relationship between creator, object and recipient.

While gems may be part of the jewel for an ordinary jeweller, they become the centre of attraction for the designer of fine jewellery.[4] From antiquity through to the 14th–15th centuries, gemstones were polished to a greater or lesser degree and used in their original shapes or cabochon cut, before being cut over the following centuries into as many as fifty-six facets. The art of jewellery design could not have developed without the increasingly sophisticated techniques of gem-cutting, or without the supply of raw material from the more recently discovered mines in Brazil or South Africa. From the mid-1960s, other jewellers also set up shop, inaugurating different styles and themes and aiming at a different audience. Principal amongst them were: Fred (since 1936), the 'Force 10' boutique collection, which has been inspired since 1978 by the sea, with rings combining 18-carat gold with steel cables and nautical motifs; O.J. Perrin 'bamboo' rings in gold and semi-precious stones (produced since 1961); or the ever round and generous lines of Pomellato's cabochons (produced since 1957); but especially the uncluttered and open 'modern' gold lines of a pretty 'two-claw rubellite pear' by Poiray from 1994 (Figs. 139 & 137).

Mass-produced French rings include three sets from the house of Bellon (Figs. 140–142), which have gold on an impressive scale. Some of them bear semiprecious stones, such as amethyst, citrine, blue topaz and green tourmaline. Three other sets of rings, by Charles Perroud (Figs. 143–145), are finer, lighter pieces, of neo-classical or more modern inspiration.

140 BELLON *Gold and semi-precious stone rings (amethyst, citrine, blue topaz and green tourmaline).*

141 BELLON *Gold rings.*

142 BELLON *Gold and semi-precious stone rings (amethyst, citrine, blue topaz and green tourmaline).*

143

144

Metal and the many ways of processing it, in addition to the effect and combinations of multi-coloured materials, determine the focuses favoured by jewellers since antiquity. Today most rings with more conventional shapes, which have been omitted here because they are of lesser aesthetic and artistic interest, are manufactured on the production line. However, a few, more daring European industrialists are continuing to perpetuate more traditional working methods, combining their mass-production imperatives with efforts to create a hand-finished look and reflect aesthetic concerns. The most persuasive examples are: in France, Bellon (from 1907), Charles Perroud (since 1880), Caplain Saint André (since 1823) and A. Augis (since 1830); in Germany, Niessing (since 1873); in Spain, Octavio Sarda; and in Italy, Uno A. Erre (since 1926).[5]

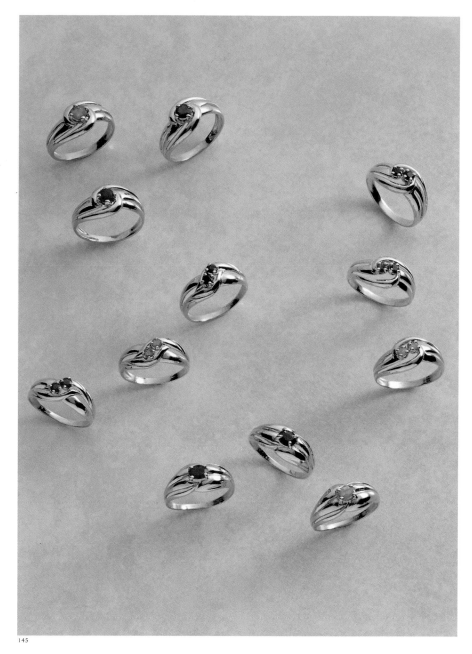

145

144 CHARLES PERROUD *Rings and precious stones (diamonds, rubies, sapphires and emeralds), neo-classical inspiration.*

145 CHARLES PERROUD *Rings and precious stones (diamonds, rubies, sapphires and emeralds).*

143 CHARLES PERROUD *Ring and earrings (gold and precious stones).*

146 CHARLES PERROUD *Machine dating from the early 1900s.*

Constraints:

The French Example

CREATION AND MANUFACTURING TECHNIQUES

The choice and purchase of precious stones constitute the first hurdle for a fine jewellery house. They are brought in to swell stocks or meet a specific order. Designs intended for such jewels are conscientiously submitted to a creative committee that decides whether or not the piece will be manufactured. Once selected, the head of the workshop does the costing on the basis of an approximate estimate of the work involved. After the costing is accepted, the design (always to scale) becomes a wax model so that the lapidary may work on the fit, the harmony of forms or colour match. Once all these parameters have been brought together, meticulously checked and perfectly mastered, the jewel is made. It must be as close to perfection as possible. In order to preserve the cohesion and unity of the combination of trades involved in making the jewel; the setters, polishers, specialists in guilloche and the casters, must work – as far as is possible – under the same roof.

Similar constraints affect mass-produced jewellery: from ideas, through conception, designs and models, to production. All these stages must be gone through before the metalworking techniques can be implemented. Using some European examples: gold, carefully worked in intaglio by Caplain Saint André, allowed this French company to introduce some element of craft-working into the mechanical production process of its jewellery. As the 'Iris' ring (Fig. 147) shows us, work on the subtle nuances of metals and the surface appearance of the metal are not just the result of sophisticated machinery and advanced technology developed by the German company Niessing, but the result of hand-finishing of irreproachable quality. Electroforming, where a film of 18-carat gold is placed on a mould and then dissolved, is the technique favoured by the Spanish firm Octavio Sarda and many French manufacturers. This technique is highly developed, making it possible to produce rings and jewellery of a substantially greater volume. Granulation, a technique dating from 3000 BC, which uses minute decorative gold beads, obtained by melting and splitting, has been magnificently brought in line with modern taste by Uno A. Erre in Italy.

As regards the creation of new models, it is important to note that all kinds of jewellery houses often call in designers or artists from outside the company. Where the artist transfers his rights, the design may be re-interpreted by the product manager or the director of the company.

ECONOMICS

The economic constraints that encompass design, production, marketing, distribution and resale costs mean relatively heavy investment for a company. This greatly influences company policy in the fields of both fine and mass-produced jewellery. Like *haute couture*, fine jewellery is concerned, above all, with maintaining its prestigious image. While continuing to design rings and jewellery intended for a privileged but increasingly rare élite, marketing constraints mean that fine jewellery houses have for many years been obliged to diversify their production into perfume, leather goods, pens and other products. In addition, they have developed less costly lines: such as Cartier's 'new jewellery' range, illustrated by a very beautiful 'bamboo' gold ring, with its very modern design (Figs. 148 & 149), the 'Two Ducks' and 'Vanessa' rings from the 'boutique' range of Van Cleef & Arpels (Figs. 150 & 151), or a 1971 gold and elephant hair ring from Boucheron (Fig. 152). These more affordable products do not harm the reputation of the house – quite the opposite. The effect of this commercial strategy is to maintain the luxury brand image intact at international level.

Industrialists, producing rings and jewellery by machine in their factories – in some cases with hand-finishing – display their wares at professional salons in order to seek new sales outlets. They are able thereby to distribute their wares using a commercial network of salespeople who can travel and visit clients. However, in commercial terms and in relation to other types of jewellery, rings made in small series involve problems of immediate availability. Such jewellery quickly loses the charm of the impulse buy when it does not fit comfortably. This means that however well-equipped the manufacturer may be, some delay is involved.

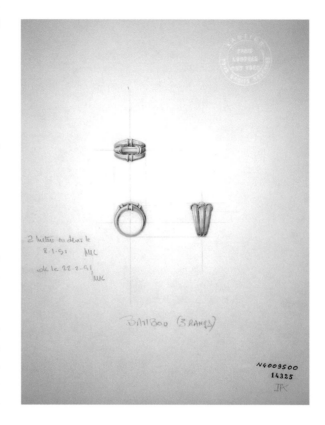

148 CARTIER *Design for 'Bamboo' ring.*

REGULATION

Another drastic constraint is regulation. Following on the sumptuary laws, which codified and regulated the wearing of rings and other jewellery in precious stones and metals over many centuries,[6] the French Revolution instituted new laws that are still in force today. In France, the 'law of the 19th Brumaire year VI' (instituted on 6th November 1797) organised all jewellers' and goldsmiths' work and trading. It obliged the two corporations to place a personal mark or stamp on each of their pieces (a diamond shape bearing initials), and then to have them checked at an assay office, in order that the latter might mark its own stamp on the pieces. Since 1838 the hallmark for gold has been an eagle's head, while since 1985 the hallmark for silver has been a small representation of Minerva.[7] This guaranteed that the gold was at least 18 carat.[8] Precious objects imported from abroad were

149 CARTIER *'Bamboo' ring, gold.*

also subject to similar controls, but these were much less strict.

The hallmarking on jewellery thus guaranteed a gold content that varied from country to country, while the jeweller's stamp indicated the origin. Denmark and Belgium enjoyed almost total freedom. As of 1993, European harmonisation was to alter the situation with regard to the guarantee of gold content, which could then go from 8 to 22 carats depending on the country. To continue to guarantee a degree of quality in gold, European professionals decided to bring these standards down to four (9, 14, 18 and 22 carats).

This raised many fears and questions as to the possible democratisation of jewellery, and the level at which the classification of gold should be set. The decision was that any jewellery containing at least 50% gold – or 12 carats – can be described as gold.

While this great debate about free competition in gold is primarily of concern to manufacturers, the consumer must also understand what they are purchasing.

Although the gold standard has not, since the first world war, been the undisputed mainstay of the economy, we can nevertheless see how gold still arouses strong passions and how great importance is attached to its trading. Professionals are aware that the purchase of jewellery in precious metal is rarely undertaken lightly and always reveals a certain ideal of consumption and a strong desire for social identity, with heavy symbolism involved in the choices made.

This is probably why almost a third of jewellery professionals have, since 1991, adopted the collective name Emagold. It is a quality label, which ensures that the gold assay mark (a sun) is visible, along with – in the case of French production – the maker's mark.

150 VAN CLEEF & ARPELS *'Two duck' ring, carved coral mounted on gold, brilliants and emeralds, 'Boutique' collection, 1987 (first created in 1970).*

151 VAN CLEEF & ARPELS *'Vanessa' ring, gold, rose-cut rubies, emeralds and brilliants, 'Boutique' collection, 1992.*

These industrialists thus continue to state the gold content clearly and, (in France), to indicate exactly where the jewellery has come from. At the other end of the production line, there is Engelhard-Clal – who are suppliers of raw material. This company, associated with the Emagold tendency, is now the world leader in refining and processing precious metals. For more than a century, Engelhard-Clal have been known and acknowledged for their metallurgical activities and as suppliers of precious metals. They merged in 1995. Engelhard-Clal has diversified its field of operation to include aeronautics, aerospace and various industries, and also manufactures semi-finished products for the jewellery sector; ready to be personalised by jewellers.[9]

As regards to precious stones, De Beers continues to dominate the diamond industry despite everything.[10] They have operated many mines, especially in South Africa, for almost a century. It also controls the various stages in processing and sale, thus ensuring a virtual commercial and economic monopoly on this rare stone.

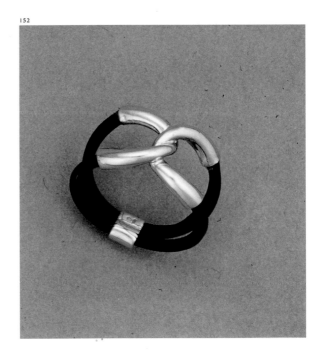

152 BOUCHERON *Gold and elephant hair ring, 1971*

Consequences & strategies

These constraints produce a number of consequences. On the positive side, the French state's strict controls ensure a high level of quality in the materials used for the national market. This also gives exports a great reputation for quality and reliability, even though Italy still has by far the largest jewellery turnover in Europe. More generally, consumers who like reliable references remain relatively well-protected by French quality. In addition, the efficient teamwork and skills of each of the leading jewellery houses provide a guarantee of efficacy at all levels. The internal design office means that new models can be worked out, or designs from external designers can be re-interpreted in accordance with specifications. Training in the art of jewellery – always of very good quality and provided either by direct apprenticeship, or at technical schools or private colleges – stands as guarantor for the safe transmission of the skills and traditions of the craft, as well as the quality of the work. On the negative side, this excessive state control and especially the lack of artistic training are the effects and limitations of a system that is guided by economic constraints rather than by genuine sensitivity.

For fifteen years, certain makers of jewellery have been trying to escape this stifling atmosphere: Jean Dinh Van, François Paultre, François Hérail, André Bénitah, Claude Benamosi, Thérèse Sudre, Patrice Fabre, David Vangelder and Xavier Pénichot are the best representatives of this movement in France. This also includes Maria Joao Bahia in Portugal and Ilias Lalaounis in Greece. They design, create and manufacture their jewellery in their own workshops and distribute their jewellery directly – either in their own boutiques or by taking part in professional salons. They embody a kind of 'ready-to-wear' tendency in jewellery. Starting from an idea, they work with and explore all the possibilities this offers in a masterly fashion.

Figs. 154 & 155 show the extreme sobriety and balance of Jean Dinh Van's rings: in both cases gold and precious stone cabochon rings. There was also his famous 'two pearl' ring made for Pierre Cardin, which had already greatly impressed the world of jewellery with its innovative design in 1967. This designer, who trained at Cartier's between 1945 and 1958, opened his own workshop in 1965. André Bénitah prefers to use resin for his rings – always round and sensual as in Fig. 157 – which he may or may not mix with gold and fine stones. Thérèse Sudre uses coloured titanium in a surprising manner – Fig. 156 shows a ring in gold, pear-shaped diamond and blue titanium.

Maria Joao Bahia believes that rings should transport the memory of the wearer: seen as a symbolic link between God and Man, the objects in Figs. 166–169, with their soft, rounded gold structures and volumes are made to echo the semi-precious or precious stones used. She sees jewels as resonating with the dreams and luxury of an aristocratic past – both hers, as she is a countess, and that of her country.

Ilias Lalaounis seeks his inspiration more directly in the historical, mythological and artistic memory of the entire Mediterranean basin. Produced in 1957, the very beautiful ring in Fig. 164, in granulated gold and sodalite, referred to the Hellenistic motif (Hercules' knot).

The 1975 group in Fig. 165 shows a Byzantine stamp. In 1994, Ilias Lalaounis inaugurated his own museum in his native town, Athens, where the most representative pieces from his thirty-five years of creation are exhibited.

Despite what is said to be a difficult economic situation,[11] these rings, with their more original designs, now find a genuine rationale, reinforcing the importance of individual style. They seem to come closer to those for whom they are intended, and take on a determinedly aesthetic meaning.

Communication and dynamism seem to be the main assets deployed by some European industrialists, who are keen to demonstrate their determination with regard to jewellery revival. My own 'evolutionary' rings, in 18-carat gold and using four interchangeable colours, have been produced since 1990. These double-reeded rings, in which the metal hoop and the

154 JEAN DINH VAN *22-carat gold and precious stone cabochon ring (ruby).*

155 JEAN DINH VAN *22-carat gold and precious stone cabochon rings (sapphire and emerald).*

155

156

156 THERESE SUDRE *Gold, blue titanium and pear-shaped diamond ring.*

157 ANDRE BENITAH *Rings in gold, resin and semi-precious stones.*

157

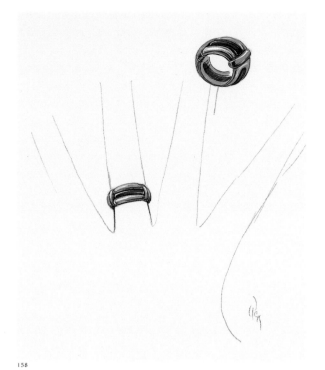

158

159

160

161

159 SYLVIE LAMBERT
*'Evolutionary' rings in
18-carat gold with stones
(black onyx, green agate,
blue agate and cornelian).*

158 SYLVIE LAMBERT
*Design for 'evolutionary'
ring.*

161 CHARLES PERROUD
Gold and diamond ring.

160 CHARLES PERROUD
Hammered gold ring.

four adjustable stones are inserted, are sold in a lipstick tube. (Figs. 158 & 159.)

Charles Perroud, for his part, has decided to open up his designer workshop to younger talents coming out of art and design schools. He is fully aware that this will revive and update his style, as shown by the gold ring in Fig. 161, with its very refined lines in which the split hoop reveals a glimpse of the diamond. The ultra-sophisticated mechanisation of this venerable jewellery house means it can combine new technology with traditional skills. Fig. 160, in hammered gold, perfectly illustrates this successful understanding between past and present. A. Augis has also preferred to opt for wider communication in order to promote his very symbolic jewellery.[12]

In Paris, the three-yearly contemporary jewellery fairs held since 1987 under the direction of Jean-Yves Le Mignot play an important role. In seeking to bring together two radically opposed worlds – industrialists and artists – they have openly stimulated jewellery design in the relatively 'closed' environment of industry. It is also in this connection that the Milan-based World Gold Council of Europe – seeking to give an even greater boost to creativity in ring and jewellery design – has been drawing up and publishing a Register of Trends every two years for the last ten years.

The World Gold Council is an international association of the mining companies from the main gold-producing countries in the world. In association with professionals, its jewellery division aims to boost gold consumption in the form of jewellery. As in the field of fashion and as its name indicates, this Register of Trends is responsible for bringing out fashion themes and tendencies in advance and anticipating future consumer needs. It is then made available to professionals and others who use it to predict tomorrow's fashions.

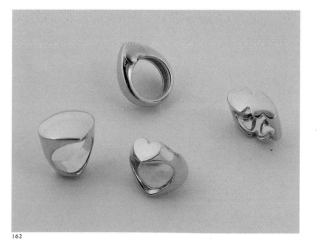

162

163

162 BELLON *Gold 'Heart'
rings, made in co-operation
with Florence Lehmann.*

163 BELLON *Gold 'Heart' ring,
made in co-operation with
Florence Lehmann.*

As in fashion design, a style bureau is set up for a few weeks in order to determine the strong trends for the coming seasons. Made up of designers and jewellers from various countries with different approaches, its great capacities for anticipation enable professionals to prepare fashionable jewellery collections in the spirit of the time. More concretely, these 'trend explorers' suggest formally and semantically relevant jewellery lines, worked out on the basis of general influences. Unlike what happens in the world of fashion, they cannot be reduced to the status of style advisers, but should be considered as real artists. They design and produce their own jewellery and devote themselves exclusively to their creations. They see jewellery as a means of expression. Key names here are Giampaolo Babetto and Paola Valentini (artistic directors of the Register of Trends in 1994/95 and 1996/97 respectively), Giorgio Cechetto from Italy, Jacqueline Mina from the UK, and Florence Lehmann and Cathy Specht from France.

Far from dictating new jewellery collections in an irrevocable and uniform manner, this profusion of ideas has the advantage of exploring various possible ways of playing on the many different aspirations of today's consumers. 'Balance and harmony', 'symbol and identity' and 'spirituality and nature', for example, were the three main themes brought out by the 1996/97 Register of Trends. Thanks to this invaluable working tool, certain jewellery manufacturers have been engaged in revising jewellery design for some years now. As far as rings are concerned, Bellon has contributed towards its substantial remodelling.

Since 1990, he has been working with a young artist-jeweller, Florence Lehmann, who is much attached to this particular item of adornment. Together they have come up with some very pretty pieces to be worn on the index or little finger, as in Figs. 162 & 163, and have steadfastly developed innovative designs.

164

164 ILIAS LALAOUNIS *Granulated gold and sodalite ring, 1957.*

165 ILIAS LALAOUNIS *Gold rings set with precious stones, 1975.*

168 MARIA JOAO BAHIA
Gold and diamond ring. Photograph by Homen Cardoso.

166 MARIA JOAO BAHIA
Gold, diamond and stone ring. Photograph by Homen Cardoso.

167, 169 MARIA JOAO BAHIA
Rings by the same jeweller.

166
167
168
169

165

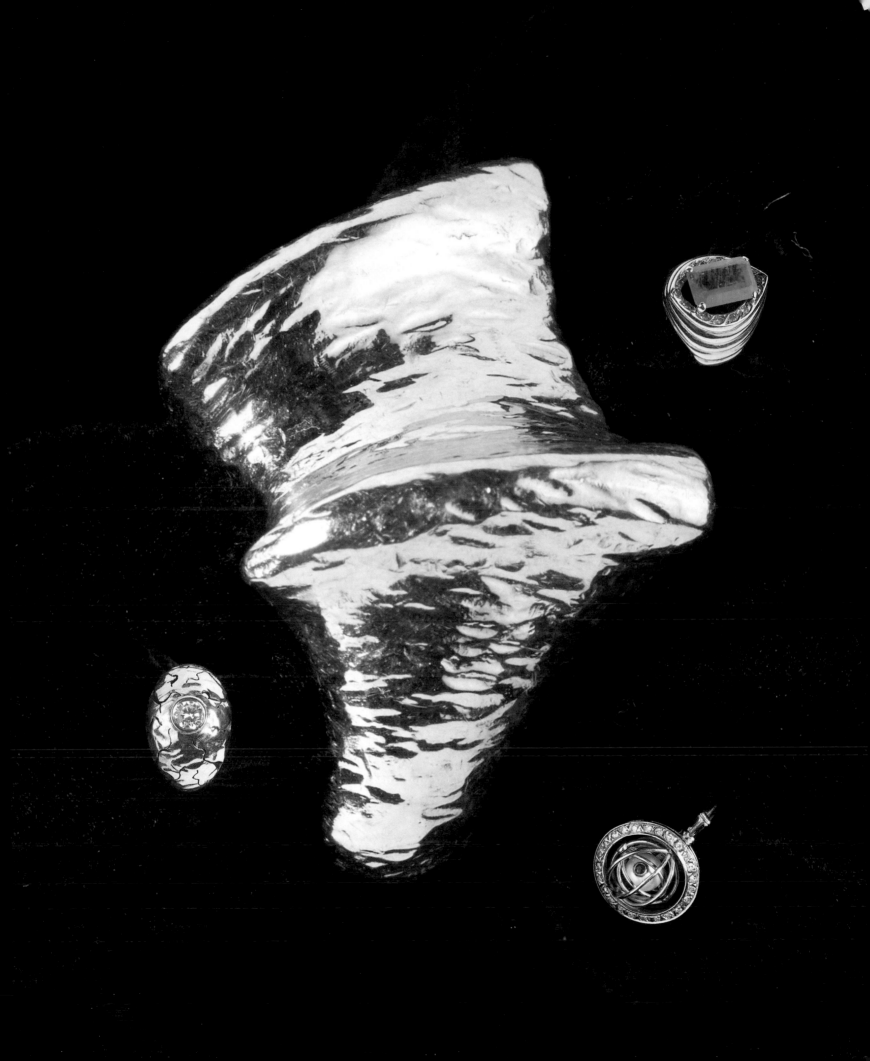

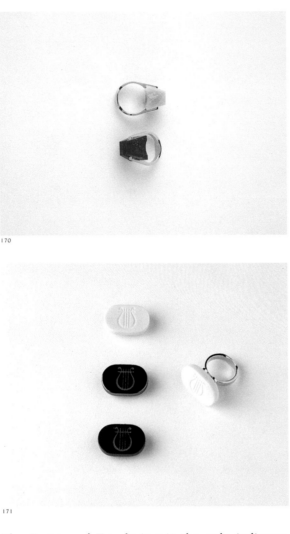

170

171

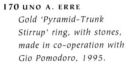

170 UNO A. ERRE
Gold 'Pyramid-Trunk Stirrup' ring, with stones, made in co-operation with Gio Pomodoro, 1995.

171 UNO A. ERRE
Gold 'Apollo' ring, with stones (haematite, sanguine and white agate), made in co-operation with Gio Pomodoro, 1995.

The Register of Trends is not the only indicator. Buying a ring represents a relatively large outlay and the object must not only embody a style, but also last through time. The production of a few very dynamic European manufacturers has thus leant towards aesthetic and artistic symbiosis. For example, Uno A. Erre, while remaining attached to the technical (specifically granulation) and cultural (particularly Etruscan) legacy of its country,[13] has quite logically co-operated with Gio Pomodoro, the famous Italian sculptor. Between 1991 and 1995, the artist and manufacturer together worked on a few very original series or models of rings, with simple, pure forms and explicitly archaeological and mythological references. For the 'sphere stirrup', 'pyramid-trunk stirrup' and 'Apollo' rings, the lost wax technique was used and the interchangeable stones (turquoise, lapis lazuli, jade and white agate), have been engraved with technological precision.[14] (See Figs. 153, 170 & 171.)

The co-operation of a manufacturer and an artist is a very real phenomenon. The few examples are quite

judicious and successful. They demonstrate the firm desire of this very closed sector of jewellery designers – and, more precisely, a few daring manufacturers – to seek a more personal way, creating an image of quality and efficiency. Thus, creative talent and industry have been trying to come together in France since 1987. This is a positive consequence of the three-yearly fairs, as well as of many travelling and themed exhibitions organised jointly with – and supported by – the World Gold Council.

It is this philosophy combining art and technique that the German firm, Niessing, has been developing since the end of the 1970s. Already highly specialised in the manufacture of wedding and engagement rings, this industrial firm adopted the innovative approach of co-operating with artist-jewellers to design rings produced in limited editions. Norbert Muerrle, Walter Wittek and especially Friedrich Becker, design rings with very daring lines that are simple, purified and elementary, and using techniques – for example, different alloys, in particular using platinum in a new way, with effects produced by shading and texture.

Since 1981, Niessing has developed the concept of the 'tension ring' as can be seen in Figs. 173 & 174: one in platinum with a synthetic blue stone and the other, more classic, in 18-carat gold with a diamond. Both of the hoops here are round in section but they can be of differing widths and degrees of elaboration. This concept of a wedding ring designed by Ursula Exner (daughter of Frantz Niessing) and Walter Wittek has a modern design that reduces the form to its function. As proof of its success, this process – although it has been registered and protected by Niessing – is nowadays much copied.

Figs. 172 & 175 show 'architectural' rings in gold and platinum which illustrate this attachment to sober design: here the line, colour and treatment of the metal in the two rings, which could be described as 'masculine' and 'feminine', take on a symbolic dimension. It is possible to see to what extent this manufacturer still remains much attached to working metal: distorting, compressing, pressing and stretching it, seeking all the possible shades, from red to grey. Niessing has been working with an outstanding integrated design office since 1986, proving once again its characteristic dynamism and efficiency.

However, this avant-garde approach remains isolated in Europe. It is true that the bourgeoisie in Germany had by the 19th century already imposed the values of hard work and commercial efficiency, taking advantage of the most recent technology. Then, from the 1920s, the analysis of modernity stripped of decorative trim shown in the work of the Bauhaus, followed by functionalism, as shown in the work of the Ulm School, sought to bring out the truth and rigour of the object. Niessing is thus the talented heir of Germany's aesthetic and cultural tradition, proving that an effective and very personal guiding concept is a measure of temperament and success.

Other than these examples which are not representative of those most commonly purchased, the design of the great majority of mass-produced rings is not very innovative.

Recent consumer surveys conducted by the World Gold Council[15] show that whereas rings remain by far the most popular item of jewellery, the most common models are the 'half reed' (a fine, rounded ring), the domed wedding ring (with a broad, domed body) and the flat (or ribbon) wedding ring. These models of rings could not be more classic or traditional. It should be pointed out that 80% of sales of gold rings involve relatively low-cost items (between about £80 and £150). This paradoxical attitude continues to characterise our entire current society and culture: the ring is both an object with very strong resonance or symbolic and mythological appeal, and yet can also be an easily purchased, ordinary, almost 'soulless' one.

The very high price of fine jewellery rings is an obvious selection criterion, thereby perpetuating inaccessible but necessary luxury and desire. As Philippe Perot writes: 'Luxury, [is] an object of desire above all,

and inseparable from the social relationships that give it shape: it is always, despite changing modalities, what others are not to have'.[16] Price alone is not a satisfactory excuse for the preference of the majority for these rings with their classic lines. These objects have certainly become less exclusive thanks to the marvels of technical and industrial progress. Yet they may be seen as 'copies' or 'imitations', standardising unattainable luxury.[17] By going back to the 'handmade' jewellery approach, the industrialists are trying to fight against this uniformity. They are endeavouring to introduce a degree of creativity, proving that, even in this field, money does not direct everything.

Jewellery is, in essence, a way of marking oneself out. But there are also other rings of accessible 'luxury', in different shapes, designed certainly with precious stones and metals, but also with other materials and other techniques, which convey perhaps

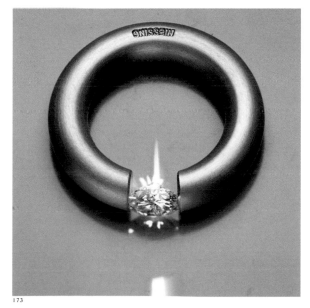

174 NIESSING *'Tension' ring, platinum and synthetic blue stone.*

173 NIESSING *'Tension' ring, 18-carat gold and diamond.*

172 NIESSING *'Architecture' ring, gold and platinum.*

even more emotion. Whether one-off pieces, or produced in limited editions or to order – designed and made by a single person – they are today real reference points, more in keeping with the function and meaning of this small jewel. They fit in with a genuine aesthetic and artistic approach and contribute towards a technical, formal, functional and semantic progress in the history of the ring.

Notes

[1] Costume jewellery or fashion accessories are not covered in this. See Jane Mulvach, *Fantaisies. Les bijoux chic et choc*, Chêne, Paris, 1989 and the joint work, *L'art du bijou*, Flammarion, Paris, 1992.

[2] Sylvie de Chirée, 'Commedia dell'arte chez Mauboussin', in *Bijou*, no. 2, summer 1992, p.18.

[3] Eveline Possémé, *Bijouterie. Joaillerie*, Massin, Paris, 1996, p.76.

[4] The following technical sources were used for this section:
   Jacques Lenfant, *Bijouterie-Joaillerie*, Chêne, Paris, 1979.
   Catalogue, *Les arts du métal*, Bibliothèque Forney, Paris, 1976-1977.
   Evelyne Possémé, *Bijouterie. Joaillerie*, Massin, Paris, 1996.
   Claudette Joannis, 'Les bijoux s'observent', in *Les bijoux des régions de France*, Flammarion, Paris, 1992, pp.106-125.
   'Techniques et matériaux', in *L'art du Bijou*, Flammarian, Paris, 1992, pp.369-400.
   Jacques Arax, *Le guide pratique des bijoux et des pierres précieuses*, Sand, Paris, 1988.
   Robert Maillard (ed.), *Le diamant, mythe magie et réalité*, Flammarion, Paris, 1979.

[5] Gori and Zucchi, *Sessanta anni di arte orafa*, Grifo, Montepulciano, 1986.

[6] Philippe Perrot, *Les dessus et les dessous de la bourgeoisie*, Fayard, Paris, 1981.

[7] Fédération Française BJOC, *Bijoux de France. La garantie française*, Azur, Paris and Jean-Louis Lemarchand, 'La guerre des carats', in *Bijou*, No.1, spring 1992, p.13.

[8] The carat is the unit of measure for gold: it is the universal standard and also refers to the fine gold content of an alloy, divided into twenty-four parts or carats. Twenty-four carats therefore represent pure gold: fragile and delicate to manipulate and fashion, it is not much used in this state in jewellery. An 18-carat jewel contains eighteen parts of gold out of twenty-four, namely 75% of fine gold. The term 750 thousandths (0.750) is also used. Although 24 carats may represent the finest of the fine in gold, 18-carat gold has maximum resilience and malleability, ideal for making jewellery. This is also the standard that the French state has guaranteed since the time of Napoleon.

[9] Françoise-Claire Prodhon, 'Engelhard-Clal: le conseil et l'assistance technique au service du plus grand monde', in *Bijoux, montres & vous*, May/June/July 1996, pp.16-17.

[10] Marc Roche, 'La bataille du diamant' in *Le point*, 4 January 1997, No.1268, pp.50-57.

[11] Françoise-Claire Prodhon, 'Création et marché', in *Bijoux, montres & vous*, February/March/April 1996, pp.22-23.

[12] Françoise-Claire Prodhon, 'Des profils différents...' in *Bijoux, montres & vous*, February/March/April 1996, pp.18-19.

[13] Gori and Zuchi, *Sessanta anni di arte orafa*, Grifo, Montepulciano, 1986.

[14] Giuliano Centrodi et al., *Gio Pomodoro. Ornamenti 1954-1996*, Artificio, Florence, 1996.

[15] *L'or et les bijoux*, World Gold Council, 1994–1997,

[16] Philippe Perrot, *Le luxe, une richesse entre faste et confort, XVIII-XIX ème siècle*, Seuil, Paris, 1995, p. 33.

[17] Ibid., pp.126-127.

175 NIESSING *Gold and platinum rings.*

3

Modern and
Contemporary Rings

The modern ring: first-generation designers of the 1960s

The difficult post-war years were followed by a much more optimistic and prosperous period. The rapid expansion of modern technology continued to bring down manufacturing costs. In contrast to the Arts and Crafts and Bauhaus movements – which sought to reach the masses, without necessarily being visually pleasing – American design stressed smooth, aerodynamic and seductive presentation. Backed by a great deal of advertising, it stimulated the desire to possess the material goods increasingly available to users: television sets, refrigerators, washing machines and other products were now accessible to everyone.

The phenomenal implications of people's changing attitudes towards objects was reflected in the ironic, sometimes bantering, artistic response of Pop Art. Andy Warhol, Lichtenstein and Oldenburg, for example, made abundant use of the new images from advertising, TV and cartoons, and objects, challenging the existing artistic boundaries. These mainly American artists strove to have everyday consumer goods considered as works of art. This tendency to bring art down to the level of daily life, which had already been seen in the 1950s, was simply becoming more refined and accentuated, even if that made it almost subversive.

The New Realists, such as Christo, César and Arman, also took as their starting point the relationship each individual can have with the objects, product and waste of the consumer society. Without hierarchy or aesthetic harmony, this reflected a new image of man and his environment.

In addition, the new opportunities for young artists to acquire training and skills were also to bring about significant changes. The education gained led young men and women towards artistic as well as social and political questioning. In the United States and in Europe too, there were many art schools whose artistic curriculae included courses in goldsmithing and jewellery-making; a field of instruction that had hitherto been traditional and ultra-specialised. Under the guidance of highly-motivated and determined teachers, these young students could then bridge the gap between the various arts: they were able to discover and fully exploit the formal and aesthetic potential offered by the field of jewellery. This very strong move back towards tradition and the new esteem for the craft of the jeweller, far from being traditionalist or protectionist, was to set the stage for the gradual development of a new concept of jewellery.

SCHOOLS AND FORMATIVE INFLUENCES

The geometric and analytical tendency

As a reaction to the hedonist, 'kitsch' design coming from America, Germany deliberately continued either in the philosophical vein of the Bauhaus,[2] Soviet Constructivism, or in the vein of 'objective' and social realism. This rationalist aesthetic – the close relationship between form and function – sought to unite art and science. It was widely preached by the Practical Aesthetics College in Ulm, which was set up by the Swiss Max Bill and operational from 1953 to 1968. This progressive school aimed to work in close co-operation with industrialists in creating objects of all types: it linked up architecture, the plastic arts and design.

It was within this educational and political sphere of influence based on social criticism that a specific type of teaching about jewellery and costume spread throughout Germany. Very active schools of art and advanced colleges came into being in Pforzheim, Munich and Halle – near Dresden.

This first generation of teachers and artists, all born between 1915 and 1930, was then very prolific and committed. Rheinhold Reiling (1922–83) and Klaus Ullrich (b. 1927), both of whom were great teachers and jewellers, taught at the Fachhochschule für Gestaltung in Pforzheim. With factories that had temporarily gone over to arms production during the Second World War, Pforzheim was again forging itself

a new image in terms of jewellery. Moreover, it was in that town in 1960 that the first museum of jewellery was opened. In the late 1990s it is still the only museum in the world that is entirely devoted to this form of artistic expression. The museum is headed by Fritz Falk, a fervent supporter of the art of jewellery, who organises exhibitions on an international scale.

Reiling and Ullrich were both traditionally trained: the former as an engraver and chaser, and the latter as a goldsmith and jeweller. Often using precious materials, Reiling and Ullrich developed a genuinely personal and novel body of work involving items of adornment. The formal structures and the combined pure materials and surfaces of their jewellery prove that they have been able to free themselves from the forms of tradition. The way the metal is treated, the interplay of levels and the assemblies of forms and elements are all ways for these two artists to look afresh at the work of the jeweller, and are techniques and forms which can be related to the approaches of abstract expressionism and Pop Art.

At the Munich Academy of Art, the figures of Frantz Rieckert and then Hermann Jünger (b. 1928) also dominated this generation. With much more graphic and, to some extent, more primitive work than Reiling or Ullrich, the gold, enamel and precious stone jewellery of Jünger seems to be drawing or painting in space and his symbolic objects seem to embody a gesture or trace. His unconventional influence, tending towards a very personal expression and interpretation of jewellery, was to encourage his pupils to work as far as possible within an individual aesthetic.

The former East Germany, represented by two women, Dorothea Prühl and Renate Heintze, was also developing a much colder art of jewellery at the Halle School of Art and Design. It was stripped as far as possible of colour and sensuality and based on silver, copper and brass. Their art, greatly influenced by Russian Constructivism, was also reactionary and feminist.

Friedrich Becker (b. 1922), who is also an outstanding and decisive figure in former East Germany, constructed part of his work around the single motif of the ring. Like Jean Desprès in the Art Deco period, his wide-ranging technical and aeronautical experience brought him to reflect on the expression of movement.

As in the examples in Figs. 177–179 & 181, his rings are made of steel and precious metals which always fit together very precisely. Harmonious in proportion, these rings were designed and made for their visual

177

178

177 FRIEDRICH BECKER
Gold, pink quartz and haematite ring, 1962.

178 FRIEDRICH BECKER
Gold and moonstone ring, 1956.

179

180

180 MARIO PINTON *White and yellow gold, diamond and ruby ring, 1976, private collection.*

181

181 FRIEDRICH BECKER *'Kinetic' ring for two fingers, stainless steel, 1981.*

179 FRIEDRICH BECKER *Stainless steel rings with corundums and spinels for one or two fingers, 1989.*

and kinetic effect and thus take account of the fact that they are placed on the finger and become part of the movements of their wearer. Their design is thus closely related to the Bauhaus philosophy, and the more contemporary philosophy of the Ulm School, but is also close to the kinetic research of Op Art. Using almost mathematical means, his rings seek to destabilise visual perception and to give the illusion of movement. The design of the ring is, here, steadfastly simplified, purified and made using a technique and laws inherent in the object itself; as if striving for a logical, but 'human' work.

The way that the form and visual and geometrical interplay are highlighted – as well as the freer use and treatment of the materials, such as casting, assembly or combinations of surfaces – gave German jewellery and rings of the 1960s an unconventional direction. All these centres of creation, which were very active in studying and creating jewellery, combined to restore the country's dominant artistic position. This very high-quality teaching continues to influence the younger generations of today.

During the 20th century, a very strong rigoristic tradition, close to the Bauhaus philosophy, has also developed in the Netherlands. From 1917, the De Stijl movement devoted itself to promoting, applying and transposing to the Hague, the pictorial, neo-plasticist and spiritualist thinking of Mondrian or Van der Leck. With its ideal of extending the abstract movement throughout the country, this tendency sought to attain harmony and universality to the detriment of individualism. It was thanks to Rietveld that neo-plasticism was to enter the field of decorative arts and jewellery design.

Furthermore, the Second World War had led Dutch architects, much influenced by the town-planning ideas of Berlage, Dudok or De Klerk, to rethink the construction and image of the nation. Holland was home to the diamond industry, but remained open by tradition towards foreign artistic influences. Artist-jewellers such as Riet Neevincz (b. 1925) or Chris Steenberg (b. 1920) were consequently able to design and make jewellery with modern forms and concepts. Neevincz used organic forms directly influenced by

182

183

184

ANELLO A FASCIA BATTUTA
gen. 4/10 o 2/10 doppia.
Ampiezza 12 mm.

Pin.
10.02.83.

ANELLO IN LAMINA SOTTILE (BATTUTA).
larghezza mm 10 - gen. 15/100-
Pin
ag.83.

struttura portante
per struttura
ossamentale.

186 MARIO PINTON *Ring designs.*

187 MARIO PINTON *Idem.*

185 MARIO PINTON *Idem.*

187

the solid-void issue raised in English sculpture, as in the work of Moore and Hepworth, whereas Steenberg was influenced by Constructivism in his metal assemblies and patterns echoing Gabo, Pevsner or Tatlin. These two jewellers thus opened the way for a second generation of artists, who became active as of 1965, especially the duo Emmy van Leersum (1930–84) and Gijs Bakker (b. 1942).

After traditional training as goldsmiths, these two artists, who were husband and wife, adopted a jewellery

188

188 MARIO PINTON *Gold and ruby ring, Museum für Kunst und Gewerbe Collection, Hamburg.*

183 MARIO PINTON *Gold and ruby ring, 1983, private collection.*

182 MARIO PINTON *Gold ring, 1988, private collection.*

184 MARIO PINTON *Gold and sapphire ring, 1988, private collection.*

aesthetic that was perhaps even more peremptory. With regard to the ring motif particularly, white gold and aluminium – both solid and malleable – enabled them to design and make objects with purified lines in grey and blue tints. However, far from being purely and strictly geometrical, these forms played especially on the suppleness and fluidity given by slightly domed or hollow surfaces and planes. These objects were intended to wed the finger; to appear to melt into it like a second skin.

This work involving the potential offered by cold matter and colour can be related to the issues raised in American minimal art over the same years. In their mutual desire to break definitively with a traditionalist conception of adornment, Leersum and Bakker studied the interrelationship and interdependence of such an object with the physical and real. The human body thus became an integral part of the jewel and was no longer reduced to merely being the peg on which it was hung. In exploring this issue, they subsequently worked on objects taking in the whole neck or the whole arm. 1966 and 1967 mark two important moments in their artistic itinerary: 'Sculpture to Wear' was a travelling exhibition which, moving from Amsterdam to London, provided an opportunity to stimulate the thinking of English artists and was the beginning of many exchanges and reciprocal influence between the Netherlands and Great Britain.

It does not therefore seem surprising that the Netherlands took such an avant-garde position. As further evidence of this, by 1969, a time when art was being challenged and redefined, the Stedelijk Museum in Amsterdam had the reliable reputation and all the perspicacity to pick out the emerging new trends. 'Of Losse Schroeven', organised by Wim Beeren, presented conceptual and minimalist work. It should be noted also that the Dutch public authorities have always been closely interested in creativity, encouraging many artists to settle and present their ideas.

Lyrical and spiritual tendencies

In Italy the work of goldsmiths and jewellers refering back to Cellini, Ghirlandaio, Mantegna, and Da Vinci immediately places jewellery design within a necessarily artistic national tradition and affiliation. The Pietro Selvatico Art Institute in Padua – initially a small, aristocratic, private arts and crafts school – had been training artists since 1826 before becoming a

well respected national arts school. However, when its courses on working and treating metal had become the mainstay of a renewed approach to jewellery, Mario Pinton (b. 1919) was encouraged to develop an entirely original and unique body of work. Following studies in Venice and Milan with the sculptor Marino Marini, this son of a chaser-engraver became a jeweller and a teacher who was to make a mark on students at that school over a period of thirty years. He was the sole instigator of what was to become known subsequently as the Padua School.

As in the 1950s, his rings – made with precious stones and metals – used simple, very supple forms. His pieces are always refined, sometimes figurative and may take their references from antiquity – refering back to Etruria and Egypt – as well as 14th-century Italian art. In this regard, Mario Pinton was not the only one to explore the resources of the past: Anton Frühauf, who was born in Germany in 1914 but chose to work in Italy, was also heavily influenced in his early days by Greek mythology, before developing a more abstract style. Even though the very beautiful 1976 ring in Fig. 180 shows us a metal structure in matching geometrical forms, it is a desire to use forms to render the essence of movement that predominate in the work of Mario Pinton. (See also Figs. 176 & 182–190.)

Along with the opening of a kinetic art school in Padua, Op Art set Mario Pinton along the road to movement and geometry in the 1960s. Thus, the issues that concerned him were in perfect symbiosis with an artistic concept which was rich in emulation and exchange, and led to circulation of ideas between various other countries. In the field of jewellery, this theory and approach to form through movement led him towards more elaborate volumes, planes and treatments of metal and its sparkle. Moreover, it also led him towards distinct interpretations, combinations and configurations, which always took into account the observer and wearer of the object.

It is interesting to compare here the rings of Friedrich Becker with those of Mario Pinton, since both of them were concerned with simplicity, precious stones and materials, and movement. However, one radicalises and analyses form in order to adapt it to its function, while the other coils and uncoils movement within the object itself. Becker moves away and becomes distant from the object, Pinton sees himself in it, revels in it and lives it from the inside. In order to express the same idea of 'modernity' and metaphysics,

189

190

189 MARIO PINTON *Gold and green tourmaline ring, 1955, private collection.*

190 MARIO PINTON *White gold and ruby ring, 1969, private collection.*

191 BRUNO MARTINAZZI
*Gold 'Narcissus' ring,
1994.*

192 BRUNO MARTINAZZI
Ring designs.

one seems to assert sincere faith in the expression and philosophy of technically and totally-mastered abstract and geometrical forms, while the other, considering technical limitations more as a means than an end in themselves, seems to be using them to move towards a kind of poetry of form. Neither of these two formal responses is better than the other, they simply show the aesthetic richness that can arise from the same initial desire to experiment.

Since the 1960s, the gold and silver rings of Bruno Martinazzi (see Figs. 191–198), have drawn direct inspiration from precise parts of the human body: belly, buttocks, eyes, mouths and fingers – namely those characteristic of human sensuality and perception. The very precise and recurrent reference to fingers – and by extension, the hand – implies a giving out and receiving of sensation. This may also symbolise the creative act or instant, and knowledge, invention and communication with other people.

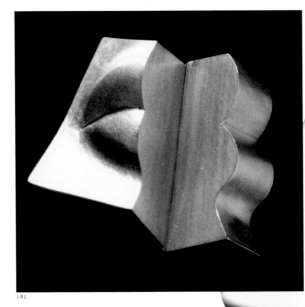

191

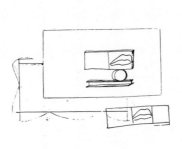

192

193

194

193, 194 BRUNO MARTINAZZI *'Venus' ring, back and front view, 1979.*

197

195

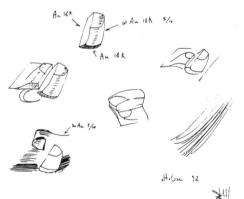

198

196

The entire work of this jeweller and sculptor (b. 1923) thus hinges around the human body in symbolic, sexual fragments. This very sensual work on living matter brings jewellery back to its primitive function, as it is in direct contact with a precise part of the human body.

The ring is no longer just an object which adorns a finger or the hand, it becomes part of the finger. Martinazzi tends to work through synecdoche (that is, a figure of speech in which a part is used to refer to the whole).

As in other countries, Italy had strong mutual influences and emulation between jewellers and artists: Giorgio de Chirico was making jewellery in Rome in his surrealistic, enigmatic style; Lucio Fontana was applying and developing his thinking about 'space matter' and monochromy in terms of jewellery; the rings and jewellery of Pol Bury are also, like his monumental pieces, based on simple forms seen in relation to movement; in Milan, the ring was, (as Figs. 199–204 demonstrate), in the hands of Arnaldo Pomodoro (b. 1926) and his brother Gio, a successful means of plastic and artistic expression.

198 BRUNO MARTINAZZI *'Echo' ring in 20-carat yellow gold and 18-carat white gold, 1994.*

197 BRUNO MARTINAZZI *Yellow gold and white gold ring, 1996.*

195 BRUNO MARTINAZZI *Ring designs.*

196 BRUNO MARTINAZZI *Ring designs.*

199 ARNALDO POMODORO
Ring with circle, white and red gold (1964 design), 1966. Photograph by Giorgio Boschetti.

201 ARNALDO POMODORO
Yellow, white and red gold and ruby ring (1964 design), 1966. Photograph by Vincenzo Pirozzi.

200 ARNALDO POMODORO
Red and white gold ring. Photograph by Vincenzo Pirozzi.

202 ARNALDO POMODORO
Ring design, 1965. Photograph by Gianfranco Gorgoni.

203 ARNALDO POMODORO
Ring design, 1968. Photograph by Gianfranco Gorgoni.

204 ARNALDO POMODORO
Ring design, 1968. Photograph by Gianfranco Gorgoni.

199

200

201

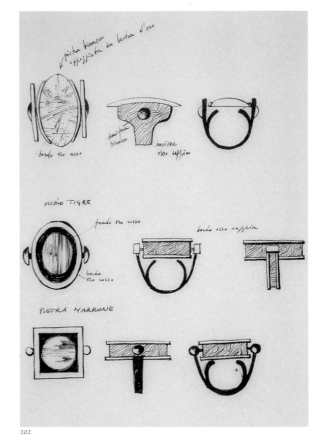
202

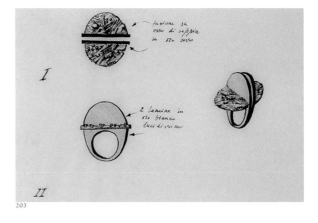
203

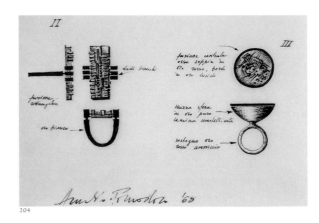
204

By means of these two aesthetic approaches – Mario Pinton's purity of line and Bruno Martinazzi's rhetoric – rings opened the way, in Italy, for other typologies and symbolism that existed elsewhere in Europe, and especially in the United Kingdom.

The craft revival in post-war Europe, which took a 'popular' form in the UK, was also a marked tendency in the 1960s. This movement was rooted in the whole tradition of arts and crafts specific to that country which had developed since the end of the 19th century. This 'handmade' philosophy, as opposed to cold, mechanical execution, continued to react against the products and objects of industry, finding perfect application in jewellery. This phenomenon also fits in more generally with the revival of interest in Indian, African or South American cultures, and jewellery whose symbolism and magic fascinated that entire generation of artists.

The 1958 ring in Fig. 205 by Alan Davie (b. 1928), made entirely of silver, comprises a broad flat hoop topped with a sphere of approximately the same diameter, on which three elements of rectangular and convex shapes seem to sit, along with a long curved stalk. Three pairs of small silver pearls arranged one beneath the other also decorate the object and give it a figurative character. Placed on a similar series of small silver balls – which act as a stand when it is not being worn – this ring almost takes on the nature of a neo-primitivist idol.

In order to revive jewellery creation within that artistic and symbolic tradition, painters like Alan Davie (himself a great admirer of the work of pre-Columbian goldsmiths) came to teach at the jewellery section of the Central School of Art and Design in London. At the beginning of the 1960s, one of his pupils, Gerda Flöckinger (b. 1927), who had then been living in the UK since 1938, was one of the very first artists of this generation to follow him along this road and to consider jewellery as a genuine form of artistic expression.

Using fine, delicate assemblies of gold or silver structures, accompanied by fine stones that she cut and polished herself, she has been taking a new look at rings since 1953 in accordance with very individual mythology and artistic influences. Her frequently offset stones, often cabochons without claws, are mounted on broad metal structures. Their overall form, the deliberate irregularity in execution, dimensions and polychromy, as well as implicit symbolism, are reminiscent of rings from the Middle Ages and the East. She taught jewellery at the Hornsey College of Art in London between 1962 and 1968, and she was the first woman to exhibit at the Victoria and Albert Museum in London in 1971. (See Figs. 206–214.)

This symbolistic and primitivist English tendency is far from the exotic attitude characteristic of the early part of the century towards non-Western art. It should instead, be related to the rediscovery of so-called 'popular' art, initially defined by the Frenchman, Jean Dubuffet, under the concept of 'Art Brut' (art in the raw state). Secondly, it was a reaction against British Pop Art, a movement convinced of the richness of pop culture, which was ephemeral, consumable (as in easily forgettable), sexy, crafty and seductive, to paraphrase the words of the pop artist Richard Hamilton in 1957.

IN SUMMARY

This presentation of so-called modern jewellers and rings thus shows two main graphic tendencies: the design being based on geometrical construction in one case and, in the other, on lyricism. These two

205

205 ALAN DAVIE *Silver ring surmounted by a stylised bird, 1958. Victoria & Albert Museum, London. Photographer: D.P.P. Naish.*

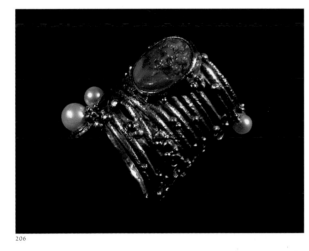

206

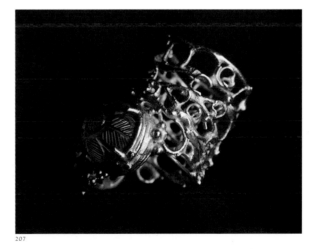

207

208

209

206 GERDA FLOCKINGER *Oxidised silver ring with coral cameo and pearls, 1975. Artist's collection.*

207 GERDA FLOCKINGER *Gold ring with carved citrine and pearl, 1969. Private collection.*

208 GERDA FLOCKINGER *Gold, amethyst and moonstone ring, 1970. Artist's collection.*

209 GERDA FLOCKINGER *Gold ring with pink and blue pearls, 1990. Artist's collection.*

aesthetic trends, however – far from being classifiable with certainty within one or other category – could also coexist. In the following years, with better distribution and knowledge of this 'new jewellery', the two aesthetic trends were to become organised less in accordance with national constraints than following individual lines of enquiry.

It is certainly true that, in order to be able to redefine an area of expression in which to work, jewellers in the early part of the century had already attempted to get away from the ultra-conventional framework in which rings had been trapped until the 19th century. Art Nouveau and the bi-polarities of Art Deco and the 1950s also aided this: although this was not without difficulty, since jewellery was not at the time either recognised or envisaged as a form of artistic expression.

Thus, in order to steer rings towards determinedly meaningful and relevant, 'modern' design, these artists had to find other fields of reference. 'Cultural' references could be based on contemporary discoveries, while retaining a certain idea of the present day, modernity and progress, while 'natural', more timeless, references could be sought in popular, primitive, archaic or mythological cultures.

This dialectic may, to some extent, be seen as an essential feature of the history of forms, swinging back and forth between 'classicism' and 'baroque', 'order' and 'disorder'. Reference can be made to the concept of the 'What is Modern Sculpture?' exhibition, as well as to the Nietzschean dialectic of tragedy, embodied by Apollo who represents light, wisdom, words and poetry on the one hand and, on the other, Dionysius who represents darkness, intoxication, instinct and music.[3]

In terms of the materials and techniques used, all these artists were to opt for the malleability and randomness that they offered. Although they varied in accordance with the great diversity of sources of inspiration: either abstract, moving forms intended to objectivise a construction of the mind, or more organic forms, with spiritual, universal and timeless dimensions.

American jewellery had been gaining its artistic independence from Europe as long ago as the 1940s; coming initially in a surrealistic and symbolic vein, as in the work of Margaret De Patta (1903–64), Sam Kamer (1913–63) and Arthur Smith (1917–82) and then in a more Pop Art, playful and subversive vein, the most representative artists being Arline Fisch

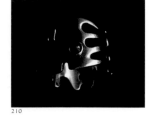

210

210 GERDA FLOCKINGER
Silver ring with cabochon amethyst, 1956.
Goldsmith's Hall Collection.

211 GERDA FLOCKINGER
Ring in silver, 18-carat gold and pearls, 1990.

212 GERDA FLOCKINGER
Ring designs.

213 GERDA FLOCKINGER
Ring designs.

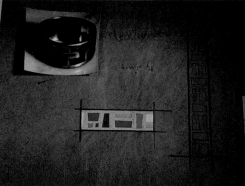

212

213

(b. 1931), Fred Woell (b. 1934) and Marjorie Schick (b. 1941). Often made using the technique of assembly from precious and scrap materials, American jewellery was thus approached and developed like a real physical sculpture. It deliberately opened jewellery up towards an enlarged, almost theatrical conception of adornment.

In this way, in the 1960s, breaking with the formal history of rings, modern European jewellers had two possible fields of plastic activity and expression. A brief cultural overview of this formal, stylistic phenomenon may demonstrate that this decisive change affected all forms of expression. It bore witness to a change in the behaviour of an entire society, with direct influence on the function of rings.

Echoing the anti-establishment youth of the 1960s, who no longer accepted immobile structures, garment designs were to develop a fashion with no reference to the past. They were democratic, liberated and unisex: with the mini-skirt, Courrèges launched an image of the young emancipated woman; Paco Rabanne created the first close-fitting garments using new materials; and Pierre Cardin designed a cosmonaut line and dresses with geometric decoration.[4] Alongside this original, futuristic style, more comfortable, 'natural' clothing was also developed for hippie clients. In this way, 'plurality followed centuries of uniformity... People began to choose their clothing no longer in accordance with the criteria of dominant fashion, but according to those dictated by the feeling of belonging to a particular political or social group'.[5] Women gained the most from this emancipation.

Since the 19th century, women had worn the jewels and been mainly responsible for seduction through dress. They were also able to make freer play of their bodies. In the 20th century, the ring then became a mark and a sign that was as much aesthetic as a vector of sexual seduction; for men, it became more a mark of distinction and identification.

214 GERDA FLOCKINGER
Silver ring with amber, 1983/4. Artist's collection.

It was thus on the basis of this radical development observed in the behaviour of the new society that artists and jewellers were able to think about rings in a different way: either by remaining receptive to progress in mind-sets and civilisation, or by escaping to another time with mythical and cosmological references. The 1960s were therefore, in the field of jewellery and fashion, a period of total innovation and creativity, marking the beginnings of manifest pluralism and individualism.

The modern ring: second-generation designers of the 1970s

The 1960s seem to have broadened the horizon for the following decades to a considerable extent, enabling the aesthetic and social changes to be echoed by new artistic aims and forms of plastic expression. The first generation of jewellery designers did, of course, continue to work, gaining maturity and passing on its teachings and influence to the following generations. The youngest of them were able, thanks to the now much more extensive and specific approaches and artistic training, to free themselves from the traditional conventions of form and function. An extraordinary diversity and plurality of themes and plastic responses were thus to dominate the 1970s at an international level. A new design environment surrounded rings.

EXHIBITIONS, GALLERIES AND MUSEUMS

The frantic growth characteristic of the 1960s was to give way to a rather more disturbed economic and world environment. However, paradoxically, it was during the early stages of the financial and oil crisis in 1974 that the number of museums, galleries, exhibitions and events connected with contemporary jewellery increased.

The appearance of independent galleries, free to exhibit and devote themselves to a personal view of contemporary jewellery, also dates from the 1970s. In Germany, this phenomenon followed in the train of the Pforzheim Schmuckmuseum. The Map Sauer Gallery was opened in Cologne in 1968, followed by Marie and Peter Hassenplug's gallery in Düsseldorf in 1969 and then, in 1981, the Spektrum Gallery of

Marianne Schliwinsky and Jürgen Eickhoff in Munich and Wilhem Mattar's gallery in Cologne. Germany had also reached the pinnacle of the artistic avant-garde: the 'Conception' and 'Prospect 69' exhibitions held in Leverkusen and Düsseldorf in 1969 were displaying minimal and conceptual art, Arte Povera, Process Art, Anti-Form and Land Art.

In England, a country with a tradition of arts and crafts that had always enjoyed public sponsorship, the same phenomenon could be seen: the Victoria and Albert Museum gathered a collection of contemporary jewellery and, in 1971, held an exhibition of Gerda Flöckinger's work. In the same year, the famous Electrum Gallery opened its doors, with a select programme of then relevant artists and exhibitions. In Holland, in 1976, the Râ Gallery in Amsterdam and New Images Gallery in The Hague were opened; the same happened in Vienna with the Am Graben Gallery and in Basle, the Atrium Gallery. Exhibitions were also held in New York, California and Australia. Most of these independent galleries, firmly committed to their aesthetic options and criteria, still exist today. They are proof of their founders' intuition and good understanding of contemporary jewellery. Some of the very first advocates were: Barbara Cartlidge and Ralph Turner in the United Kingdom, Paul Derrez, Louise Smit and Marzee in Holland, Graziella Grassetto in Italy, Marie Zisswiller, Claude Chéret, Ornella Gagliardi, Hélène Porée and Bruno Livrelli in France, Bernard François and Sophie Lachaert in Belgium, Veronika Schwarzinger and Léa Tudosze in Austria, Margarita Kirchner in Spain and Michèle Zeller in Switzerland.

Museums also played a decisive role during those years in the scene that was gradually being set and organised around jewellery: the Pforzheim Museum, the Victoria & Albert Museum and the Crafts Council in London, the Musée des Arts Décoratifs in Paris, the Kunstgewerbemuseum in Vienna, the Stedelijk Museum in Amsterdam, the Galleria Nazionale d'Arte Moderna in Rome, as well as the National Gallery of Victoria in Melbourne and the Museum of Art in New York. Contemporary jewellery thus gradually became internationalised: from then on it was shown and exhibited; it flattered and provoked.

It would be interesting here to draw briefly a parallel between the appearance of contemporary jewellery galleries and museums and the first modern art museums at the very beginning of the 20th century. With the exception of the Russians, it was in Germany that the very first museum collections were set up, purchasing and displaying contemporary art, even though the United States were the first really to popularise modern art. This simple comparison shows the role of museum institutions when a new form of art appears: purchasing, exhibiting, promoting and giving official approval. The responses and retorts of Dadaist artists like Picabia or Duchamp – whose deliberately provocative gestures and acts broke down, to a large extent, the concept of the work of art as something sacred or aesthetically pleasing – are well known. By declaring, in effect, that anything at all could become art and that anybody at all could be an artist, they challenged the artistic act, as well as the limits and powers of the institution and preservation of works of art. This touches on the interrelationship between art, politics and power.

The second-generation jewellery designers (all born between 1930 and 1950), reflecting in their turn on the possible value and function of rings or jewellery in the modern world, had to make their response bearing in mind this historical situation. Like painters and sculptors, these new jewellers were, above all, independent artists trying to make a living from their own creations.

This introduces a question about the real artistic or aesthetic status accorded to jewellery. Museums and institutions accord painting or sculpture from this period – which used this particular form of expression – the status of art; whereas, from the second half of the 20th century, jewellery, and rings posed a real problem of definition.

As its history shows, the ring has always come in many forms – relating to functions and fields as diverse as *haute couture*, fine jewellery, industry, crafts, entertainment and fashion accessories. Could it also be considered as a work of art? To decide that, one must establish what is a work of art and under what conditions or criteria does a given object take on that quality or find itself refused that high distinction?

This debate is tackled in the excellent essay by Jean-Marie Schaeffer.[6] He demonstrates that no final definition is really acceptable and that all those who pride themselves on having openly and indisputably classified artistic boundaries come up against a great deal of objection and historical ignorance. The example of Egyptian, African or Roman statuary shows that the magical, as well as aesthetic, value of these objects is undeniable. 'Recognising that commits us to taking the drama out of the issue of the frontiers of art: it has neither the cognitive interest nor the axiological importance too often accorded to it. The question of the "value" of various works does not refer to setting the boundaries of the artistic field, but to the analysis of the relationship between us and them.'[7]

The jewellers of the 1970s worked precisely on the emotional bond that the artist, jewel and recipient – the wearer or spectator – can mutually maintain, both visually and sensually. It is vital however, that the presentation of two aesthetics – cultural and natural – should be understood not in the sense of mutual opposition, but as an approach that can be addressed by the same artist, who may sometimes even go beyond it.

The geometric and analytical tendency

Germany, Austria, France and the Netherlands

While Friedrich Becker was continuing to refine his technical and analytical research into the movement that he saw as inherent to his rings, the Austrian Peter Skubic (b. 1935), who was then working and teaching in Germany, approached rings from an angle that he initially saw as fundamentally plastic – that is, considering them as architectural and 'autonomous' forms.[8] From 1969, he made some rings with geometric tendencies, which develop from a relatively impressive bezel or a very noticeable base. When they are not worn, the hollowed-out circular part then becomes

216 PETER SKUBIC
Gold 'split' ring, 1978.

217 PETER SKUBIC
Gold and synthetic ruby ring, no date.

216

217

In 1974, Peter Skubic organised 'Schmuck aus Stahl', a symposium on the use of non-precious metals, and particularly steel in jewellery. A militant, who considered that the intrinsic value of a ring is not determined on the basis of carats, he theorised that artist-jewellers should use and abuse this so-called 'non-noble' material. This great Austrian and Germanic jeweller attached as much importance to the exterior – the surface – as to the structures – or forms – which, according to him, are related to the working and treatment of the material. He also worked out mechanical links that enabled him to make jewellery without soldering. Although strongly committed to this great debate about materials, this jeweller nevertheless continued to use gold. (See Figs. 216–223.)

an integral part of the object, in which the void mocks the solid and vice versa. He worked out a system of fluting or grooves so that the object would remain well positioned on the finger, minimising discomfort.

His research was thus mainly based on inner feelings and physical tension. However, far from being strictly analytical, it was the intimate nature of the wearer's body that Peter Skubic sought to reach both its spiritual aura and its sensual side. Throughout this period, his rings – made of precious or other metals – thus took an abstract form with strong phallic connotations.

The beautiful ring in Fig. 217, with its Ionic capital, bearing a red synthetic stone, is rather 'post-modern' in appearance. Since 1991, Peter Skubic (who has been exhibiting since 1969) has developed his entire work around the concept 'the black hole is the inside of the ring of God'. After having tried in 1975 to implant a jewel under the skin, so that it would not be visible, in 1993 he created the 'stand for an invisible

222 PETER SKUBIC
  Granulated gold ring, 1970.

218 PETER SKUBIC
  Steel and synthetic ruby ring, 1975.

219 PETER SKUBIC
  Steel, chrome and nickel ring, 1976.

220 PETER SKUBIC
  Steel, chrome and nickel ring (7 position bezel), 1976.

223 PETER SKUBIC
  Gold and glass ring, 1989.

221 PETER SKUBIC
  Silver 'anamorphic souvenir' rings, 1971.

224

225 FRITZ MAIERHOFER *'His and Hers' rings in yellow and white gold, no date.*

224 FRITZ MAIERHOFER *'His and Hers' rings in yellow and white gold, no date.*

228 FRITZ MAIERHOFER *Gold and acrylic ring, 1971.*

227 FRITZ MAIERHOFER *Gold and silver ring, 1993.*

226 FRITZ MAIERHOFER *Gold 'Match Stick' ring with three diamonds, 1995.*

229 FRITZ MAIERHOFER *Gold and acrylic ring, 1972.*

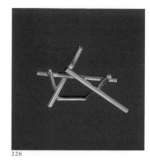

226

225

227

ring' – an immaterial, impalpable and elusive object. Since 1979, he has been a teacher and lecturer at many colleges and institutions.

With regard to the use of plastic materials in designer jewellery, 1971 had already been a year to remember, since the Electrum Gallery in London had held an important exhibition. For the first time, it showed the use and the formal and aesthetic potential of acrylics. The Austrian Fritz Maierhofer (b. 1941), along with two leading Germans, Gerd Rothmann and Claus Bury, were all concerned with the same issue and took part in this gathering of artist-jewellers.

The rings made by Fritz Maierhofer in 1971 and 1972 are all objects with coloured, contrasting visual effects. They are made up of geometric volumes that fit closely together and whose simple, smooth forms, surfaces and planes, together with the combination of apparently contradictory materials, clash and match at the same time. (See Figs. 228–229.)

Fritz Maierhofer also bases his work on the tension that his finished object must reflect, as according to him this is where the whole force and the very essence of a ring or jewel lie. When they are not being worn, his rings may rest on a stand aesthetically made for the purpose or they may, as in the examples, simply rest on their hoops. The ring must, therefore,

228

229

230 FRITZ MAIERHOFER
Gold wedding rings, 1995.

be understood and grasped as much as an object as as a jewel.

This great Austrian jeweller, who has been exhibiting since 1971, has worked more recently – in 1982 and 1995 – on very graphic rings. His 'His and Hers" rings' (see Figs. 224 & 225), split into two or three and, made of yellow and white gold, were designed to be assembled and actually form the shape of a house. In 1995, he also worked on the concept of the wedding ring: he has drawn on the Turkish belief according to which the husband and wife to be are said to glimpse the columns and stairways of the Holy Temple. Of the two complementary rings (see Fig. 230), one illustrates the fluting on a column in one case, while the other illustrates the downward spiral shape of the steps. Both of them embody that ritual and initiatory ascent or transformation that marriage may represent in Turkey. (See also Figs. 226 & 227.)

The Frenchman Henri Gargat (b. 1928) was a key figure in the 1970s, since he also seems to have addressed geometrical and analytical issues. His rings entitled 'Ephemeral' (1970) (Fig. 234), in which a bead of mercury circulates in the hollowed-out area of the bezel, 'Gimmel' (1971) (Fig. 232), 'Between two fingers' (1971) (See Fig. 231) and 'Swirl' (1972), in which the bezel turns endlessly on itself, are in fact 'hand ornaments' with very sober forms and volumes. They can be fitted together as in a game with moving adjustable pieces, in which industrial materials both contrast with and match each other – these include plastics, aluminium, steel, stainless steel and Perspex©. (See also Figs. 215 & 233.)

However, whereas Friedrich Becker analyses and abstracts movement and the illusion of movement, Henri Gargat deliberately endeavours to join them to the rhythms of the body. He conceives his rings as being in total osmosis with the person wearing them. At the slightest movement of the wrist, the volumes move around – pivoting, while the general form of the object becomes animated, adopts other facets and frees itself.

From 1957 onwards, following an entirely traditional training in jewellery-making, this artist was to work in this way. As an innovator quite unique at that time in France, Henri Gargat allowed himself to be guided by form, dared to try new lines, provoked movement and the illusion of movement, as well as using all types of materials, since he sought to achieve

231 HENRI GARGAT
'Between two fingers' ring in silver and moonstone, 1971. Photograph by Edouard Rousseau.

234 HENRI GARGAT
'Ephemeral' ring, gold and mercury, 1970. Photograph by Laurence Sackman.

233 HENRI GARGAT
Gold 'Spiral' ring, 1991, Musée des Arts Décoratifs, Paris. Photograph by L. Sully-Jaulmes.

232 HENRI GARGAT
'Gimmel' ring in steel and stainless steel, 1971. Musée des Arts Décoratifs, Paris. Photograph by L. Sully-Jaulmes.

bodily communication and communion through his objects. By increasing and refining his knowledge and research on optical and kinetic interplay, Henri Gargat attempted to redefine jewellery in his own way. This resulted in rings for two fingers, a ring worn between the fingers – experiments taking ever further forward his quest for form and matter in inter-relationship and inter-dependence with anatomy. For him, the ring is not an addition to the body, it is an integral part of it.

The German Claus Bury (b. 1946) who had taken part in the 1971 exhibition at the Electrum Gallery – another artist fiercely opposed to traditional jewellery – has worked on refined alloys of acrylics and precious metals. He constructs his jewellery by adding or fitting together planes and surfaces, or by means of assemblies and adjustments of units and volumes inspired by mechanics.

In 1974, on his return to the United States, he was much impressed by the American concept of jewellery and, more generally, of art, and decided to broaden his own sphere of activity. He began to conceptualise his work and focus on the actual process of creating his objects, aiming to detail as far as possible the production of his pieces from design to finished artefact. This analytical research into the act and action of creation was intended for exhibition, while the piece of jewellery was not complete unless worn.

In the case of Claus Bury, this approach and the artist's physical engagement with matter or materials became an anti-establishment stance, aiming to remove the sacred aura surrounding art. It paralleled the aversion of artists and most jewellers of that decade to the art market, to the notion of jewellery as an investment and, more generally, the whole system in which they felt themselves to be trapped. In order to get out of that dead end, Claus Bury was to plan his objects with a much more monumental perspective. From 1975, he began to experiment, like artists in the Land Art movement, with the interdependency between the jewel-sculpture, its placing and the space surrounding it.

Since the 1970s, the Swiss Otto Künzli (b. 1948), has also played an important role on the jewellery stage. He approaches materials and the function of the ring from a conceptual, ironic and subversive angle, criticising the consumer society, especially in the United States. An acknowledged great artist, still in the public eye and much studied, he is now a professor at the Munich Art Academy.

Gijs Bakker (b. 1942), is one of the very first jewellers to have conceptualised his work on the basis of non-precious materials. He also researched the relationship between the artist, jewel, wearer and spectator; a relationship that is both cognitive and artistic. In fact, after 1970, he continued to see his creations as a kind of social debate, thereby rejecting the power, status and value traditionally conveyed by the precious materials in a ring. Although heavily crit-

235 CLAUS BURY *Gold and acrylic ring, 1971, Schmuckmuseum, Pforzheim.*

icised within his own country, he may be credited with viewing various types of jewellery as a set of problems to be solved. With deliberately simplified – almost industrial – design, using materials that could also be non-precious, and characteristic dimensions that were close to the proportions of the parts of the human body (the phalanx, forearm, neck or chest), his jewellery develops against the body of the wearer – like a garment or protective screen, or a layer of skin ready to be sloughed off.

These two lines of research or aesthetic work emphasise firstly the phenomenology of perception and the visual effects produced and, secondly, the manner in which these appear to transform the body and the space where the phenomenon is found.

Taking this concept even further forward in 1973, Gijs Bakker made a bracelet of gold wire designed initially to be wound and tightened around the wrist. In a second phase, it was to be taken off, leaving only the imprint of the absent object, the only real embodiment of an invisible presence. By working in this way, the jeweller thus commits himself to 'dematerialising' the jewel, which is present through its absence. Like

236

237

240

239

238

238 ONNO BOEKHOUDT *Illustration for steel wire rings 1995.*
Photography by Harry de Boer.

237 ONNO BOEKHOUDT *Idem.*

239 ONNO BOEKHOUDT *Idem.*

236 ONNO BOEKHOUDT *Idem.*

240 ONNO BOEKHOUDT *Sketches for ring designs.*

the minimalist and conceptual artists of those years, Bakker worked with photographs as backing. Used as tools and not as an end in themselves, they were ultimate memories of the ephemeral transformation of a person by a jewel, and vice versa.

Was jewellery no more than an idea? Did the real object have less meaning than the approach, the concept and all those questions and attempted answers it may arouse? Was the artistic product, in fact, no more than a mere reminder or thought-provoking statement? In the Netherlands, this purist, formalist and militant movement against the traditional world of jewellery and the attitude of possession and power it primarily conveys was inevitably turning towards the gradual elimination of jewellery. This radical stance was, as might be expected, to provoke very strong contrary reactions. And, as a result of this, two opposing tendencies struggled to get away from this 'ideality' of jewellery.

It was this rationalist and minimalist aesthetics that the BOE ('Jewellers in Revolt') group was the first to oppose. Marion Herbst (b.1944), a founder member in 1973, and Onno Boekhoudt (b. 1944) saw jewellery from a much more formal perspective, in which design was again predominant. Onno Boekhoudt had already envisaged producing a variety of rings on the basis of simple, circular form, fashioned in silver. Each time a ring was made, only the surfaces were palpably modified; although almost imperceptibly. This deeper study of form, as well as work on the brushed, matt-surfaced metal, tended to give the small objects a remarkable presence.

More recent rings from 1995 (Figs. 236–239) prove that design remains the mainspring of research for this jeweller. Using several steel wires, bent and curved into many open and closed circles, Onno Boekhoudt makes rings which contain references to the human form – the head, hand and foot, for example. These fine, elegant pieces with their elementary design seem to occupy and create volumes, as well as to circumscribe and open up space. The drawings and graphic research leading to the pure forms of this artist seem to suggest the desire to rewrite the story of jewellery. (See also Figs. 240.)

Robert Smit (b.1941) is solely responsible for the second line of research in the Dutch debate. A ring from 1970 (Fig. 241) fits in with an abstract analytical aesthetic: the broad, rectangular bezel, here in slightly shaded pink Plexiglas®, offers a glimpse of a repetitive series of figures probably produced by computer. On this very smooth, shiny surface or plane, a few beads of gold stand out. Everything seems to be leaning or resting on a white gold hoop, again tinted with pink acrylic.

The artistic work of this great jeweller must, therefore, be placed within that context of reaction and protest against a traditional aesthetic of jewellery. Attracted mainly by the technical, pictorial and visual potential of gold, Robert Smit envisages his jewellery like drawings and paintings, as he is also a painter. Following this experimental period after 1975, he made his mark on and explored what might be called a more 'natural' or 'spiritual' aesthetic. He set himself explicitly to work gold like paper; painting, bending, folding up, assembling, intermingling and weaving it.

241 ROBERT SMIT *Untitled ring, white gold and Plexiglas®, 1970.*

He then manipulated the form and design of his pieces, playing on their proportions. His jewellery is as much a search for – and an interplay of – rhythms and gestural, coloured harmonics, as an in depth investigation into the properties and powers of the yellow metal.

Since the 1970s Robert Smit has questioned the concept and limits of jewellery – its material, form and function. He is convinced that jewellery goes far beyond its ornamental function, since it can, according to him, also exist in the plastic and aesthetic sense as 'autonomous' art and thus go far beyond a simple connection with the body. Robert Smit approaches jewellery as a painter and almost an alchemist.

In this debate, the United Kingdom was to play a remarkable role; finding completely original artistic and aesthetic solutions or proposals from its own unique references and resources. It should be noted that the many exchanges that took place then between the Netherlands, the United Kingdom and Germany in particular, thus dynamised and revived the whole creative scene.

United Kingdom

The twenty or so rings made at the very beginning of his career by the British jeweller David Watkins (b.1940) are probably his only ventures into this specific field of jewellery. They are all, with the exception of a few details, composed from the same basic structure: tall, elongated elements, sometimes bearing precious or semi-precious stones, and all develop from a broad, flat, metal hoop in gold or silver. These rings are airy, while still conveying an impression of stability. They function like small sculptures, but are also designed to react to the curves of the body. As in the case of most pieces made by this jeweller, they can be sketched out with the aid of a computer and finished by hand. They make up a perfectly coherent experimental whole, as do his necklaces.

The work of David Watkins cannot be ignored in the world of contemporary jewellery and does not fit in with the Arts and Crafts tradition of his country. After studying sculpture, this jeweller – who is also a professional jazz musician – has been teaching at the Royal College of Art in London since 1984.[9] He has maintained his interest in the new techniques, in particular, computer-aided design, and in the use and relationship of traditional and more modern materials like Plexiglas®, Neoprene, acrylics and steel. He has also developed new techniques for colouring and bending the long stalks of his objects. Influenced by aeronautics, astrology and musical improvisation, as well as by the theoretical, analytical and anti-establishment sentiments found in Holland, he gradually came to work out a very personal and completely original approach – geometric, purist, rigorist and abstract. Only simple shapes, line, the combinations of minimal

elements, as well as their relationship to the various materials – are used, perfectly echoing the curves, volumes and movements of the body (see Figs. 244–246). The fact that he has made so few rings may perhaps be explained by the fact that his wife, Wendy Ramshaw (b.1939), herself a leading British jeweller, has been developing her entire work around this specific motif since 1970.

Wendy Ramshaw produces impressive cylindrical structures or stands made of Plexiglas®, acrylics, nickel or copper. These unscrew at the centre, so that groups of rings can be threaded on, bearing fine stalks that are usually encircled with enamel in delicate shades of colour. The stalks are also capped and sometimes decorated with precious or semi-precious stones such as amethyst, sapphire, agate, cornelian and turquoise. When the rings are not being worn, they seem to rest on these tall shapes which look like elongated turrets with the stalks of the rings stretching out like headlights pointing towards the sky.[10] (See Figs. 242, 243, 247–251).

All Wendy Ramshaw's work is based on the infinite interrelationship between simple abstract forms. Using these basic, formal, coloured units again and again, she succeeds magnificently in creating new complex and homogeneous pieces. Like Friedrich Becker, this English jeweller devotes herself primarily to the concept of the ring. In this way, all her objects are made up of series of pieces each more surprising and unexpected than the last. In each composition, the rings alternate on stands which look like minarets or even phallic emblems.

When in 1978 she discovered the 'primitive art' of Australia, with its vitalist forms and magical references, she became deeply influenced by it. Furthermore, her research and pictorial preferences were subsequently to lead her, quite logically, to work from portraits of women painted by Picasso. For example, the two paintings *Woman Sitting by the Window* from 1937 and *Woman in a Rocking Chair* from 1977 provided an opportunity for this artist to reflect on geometrised and colourful planes and rhythms, as well as on the relationship between forms and sensual and erotic elements. Having devoted herself since 1968 to the relationship and cadence of forms, materials and colours that can at any time be altered and interchanged in rings that are at once ornaments, objects and sculptures, she is now working on the transparency of her Plexiglas® stands and on rings made entirely of gold and diamonds (Figs. 251).

242

242 WENDY RAMSHAW
Ring 'For a woman sitting at the window', coloured nickel base and 12 silver rings with semi-precious stones (yellow and dark blue cornelians), 1989.

243

243 WENDY RAMSHAW
'White Lady' ring, stand and 16 rings in yellow gold, pale sapphire, moonstone and white enamel 1976, artist's collection.
Photographs: Bob Cramp.

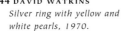

245 DAVID WATKINS
Silver ring with white/yellow pearls and black pearl, no date.

247 WENDY RAMSHAW
'Pillar' ring, Plexiglas® stand and three 9-carat gold rings with blue enamel and lapis-lazuli. No date.

244 DAVID WATKINS
Silver ring with yellow and white pearls, 1970.

248 WENDY RAMSHAW
'Pillar' ring: 5 silver rings with semi-precious stones (green cornelians and amethysts), 1972, private collection.

246 DAVID WATKINS
Gold ring with semi-precious stones (amethyst, yellow and grey agates, red ruby), c. 1970.

249 WENDY RAMSHAW
Ring designs, 1993.

250 WENDY RAMSHAW
Yellow gold stand and ring with green and blue cornelians, 1971.

251 WENDY RAMSHAW
Transparent Plexiglas® stand and four 18-carat gold rings with diamonds, 1996.
Photographs: Bob Cramp.

Echoing Picasso, who transformed the identity of his models – reflecting both his personal feelings and visions metamorphosed into other people – Wendy Ramshaw also designs and makes rings with multiple meanings.

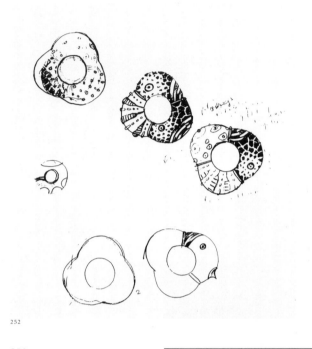

255 JOEL DEGEN *Ring in 18-carat white and yellow gold, blue anodised titanium and baguette-cut diamond, 1983.*

254 JOEL DEGEN *Ring in white gold, titanium, yellow gold, wide faceted emerald and four diamonds, 1985.*

253 PETER CHANG *Gentleman's thumb acrylic and polyester ring, 1993, Louis Koch Collection, Switzerland.*

252 PETER CHANG *Ring designs.*

253

The design of a very colourful ring in acrylic and polyester (Fig. 253), made by the British jeweller Peter Chang (b. 1944), takes the central, hollowed-out circle reserved for the thumb as a basis. It is subdivided into three rounded shapes of equal dimensions, themselves separated by three red hoops clearly distinguished by the way their surface and motifs are treated. First there is a set of four translucid blue and red annular shapes, then a darker-patterned section with bright green circles. Finally, there is a section with black and white geometric shapes of varying sizes with a small black eye on a white background which might symbolise a bird's head. Despite its formal and iconographical diversity, the whole is harmoniously proportioned. It makes up a compact, homogeneous, playful piece, completely original in design and execution. (See also Fig. 252.)

The materials that Peter Chang endows with unusual shapes are fully explored since they are, for him, inseparable from his approach. This is a conceptual approach and very much of his time. However, in comparison with Wendy Ramshaw or David Watkins,

254   255

256

256 JOEL DEGEN *Four rings in 18-carat yellow gold, titanium, steel and precious stones (emeralds and rubies), 1986.*

his object-sculptures are always full, round, sensual volumes, which are deliberately conceived with playfulness and irony. This jeweller seeks to establish a balance and harmony between the cultural domain of knowledge and the intellect, and the natural one of intuition or sensation. A comparison might be made with the 'glamour' sculptures of Niki de Saint-Phalle.

France, Belgium, Switzerland and Denmark

When he arrived in London in 1965, the Frenchman Joël Degen (b. 1941) approached the creation of rings and jewellery from the opposite viewpoint to that of his fellow countryman, Pierre Degen. His rings, made of stainless steel and titanium, sometimes with touches of gold, have simple geometric forms. These objects, in which impressions of cold and heat alternate, are like small architectural structures that may also, at their focal point, hold a precious stone. (See Figs. 254–256.)

He was also much impressed during the 1970s by Scandinavian design and the artists Claus Bury and Fritz Maierhofer, but developed his own research into the necessary dialogue between extreme simplicity of design, three-dimensional combination of metals, and the desire to achieve perfect balance with the part of the body to be adorned. Because it is placed next to the finger and thus, according to him, the tip or edge of the body, the ring is said to be like a lamp or a distinct sign. It would therefore be the most 'independent' of all types of jewellery; the precise point where both past and present symbolism could still be developed. Joël Degen's rings are often purchased by men – architects in particular – frequently for themselves, and sometimes used as wedding rings.

The 'Tube' or 'Carapace' rings (Figs. 261, 262, 263 & 264) by the Belgian jeweller Claude Wesel (b. 1942) are of simple design and structure. They cover a part of the finger or hand – the phalanx – which, according to this jeweller, is very exposed, in a manner reminiscent of a protective shield. This theme of the 'jewel that protects and isolates' was also to be amply developed by other artists. The whole of his work appears to be moving towards a cultural focus.

The French jeweller Henri-Morand Boltz (b. 1936), approaches ring design from a geometric angle, but using historical references. He designs and makes objects, from gold, silver, precious stone, enamel or cloth, whose lines and structures are graphically woven in space and build up momentum like miniature compositions (Figs. 257–259). His 'Architecture' or 'House' rings are designs with personal touches intended to illustrate the behaviour or identity of the wearer and remind us that, in antiquity, this small item of adornment could represent the residence of the individual, as well as his own coat of arms or

257

258

259

257 HENRI-MORAND BOLTZ
Designs for 'Architecture' rings.

258 HENRI-MORAND BOLTZ
'Architecture' ring in painted silver.

259 HENRI-MORAND BOLTZ
'Architecture' ring in 18-carat gold and diamonds, no date.

260 JOHANNA DAHM
'Between two fingers' rings in opaque and transparent Plexiglas® and rubber, 1985, Musée des Arts Décoratifs publications, Lausanne.

260

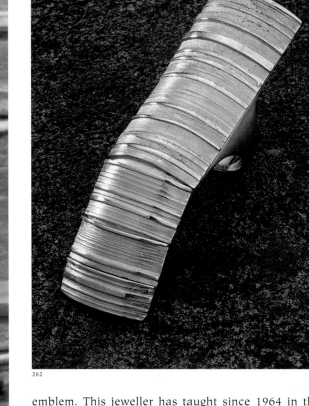

262

emblem. This jeweller has taught since 1964 in the jewellery section of the famous School of Decorative Arts in Strasbourg.

The 1985 series of 'Between two fingers' rings by the Swiss jeweller Johanna Dahm (b. 1947) – four rings and four squares of different colours in matt Plexiglas®, tied together with a black rubber strip – was ordered and produced by the Museum of Decorative Arts in Lausanne[11] (Fig. 260).

The study and development of this concept provided an opportunity for this jeweller to reflect on 'effective' design and on the concept of 'multiples'. Johanna Dahm is also a professor at many schools of art and is now working on light as a transforming element in her jewellery.

261 CLAUDE WESEL *Gold 'Tube' ring, no date.*

262 CLAUDE WESEL *Gold 'Carapace' ring, no date.*

263 CLAUDE WESEL *Gold 'Tube' ring, (detail).*

264 CLAUDE WESEL *Gold 'Carapace' ring, (detail).*

265 JAN LOHMANN *Gold ring, 1994.*

261

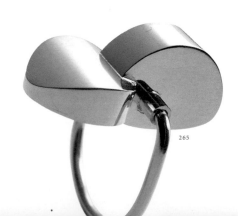

265

Since 1970, the Danish jeweller Jan Lohmann (b. 1944) has always made his rings, seen here in gold (Fig. 265), on the basis of arrangements of geometric planes and volumes. He also works on the different shades of colour of anodised titanium and makes his jewellery mainly by means of constructions and assemblies of stylised motifs and elements.

These artists who have relied on the criteria of 'cultural aesthetics' have, above all, sought to explore how far it is possible to go with rings, seeking formal and functional autonomy. The ring is designed and made not just as a jewel but as a sculpture – exploring new lines, forms and compositions, as well as materials and techniques. In this way, these jewellers have redefined the interdependence between rings, the finger, the hand and movement. Their analytic, scientific and aesthetic attitudes and choices have sometimes echoed an aspect of social and even political protest, providing a way for them to anchor themselves within contemporary society and space. It is space, to be understood also as a sculptural entity, that has been at the heart of their thinking and debates.

266 GILLES JONEMANN
Ring in ebony and Altuglas®, 1975, Musée des Arts Décoratifs, Paris. Photograph by L. Sully-Jaulmes.

266

The lyrical and spiritual tendency
France

The Fontblanche Workshops are, like Strasbourg, an important point of reference in the story of jewellery creation in France. Their vice-president and founder member, Gilles Jonemann, works with every type of material – from precious ones like stones and metal, to rubber and coconut shell. These are the props and springboard for his moods and emotions. His rings alternate between geometric and organic forms, but nature – for him, the guarantor of sensual and cognitive balance – remains his major inspiration.

Catherine Noll (1945-94), the grand-daughter of the famous sculptor Alexandre Noll, was preoccupied by

267 FRANCOISE AND CLAUDE CHAVENT *'Cock' ring in gold and forged iron, one-off creation, 1992.*

268 FRANCOISE AND CLAUDE CHAVENT *'Fragment' ring in gold and forged iron, seven copies, 1993.*

volume and the direct confrontation or collision with matter, which was always of natural origin in her work. Her rings are imbued with a great spiritual force and presence. Her artistic approach may be related to that of Constantin Brancusi, who shared the same desire to restore and rediscover the essential value of matter. She also co-operated with leading jewellers and great couturiers like Chanel, Dior and Nina Ricci in their respective jewellery collections.

The whole career of Christiane Billet (b. 1940) can be summarised in the materials she uses such as shell, stone, wood, mother-of-pearl, pebbles, amber and coral, combined with yellow metals such as bronze and gold.

The rings of Françoise and Claude Chavent (both b. 1947) have been made of metal since 1978, with impressive dimensions or volumes, and forms with architectural, natural and figurative references. Considering the ring both as the essential piece of jewellery – because it is in close contact with the most 'intelligent' and 'communicative' part of the body – and as a social adornment, they also design and make rings to work as fully-fledged object-sculptures. Their very strong literary and historical references have brought them more recently to work on much more graphic objects in iron.

In this way, like the first Roman, Christian and Celtic wedding rings, their wedding rings are strongly symbolic of genuine bonds.

These two jewellers clearly distinguish their one-off pieces from those of which several copies are made. (Figs. 267–273).

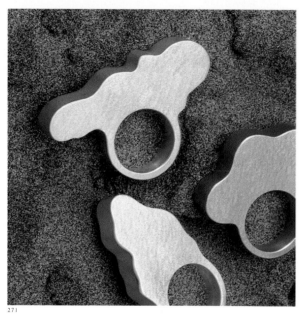

270 FRANCOISE AND CLAUDE CHAVENT *'Canyon' ring in gold and burnished steel, seven copies, 1990. Photograph by Hölzer.*

271 FRANCOISE AND CLAUDE CHAVENT *'Clouds' rings in gold or silver, unlimited production 1996. Photograph by Hölzer.*

272 FRANCOISE AND CLAUDE CHAVENT *Design for 'Clouds' rings, 1996.*

273 FRANCOISE AND CLAUDE CHAVENT *'Bridge' ring in burnished steel and nylon, one-off creation, 1983. Photograph by Hölzer.*

269 FRANCOISE AND CLAUDE CHAVENT *Design for 'Canyon' and 'Bar' rings, 1990.*

Since the 1970s, therefore, France has taken part in the great debate on jewellery. All these jewellers display genuine presence and creativity in this field, despite the obvious lack of relevant training, which is unfortunately characteristic of that country.

Switzerland and the United Kingdom

All rings by Pierre Degen (b. 1947), who lives and works in the United Kingdom, were made during two brief periods: firstly between 1976 and 1982, and then in 1994. They fit in with the experimental approach to jewellery he has adopted since the 1970s. Made of assemblies of materials as varied and unexpected as ceramics, plastics, rubber, nickel, graphite, bread, jam, elastic and cork, his rings can be related to both the Pop Art approach and to Italian Arte Povera. Much influenced by the sculptures of Claus Oldenburg, Kounellis and Merz amongst others, as well as by the intellectual approach of Claus Bury and his use of acrylics, Pierre Degen wished in his turn to experiment with the intimate relationship that jewellery can maintain with the wearer. (See Figs. 274–275, 277–279.)

His deliberately provocative thinking, which has subsequently led him to work on light and the movement of shadows projected through 'performance' or 'environmental' jewellery, resulted in a real exploration of the body and its emotions, movements and spaces. Pierre Degen has now come to think that a ring, like any other piece of jewellery, corresponds to a particular period in the life of an individual and can represent a piece of personal or artistic history – for the jeweller as much as for the wearer. Like the Dutch jewellery-designers, but following a dreamlike, primitive and playful aesthetic, he too pushes the idea of 'wearable' jewellery to its furthest extent.

The use of scrap materials such as rusty iron, broken glass, shampoo sachets, bits of tin and paper bags – sometimes assembled with gold – are a recurrent theme in the work of the Swiss jeweller Bernhard Schobinger (b. 1946). Having been taught by Max Fröhlich, he too made his commitment and contested the 'noble materials' of traditional jewellery. His jewels, with their acerbic, sometimes violent and radical forms, visibly worn away by time, attempt to link up at a deep level with the lost primitive and popular roots of contemporary society.

The rings of Jacqueline Mina (b. 1942) are made from almost transparent platinum 'gauze', on which little grains of 24-carat gold delicately stand out. Throughout her career, this English jeweller has always tried to take full advantage of the most ancient techniques – granulation in this case. Like airy, diaphanous envelopes, these rings seem to evoke fragile weaving – particularly a fine, spun cloth like gold lamé. (Fig. 285.)

Germany

The rings and other jewellery of Gerd Rothmann (b. 1941) deliberately overturn the forms and values traditionally expected in jewellery. Since the 1970s, his metal rings have drawn inspiration from the body.

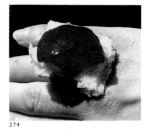
274

275

274 PIERRE DEGEN *Ring in bread, jam, elastic and ribbon, 1982.*

275 PIERRE DEGEN *Ring in nickel, ceramics and various plastics, 1977.*

277, 278, 279 PIERRE DEGEN *Rings in cork, rubber and nails, 1994.*

276 GERD ROTHMANN *'Stück Finger und Ring' rings in gold, 1994. Photograph by Annemarie Petzi.*

276

277

278

279

280 GERD ROTHMANN
Gold 'Siege' ring, 1984.

281 GERD ROTHMANN
'Auf den Finger gedrückt',
in yellow and white gold,
1987. Photograph by
Dorothea Baumer.

282 GERD ROTHMANN
'Zwischen den Finger' ring
in silver, 1990. Photograph
by Therese Hefele.

283 MARIANNE SCHLIWINSKI
'Rose' ring in silver and
pink quartz, 1993.

284 MARIANNE SCHLIWINSKI
Mourning ring in gold
(900/1000), 1995.

His rings may, for example, materialise and develop in the free space between the fingers or, as in Fig. 178 (1990), just above the fingers, making the void into an artistic and erotic solid. The 'signet' rings in Figs. 280 & 281, (1984 and 1987) bear a fingerprint on their bezels. A more recent design from 1994 (Fig. 276) is made up of a set of three rings, arranged in a box and entitled 'Piece of finger and ring', which operate like three symbolic marks or events, representing an anniversary, friendship or alliance.

After working for a whole year in 1966 in the workshop of Hermann Jünger, he developed his entire work on the concept of the personal jewel. Though his work was shown alongside that of Fritz Maierhofer and Claus Bury at the exhibition on acrylics in 1971, he was still more interested in the surfaces and volumes of metal, as well as their relationship with human beings. His experimental work is as aesthetically pleasing as it is subversive.

Their structure influenced by Japanese architecture, the rings of the German jeweller Wilhem Mattar (b. 1946) mix gold, silver, slate and, more recently, bone (1987). Although he has resorted to material that is apparently crude and rough, here it is so finely worked that one cannot fail to think of ivory. However, his pieces with their calm, majestic presence, which may call to mind those of pre-history, also recall the heavy symbolism of bone.

The rings of Marianne Schliwinsky (b. 1944) are of almost basic design. Their strong symbolism is thus expressed through minimal yet pertinent details. Whether they be simple metal hoops in gold, platinum or copper; or envelopes, coils or spirals of antique appearance with flattened but deliberately visible soldering; or rings bearing an off-centre glass bead, all these rings speak of the committed bond between two human beings. (Figs. 283 & 284).

This German jeweller opened her own gallery in 1981 with Jürgen Eickhoff, representing artist-jewellers such as Alexandra Bahlmann, Michael Becker, Georg Dobler, Winfreid Krüger and Brigitte Tendahl.

Italy

The rings of Francisco Pavan (b. 1937), which are always made in metal, adopt resolutely structured and always geometric forms, giving the illusion of an intermingling of metals of different tones, or working more specifically on the chromatic qualities of gold.

286 FRANCESCO PAVAN
Ring in gold, silver and alpaca, 1991.

287 FRANCESCO PAVAN
Ring in gold, silver and alpaca, 1991.

Through the extremely simplified construction of his objects, he seeks above all to concentrate on the effects of different materials and the colour combinations of metals in general, and gold in particular.

Thus the jewellery of this Italian artist seems to attempt to reinterpret a line that must, above all, be very pure. A graduate of the Pietro Selvatico Institute in Padua and a former pupil of Mario Pinton (he worked in his workshop for two years), he is perhaps the most sensitive of his generation to kinetic and constructivist influences. However, by experimenting and planning his method on the basis of the assembly or intermingling of elements of always simple metal

287

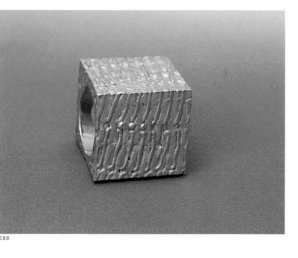

288

288 FRANCESCO PAVAN
Red gold ring, 1996.

shapes, he is trying to come up with a piece as open as possible, so that the eye and especially the light may project visual sensations on to it. This takes in Euclidean geometry and notions of false perspective; an illusion is played out, where the wearer of the jewellery or spectator alters their position and therefore their entire interpretation of it, depending on the angle from which they see it, or how they move. Even though the rings made by this jeweller have an abstract line and design, we can feel a clear desire, in the way the metals are attached and treated – woven like the threads of a tapestry – to rediscover genuine temporal and spiritual value.

The rings of the Italian jeweller Giampaolo Babetto (b. 1947) always rely on simple forms and follow a

285 JACQUELINE MINA
Ring in 24-carat granulated gold and platinum, 1996.

289

290

289 ALOIS BAUER *Gold and diamond ring, 1989.*

290 ALOIS BAUER *Gold ring, 1989.*

291 GIAMPAOLO BABETTO
*18-carat gold ring, 1991.
Picture supplied by Aurum
Press, from its series
'Contemporary Gold Jewelry
Artist Series': Giampaolo
Babetto.*

lengthened with a few stylised laurel leaves may make up the bezel of a ring. Giampaolo Babetto used synecdoche, where the objectivised part stands for the implicit whole; a kind of embodiment of presence through absence. In contrast to the perhaps more 'abstract' rings and jewellery of someone like Francesco Pavan, Babetto works on extreme simplification, looking more deeply at line and its powers, the relationship it maintains with gold (the most primordial and symbolic of materials) and its various possible alloys. Both intellectual and metaphysical force emanate from the rings of this great Italian jeweller. (See Fig. 291.)

minimalist geometrical line. Of the noble materials that he has been using since he began his investigations in 1970, the main one is gold, often in 18-carat strips varying from three-tenths to five-tenths of a millimetre in thickness and hollow for reasons of weight and visual lightness. He also uses various shades and surface treatments from yellow to red, brushed and smoothed to a matt finish, with or without the addition of various metal alloys (such as niello in 1975 and coloured synthetic resin from 1977 to 1984, or silver and copper between 1989 and 1991). Each of his rings is carefully crafted with a particular attention to the materials used and, as an architect by training, he leans towards a formal, volumetric search for balance and respects proportional values. The execution is always perfect and refined, because he seeks to transmit visual purity and inner tension to the wearer and/or spectator.

This jeweller, who is also a former pupil of Mario Pinton at the Pietro Selvatico Institute of Art in Padua, has therefore been developing work that is both abstract and spiritual. This quest for pure line and harmony by means of the 'divine proportions' so dear to the artists and architects of the Italian Renaissance, logically brings Babetto to think about gold and about light.

Since 1989, he has taken as his starting point a canvas by the mannerist Italian painter, Pontormo. He dissects and fragments each two-dimensional part, in order to reveal the extreme tension and emotion of the lines that cross and balance the picture. The detail selected then forms the basis of the jewel. For example, an outstretched arm, or legs going downstairs, may produce a brooch, or ankles and feet

Austria

From 1989 light was also the focus of interest for the Austrian jeweller Aloïs Bauer (b. 1948) in his series of rings in gold and diamonds, but in this case light in its interdependent relationship with shade. These two objects have matching geometric forms, one being the objectivisation of the shadow of the other. In this close inter-relationship, the rings are inextricably linked to each other, as the one contains the other and vice versa, like Yin and Yang, like 'me' and 'I'.[12]

292

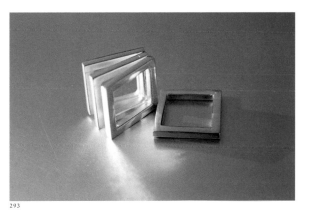

293

Finland and Denmark

The two rings by the Finnish jeweller Eila Minkkinen (b. 1945) illustrate her two lines of research – 'figurative' and 'abstract'. The 1976 ring represents a bear head and the design is still being manufactured today. The other one, which is very simple and in the shape of a hollowed-out square in geared sections, was designed and made in 1984 (see Figs. 292 & 293). It may be worn as it is, or in different combinations (up to four) of its sections, creating a different object. All the rings are made in silver.

The bear, which is both feared and respected, is Finland's national animal; a sign of power and courage. It used to form part of a large number of rites in that country and was often depicted on amulets. The 'bear' ring explicitly takes over this traditional belief. As for the extreme simplicity of the other, square, adjustable ring, its form with its purified design immediately stands in opposition to the circular form traditionally expected. Yet far from belonging to two incompatible lines of research, Eila Minkkinen's rings are symbolic. This jeweller, who has been exhibiting regularly in her country since 1969, has always taken the side of nature. Her recent works (made with real plants), moreover, take a strong ideological and ecological stance against pollution. The symbolic choice of the square, which fits in completely with the spirit of simple, sober and 'effective' Scandinavian design, could also be explained in the sense of this artist's respect for nature: the square is the geometric figure reserved for the earth.[13]

The Danish jeweller Per Suntum (b. 1944) used an almond-shaped bronze sheet to design and make the series of five 'rings of bloom' or flower rings. They all involve ovoid, flat, closed, gilded forms of decreasing sizes; this basic shape having come naturally to him. He thus quickly sorted his gilt bronze sheets by size, cutting and fashioning them to make five rings in designs which are both simple and evolutionary.

This artistic and aesthetic experience illustrates the whole approach of this great Danish jeweller and the lines of enquiry he pursues. On the basis of his encounter with materials (mainly metals), he exploits all the possible effects of surfaces and textures, in order to convey what it makes him feel.[14] Drawing inspiration from nature, he seeks to attain its essence through forms that are always fundamental and organic. Here, like a mirror of the gradual metamorphosis of a shape and of matter, Fig. 296 represents the four seasons: germination, budding, flowering and withering. They all reach their peak in the last ring in full 'maturity' (Fig. 297), which contains the four others and which seems to be pointing its stylised leaves and flowers towards the vital energy of the sun.

A ring in oxidised silver (Fig. 294), gold leaf and lacquer, like almost all the jewellery designed by the Danish jeweller Annette Kraen (b. 1945), is organised on the basis of essentially geometric forms. Here, the circle and square are arranged at right angles and play on the effects of their respective materials. This jeweller, too, is much influenced by the organic,

294 ANETTE KRAEN *Ring in oxidised silver, gold leaf and lacquer.*

oxidised and thus temporal and 'living' character of the metals that she mainly uses.

Nature seems, therefore, to be the major inspiration for the jewellers amongst this generation of Scandinavian artists – with the exception of Jan Lohmann, who seems to be taking a more analytical path. These preferences and references may be explained by the geographical position of these countries – which are extremely exposed to the elements and have relatively difficult climates – as well as by the strong presence of nature and by the influence and survival of a whole mythological and literary tradition.[15] The respect and concern of Nordic countries for their environment shows that ecology is not a policy for them, but rather a way of living.

Spain and Portugal

A great deal of delicacy and refinement emanates from the very sober rings of Hans Erwin Leicht, which, since 1991, have been mainly annular in shape and made up from different metals. This jeweller, who was born in Germany in 1941 and who works like a genuine goldsmith, has been a professor at the famous Massana School in Barcelona since 1988. (Fig. 295.)

295

Joaquim Capdevila (b. 1944) likes his rings, which are mainly in precious stones and metals, to adopt quite 'open' forms so that the spectator and the wearer may project onto them symbolism and functions, or their own aesthetic expectations. This jeweller has always defended the idea that whatever the nature and form of a jewel may be, it must arouse, above all, the most intimate feelings of its recipients; as they alone must decide how it will be used. He feels that a

296

297

298

299

300

298 TERESA CAPELLA I MARTI *'El mar' ring in silver and turquoise, 1994.*

299 TERESA CAPELLA I MARTI *'El coral' ring in silver and coral, 1994.*

300 TERESA CAPELLA I MARTI *Ring designs.*

jewel must, through its dimensions and proximity to the body, establish an intimate and significant triangular relationship between the creator, wearer and spectator. (Figs. 303–306.)

The rings of Teresa Capella i Marti (b. 1945) in metals and semi-precious stones like turquoise, coral and tiger's eye have a very elongated bezel, which develops organically on the finger. The rings in Figs. 298–300 are of Mediterranean inspiration with references to the sea. A pupil at the Massana School and then at Pforzheim under the guidance of Reinhold Reiling amongst others, this jeweller has been exhibiting in Spain since 1967.

The Portuguese jeweller Filomeno Peirera de Sousa (b. 1949) makes rings with very colourful alloys of precious metals, plastics and acrylics. Having been invited to the Massana School in 1988, he used the 'Jardin du Luxembourg' series, which dates from 1989, as an opportunity to reflect on the symmetrical elements making up the French-style garden. His jewelled objects, always with bulky bezels, are artistic

301

302

302 FILOMENO PEIRERA DE SOUSA *Gimmel ring in plastic.*

301 FILOMENO PEIRERA DE SOUSA *Ring in acrylic and plastic, 1988.*

messages as much as aesthetic anecdotes. (Figs. 301 & 302.)

In 1988, he created Contacto Directo, a school and gallery reserved for jewellery in Lisbon, which he manages and also teaches. In addition he teaches jewellery techniques at the Ar. Co, a centre for visual art and communication in Lisbon.

The rings and intentions of Spanish and Portuguese jewellers prove that in these countries, mainly in Barcelona and Lisbon, there is genuine creative talent. This dynamic process must be included and understood within a much more general artistic movement, which, in the case of Barcelona, took root at the end of 19th century. In fact, Catalan Modernism was at the time playing a leading role, just like Arts and Crafts in the United Kingdom or Art Nouveau in France. In Barcelona there was urban and regional renewal, and a most successful association and co-operation with artists and architects, as well as 'designers' as inventive as Louis Doménech i Montaner, Antoni Gaudi i Cornet and Joseph Jujol i Gibert, in conjunction with major industrialists, such as Euseibi Güell. In the field of Art Nouveau jewellery, there was Luis Masriera i Roses (1872-1958), Ramo Teixé (a colleague of Gaudi), and then, in relation to Art Deco or Noucentism (1914-36), the work of Ramon Sunyer and Jaume Mercade.

However, it was particularly after 1929 that Barcelona gradually came to make its mark as a decisive and completely original centre for the creation of jewellery.[16] It was in that year that the ambitious and enterprising Massana School undertook to conserve and promote the 'applied' and 'industrial' arts (now 'Arts and Design'). Taking advantage of the effervescence in Europe that was very propitious for the creation and conceptual revival of jewellery in the 1950s and 1960s. The Massana School was set up as a jewellery workshop in 1959 by Manuel Capdevilla. It was taken over and managed by Anna Front in 1974 and then by Ramon Puig Cuyas in 1981. The Massana School is still famous today for the quality and freedom of the training it gives in connection with jewellery, following the rational and analytical as well as the intuitive and more spontaneous tendencies. A large number of Spanish, as well as foreign artist-jewellers have passed through the gates of this institution as teachers, students, or both: they include Hans Leicht, Joaquim Capdevila, Ramon Puig Cuyas, Carmen Roher, Xavier Domenech, and Silvia Walz.[17]

To sum up, the artist-jewellers who, in the 1970s,

relied on the criteria of 'natural aesthetics' sought, above all, to find lines, materials and techniques that could defy the relationship with time. They were keen to redefine or rediscover contact with matter and try to draw out its spirit and cyclical essence. These artists gave pride of place to the sensual, irrational and almost secret relationship that wearers must maintain with their jewellery.

Preference for non-precious materials is one of the particular features of jewellers who chose a more analytical path, but was also characteristic of the artistic jewellery of the second half of the 20th century. This tendency has been present in art (Constructivism) and jewellery in the 1960s (the Dutch duo Leersum-Bakker). From 1970, technological progress made audacious effects and combinations more feasible than ever. This included new

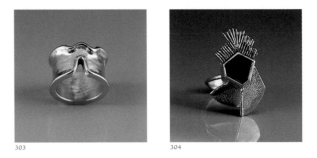

303

304

alloys to obtain a very rich range of tones and shades; new laser cutting techniques for metals; computer-assisted design; and very refined mechanical construction and casting techniques. With regard to plastics, their approach to such 'new' materials enabled these jewellers to measure up to the technology of their time and to construct other codes of reference such as abstract, architectonic, kinetic or fluid, fantastic, figurative and dreamlike. Generally speaking, it can be seen that the interest of these artists in plastics was an obvious challenge to traditional theories and approaches, but also it gave them the possibility of playing on optical illusion.

IN SUMMARY

Far from being opposed, the two aesthetic tendencies highlight the strong points and focuses shared by all the jewellers of this generation. All of them are seeking to redefine the interdependent and complementary relationship that links the designer, the wearer and/or spectator, and the ring. Some of them have even chosen to carry out their works in a spirit of social and

303 JOAQUIM CAPDEVILA
Untitled ring in yellow gold, 1985. Photograph by Ramon Manent.

304 JOAQUIM CAPDEVILA
Untitled ring in yellow gold and tourmaline, 1985. Photograph by Ramon Manent.

sometimes political protest, such as Bakker, van Leersum, Maierhofer, Bury, Künzli and Rothmann.

At a more general level and on an international scale, there was a deliberately confrontational artistic nature present during these years after 1968. On the one hand, there was the theoretical challenge of conceptual art, art and language, the BMTP groups and then Support/Surface; or the sociological and artistic challenge as in the case of Hans Haacke. On the other hand there was the Fluxus reaction or movement, with its response shown in the attitude and installations of someone like Joseph Beuys (1921-86), who had a strong influence on and opened up a broad range of unexplored opportunities to a whole young generation of artists. There was also the violent, extremist action of Body Art, including, for instance, the French artist Michel Journiac (1943-95) and his

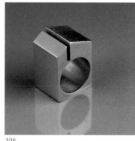

306 JOAQUIM CAPDEVILA
Untitled ring in yellow gold, 1970-72. Photograph by Ramon Manent-Ferran Borras.

306

ritual, provocative, dramatic performances. The latter saw his artistic and bodily activity not in individual terms, but as social/political/religious criticism. He also made jewellery and rings using gold-plated human 'bones'.[18] While his piece entitled 'Ritual for a dead man', which features the skeleton of a left hand, certainly represents a challenge – albeit in precious metal – to the usual expected order of things, it can also be interpreted as a wedding ring that binds the body irrevocably to Death. This ritual is there to state and to remind us that 'the body is an absolute that desire or death reveals'.[19]

In studying the design of examples of rings from the 1970s, it is apparent that these items of adornment reflect the artistic and aesthetic – as well as symbolic, social and political – choices characteristic of that decade of theoretical challenge.

305 JOAQUIM CAPDEVILA
Untitled ring in yellow gold, brilliant-cut diamonds and malachite, 1992. Photograph by Ramon Manent.

The contemporary ring: third-generation designers of the 1980s and 90s

The rings of the 1960s, and especially the 1970s, have to be understood in terms of the theoretical issues they raised, in what were regarded as artistic, aesthetic and socio-political battlegrounds. It should be noted also that the jewellers of the 1970s had attempted throughout those predominantly theoretical and 'modernist' years to advance the cause of jewellery by revising concepts, achievements and debates about the art of adornment. With their analytic attitude and more spiritual aesthetics, these artists had triggered a rethink of traditionally accepted ideas about jewellery. It was more radical than anything in the 1960s, especially regarding the intrinsic value of the materials. In their systematic use of plastics, the great originality of jewellers – reflecting cultural aesthetics – lay in finally setting adornment free from its straitjacket and trying to reveal its real meaning.

In the 1980s and 1990s, this artistic and social utopia has no longer been the first concern of the younger generation of designers, who were all born between 1950 and 1975. They apparently prefer to play on references to shapes, materials, history, meanings, and what appear at first sight to be more symbolic and metaphorical aesthetics.

Museums, galleries and exhibitions continued their activity in relation to contemporary jewellery, encouraging fairs, creativity, collections and conversation, as well as reflection and the publication of catalogues, reviews, articles and books. This ardour, which certainly shows that the art of adornment cuts across many fields of culture, does not, however, explain why it continues to address itself solely to the initiated. Rather than making an attempt to explain this, it is perhaps more helpful to analyse the nature of the design of rings in the closing years of the century. Without the benefit of hindsight, it is difficult to make a classification of the approach or thought processes of this younger generation. Nevertheless, it is apparent that all these young jewellers, in comparison with their elders, are more concerned with a multi-faceted, 'open' approach to jewels. This may sometimes be geometric, analytical and abstract and, at other times, sensual, sensory and spiritual. The main characteristic of this latter generation appears, in fact, to be its primarily personal and indeed, individual, expression.

310

308

308 GRAZIANO VISINTIN
Gold and ebony ring, 1981
Photograph: Trento.

309 RUUDT PETERS
Ouroboros 'Wunstorf' ring
in gold and silver plate and
marcasite, 1995-96.

310 RUUDT PETERS
Ouroboros 'Mibladen' ring
in silver and gypsum flower,
1995-6.
Photographs: Rob Versluys
Studio.

Third-generation designers in context

Netherlands

The very recent ring-objects (1995-96) made by Ruudt Peters (b. 1950) from precious metals like silver and gold plating, with marcasites or, as in Fig. 310, gypsum flower, comprise a more or less elongated, smooth shape, which corresponds to the bezel, and a spherical shape, the surface of which bears rough, slightly raised work and which is to be placed in the palm of the hand. The stalk of metal allows the fingers to be slipped in and to hold these 'hand ornaments' – which belong to the 'Ouroboros' collection – upright together.[20] (See also Fig. 309.)

309

The mineral, or natural, and at the same time polished, or cultural, treatment of the object, as well as the symbolic and mythological references, is quite explicit. Ouroboros does, moreover, have a dual symbol of repetition and mutation. On the one hand, there is the image of the snake biting its tail, recalling that of the circle or closed cycle of eternal recurrence. On the other, there is the idea of change or transcendence. With these objects to be worn between fingers and skin, Ruudt Peters is deliberately seeking to bring into contact the chthonian and celestial worlds, or the underworld and heaven. He endeavours to reach the point of balance of the principles decomposition and composition. In relation to his previous rings, which were always based on simple shapes, here he is going beyond the closed shape of the traditional circle. He succeeds in embodying that fragile point of contact between nature and culture, where everyone must be free to find their own balance.

This Dutch jeweller, sculptor and former pupil at the famous Gerrit Rietveld Academy in Amsterdam (1970-74) has, since the 1980s, been developing a body of work deeply imbued with spirituality and mysticism. These include 'Initiation' (1986), 'Interno' (1990-91), 'Dedicated to' and, in 1996, 'Ouroboros'; always using gold for its chemical and alchemic properties, never for its prestige value.

The 'echo' rings in metal like gold, silver, zinc, steel and copper, by Rian de Jong (b. 1951) display an impressive fine, elongated bezel. The stretched-out shape of these objects has been rigorously designed to contrast with that of the finger and the movements of the hand. However, these objects, which are made to

311 RIAN DE JONG 'Echo' ring in zinc and copper, 1992.

312 RIAN DE JONG 'Echo' ring in gold, silver and steel, 1992.

311

piece. The hoop is usually relatively broad, with a bezel resting on or spreading from it and bearing the stone – when there is one – which it draws attention to. The effect of stability provided by the volume and harmony of the proportions of these objects gives them a serenity which is both strong and elegant.[22] (See Figs. 313–317.)

Philip Sajet's main interest is in necklaces and bracelets[23] – objects designed on the basis of the circle, which are intended to clasp a precise part of the body. Since 1984, he has been able to take this formal constraint as a springboard to give free range to his personal interpretation, which is always controlled, eloquent and poetic. Again a former pupil of the Gerrit Rietveld Academy, he has been exhibiting since 1985.

Whether in glass and brass, gold and aquamarine,

316

316 PHILIP SAJET 'Parasiet' ring in gold and rock crystal, 1993

be touched and worn in contact with the skin, openly claim their autonomy in respect of the body. At no time do they seek to become one with it but, like the body, they hint at profound secrets. Also a former student at the Gerrit Rietveld Academy (1979-85), Rian de Jong has opted for forms with natural references, such as creepers, and also architectural ones. These are intended to wrap around the part of the body to be adorned and, like nature, to resonate with it. (See Figs. 311 & 312.) [21]

Philip Sajet (b. 1953) uses precious stones and metal such as gold, silver, niello, diamond, ruby and rock crystal for his rings, which are always of very simple, pure design. He always works on the basis of a circlet, which may be closed or open depending on the

313

314

315

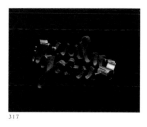

317

315 PHILIP SAJET 'Hoge Byzantijn' ring in gold, rock crystal and glass, 1988, private collection.

317 PHILIP SAJET 'Annulus vulgaris' ring in gold and diamond, 1993, artist's collection.

313 PHILIP SAJET 'Parasiet' ring in gold, silver and niello, 1989. Stedelijk Museum, Amsterdam.

314 PHILIP SAJET Jade and amethyst ring, 1994, private collection.

318 HERMAN HERMSEN *Ring
with balls in rubber and
gold plated brass beads,
1987.*

318

pearls or silver, rings designed by Hermann Hermsen (b. 1953) are real challenges to the balance between form and function. Yet without ever losing anything from their overall effect, their very considered and structured design is reduced to the minimum. As of 1986, it was from this angle that he initially rethought the concept of the finger ring, freeing it from its circular form. Structured in a T-shape, his creations are worn between the index and middle fingers, projecting and spreading the stone and the colour magnificently over the fingers (Fig. 335). In 1987, he made a small, fine ribbon of rubber with gold beads at the ends, which is to be wrapped around and attached to the finger (Fig. 318). In 1988, four black pearls arranged in a square and linked together by four

straight gold wires enabled this jeweller to balance his construction and, once again, to go beyond the enclosed circle (Fig. 320). The same goes for the flowing, pure piece for two fingers made in 1989 of gold and silver wires shown in Fig. 321. (See also Fig. 319.)

It is interesting to note that this jeweller, who studied at the Arnhem Academy of Art, worked as an assistant to Emmy van Leersum and Gijs Bakker from 1980 to 1984. While inevitably influenced by these two great personalities, he succeeded magnificently in finding and developing his own language and form of expression as a jeweller. Since 1991, this artist has been a teacher at the Arnhem Academy of Art and the

319

320

322

321

319 HERMAN HERMSEN
*'Meander-lines' rings in
18-carat gold, 1995.*

320 HERMAN HERMSEN *Ring
with four pearls, gold and
black pearls, 1988.*

321 HERMAN HERMSEN
*'Double' ring in gold and
silver, 1989. Photograph by
Franck Kanters.*

Düsseldorf Fachhochschule für Gestaltung. He has been exhibiting since 1981 in the leading galleries of his country (Marzee and Ra). Very recently, in 1995, Hermann Hermsen has been working on a ring-concept, designed in two complementary parts to be in her research: such as transparency, movement, infinity or space. A pupil at the Gerrit Rietveld Academy from 1978-83, she has been exhibiting regularly since 1982.

Ted Noten (b. 1956) has only been making rings

323

322 ANNELIES PLANEDYT
'Wind' ring in 12-carat gold, 1988. Photograph by Sigert Thomanetz.

323 ANNELIES PLANEDYT
'Font' ring in 18-carat gold, 1989. Photograph by Tom Haartsen.

fitted together like a jigsaw puzzle, leaving him free to reinterpret the circular form.

The few rings designed by Annelies Plandeydt (b. 1956) have all been made of gold wire since 1987. These three examples – 'Alliances', 'Wind' and 'Font' (Figs. 322–324) – show objects that develop graphically in space with a great deal of delicacy. True calligraphy and poetry in precious metal, they seem to allow the elements to flow through their metallic entanglements and fluidities. This artist makes her jewellery mainly from precious metals, since they enable her to express the fundamental ideas inherent

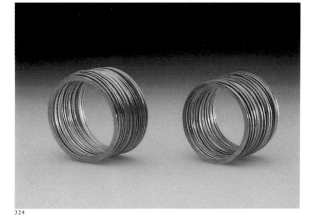

324

324 ANNELIES PLANEDYT
'Wedding' rings in 18-carat gold, 1987. Photograph by Tom Haartsen.

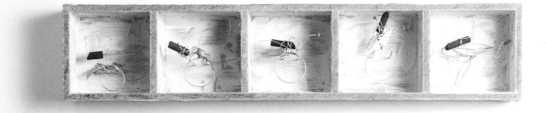

327

325

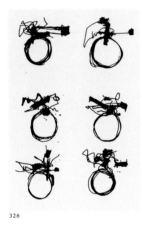

326

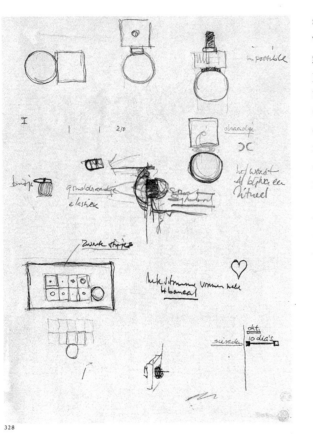

328

since 1991. He started with 'Visier' (Fig. 329), in which a flat, gold hoop – itself framed by a quadrangular form – bears a portrait, of the same proportions, photographed in black and white with a square hole in the centre. In 'Sweat with Horse' (Figs. 330&334) (1992), he drew inspiration from the game of chess in order to design and make five rings in different materials such as paper, wood, silver and iron. While offering variations on the form of a horse, they do in fact have a different history and function. In his 'Sketch in Metal' (Fig. 327), five small rings in gold, wood, plastic and charcoal – presented in their respective wooden boxes – illustrate the extreme fragility of writing. In 'Chip Ring' (Fig. 325) (1996), the transparent Plexiglas® provides [24] a delicate showcase for computer chips. Finally, 'Containering' (1996) is also a structure in transparent Plexiglas®, but with a very prominent bezel acting as a container for a multitude

327 TED NOTEN *'Sketch in metal' rings: five small rings in their box, in gold, charcoal, wood and plaster, undated.*

325 TED NOTEN *'Chip ring' in 18-carat gold and Plexiglas®, 1996.*

326 TED NOTEN *Designs for 'Sketch in metal' rings.*

328 TED NOTEN *Illustrations of 'Visier' ring.*

329 TED NOTEN *'Visier' ring or 'ring for a photographer' in 18-carat gold, iron and negative, 1991.*

330 TED NOTEN *Designs for 'Sweat with horse' ring 1992.*

334 TED NOTEN *'Sweat with horse' ring, gold, horse-skin and sheets of paper, 1992.*

329

of interchangeable coloured stones. (See also Figs. 326 & 328.)

Like Hermann Hermsen, Ted Noten has a conceptual approach to rings, but their form and function have an anecdotal side and artistic references that are very individual to him, including photography, painting, literature, chess and an interest in the fragility of matter. This jeweller, who was trained at the Maastricht Academy of Applied Arts from 1983-86, and then at the Rietveld Academy from 1986-96, has been exhibiting since 1989. He works according to an ideal concept, followed by preparatory drawings. He considers the ring as the last or 'ultimate' piece of jewellery since, for him, it is the most personal and most expressive ornament.

Rings made by Ralph Bakker (b. 1958) are finely-crafted structures of precious stones and metals such as gold, silver, pearls and niello. The careful attention paid to both the outer and inner parts of these rings is probably explained by the fact that this Dutch jeweller (a former pupil at the Gerrit Rietveld Academy, from 1991 to 1994) is interested in them from both an

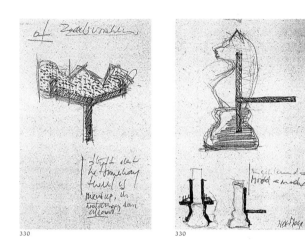

330

330

331

332

333

331 RALPH BAKKER *Untitled ring in gold, silver, niello and pearls, 1996.*

332 RALPH BAKKER *'R'A'dam' in gold, silver, niello and pearls, 1991.*

333 RALPH BAKKER *Gold wedding rings, 1995.*

334

artistic and a historical point of view. (See Figs. 331–333.)

The rings of Miriam Verbeek (b. 1960) are allegorical. There is a ring in silver and pearls that encloses or holds a poem (Fig. 338), and a silver ring to be wound around one or all five fingers linked together or held in the palm by a small spherical silver hook (Fig. 336). This can be regarded as a symbol of life, worn next to the skin enabling positive emotions to flow outwards from within. Other examples are a flower ring or eternity ring in silver lace, suggesting a piece of a church or cathedral (Fig. 339). It is from this aesthetic – as well as historical and cultural – angle that we should see the jewellery of this young 1993 graduate of the Gerrit Rietveld Academy, who directs all her work towards the embodiment of

336 MIRIAM VERBEEK 'Wikkel' ring to slip on, in silver and silk, 1993.

338 MIRIAM VERBEEK Idem.

337 MIRIAM VERBEEK 'Rouw' mourning ring in silver, silk and nut, 1993.

339 MIRIAM VERBEEK 'Eeuwig' eternity ring in silver and gold (recycled from a wedding ring), 1994. Photographs: Henri Van Beck.

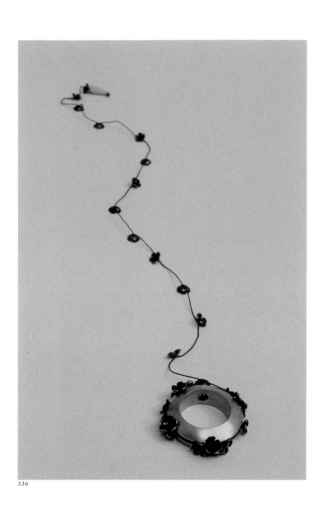

336

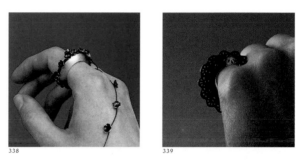

338   339

337

335 HERMAN HERMSEN 'Glass' or 'Aquamarine' ring in glass and brass or aquamarine and gold, 1986-7.

personal emotions; mainly love and grief. (See also Fig. 337.)

Lucy Sarneel (b. 1961), again a former pupil of the Rietveld Academy, designed and made 'chair' rings in 1992-93, using silver, wood and gold solder, which are symbols of personality or, in the words of the artist, 'delicate altars of repose for birds' (Fig. 340).

These young Dutch jewellers seem to prefer to work

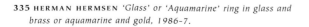

340

340 LUCY SARNEEL 'Chair' rings in silver and soldered gold, 1992-3.

341 GEORG DOBLER *Ring in 18-carat gold and a 1.51-carat diamond.*

noble materials. These are materials and techniques that were deliberately neglected and criticised in the minimalist theoretical spirit that was characteristic of the 1960s and 1970s. Undoubtedly following the well-trodden path of their predecessor Robert Smit, these young artists were able to turn a corner and bring new dynamism to jewellery in their country. With the exception of Hermann Hermsen, most of these artist-jewellers studied at the Institute of Applied Arts in Amsterdam, the academy that took the name of the famous architect Gerrit Rietveld in 1966, two years after his death.

Germany

The rings of Daniel Kruger (b. 1951) are made with total respect for the metals and stones used, recalling, in their form, those of the Middle Ages. For example, a metal hoop topped with an impressive bezel bearing an amethyst, tourmaline or quartz, or a fragment of glass. The expressive treatment of these objects gives them a great deal of presence, or even a degree of

346

'primitivism'. These effects are provided in particular by proportions, irregularities in the surfaces, offsetting and a good deal of finesse and sensitivity. (See Figs. 342–345.)

After studying painting and spending six years at

342

343

344

345

342 DANIEL KRUGER *Ring in 18-carat gold and amethyst, 1989.*

343 DANIEL KRUGER *Ring in gold and pink quartz, 1996.*

344 DANIEL KRUGER *Ring in silver, beryl, amethyst and brilliants, 1992.*

345 DANIEL KRUGER *Ring in 18-carat gold, pieces of glass and mirror, 1989.*

347

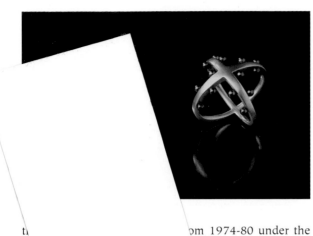

'Sissi' (Fig. 354 & 355), 'Alien' (Fig. 351), 'Brazil' (Fig. 352) and 'Blade Runner' (Fig. 353) are impressive rings, made of gold, silver and precious stones, as well as cloth and little photographs. These 'monumental', very elegant objects made by Sabine Klarner (b. Istanbul, 1957) echo the cinema. They have been deliberately designed and made in accordance with the characteristic atmosphere of the films that deeply impressed and moved this jeweller. Each of her pieces shelters, hiding like a secret, a little photograph or fetish of the main actor, such as Romy Schneider, Sigourney Weaver, Robert de Niro or Harrison Ford. The architectural, baroque and strongly oriental influence gives her work an appearance that is both theatrical and mysterious.

Sabine Klarner studied at the Berufsfachschule für Goldschmiede in Pforzheim (1976–78) and then in Munich (1978–80). She is now living and working in Hamburg, where she opened her own gallery in 1992, although she has been exhibiting since 1987.

349 MICHAEL BECKER *Three rings in 18-carat gold, 1995.*

350 MICHAEL BECKER *Ring in 18-carat gold and aquamarine, 1995.*

t... om 1974-80 under the
ar... ce and influence of
He... eller has always
app... deal of expression
and ...

The... ig. 341 is not truly
represe... ly produced by
Georg L... e, only the very
architect... l netting that
holds the... hat this great
jeweller des... t and curved
lines that t... eometrical,
abstract draw...

The 'between... old and/or
niello by Ange... heir true
artistic and aes... on the
middle finger. Th... aves or
little pearls can be... t right
angles or straining... er, seeming to
merge into and hug ... m and the forms and movements of the finger. (See Figs. 346–348.)

Another pupil of Hermann Jünger and the Munich Academy of Art from 1983-88, this jeweller's work also adorns other parts of the body. For example, the shoulder, for which she has also created brooches or 'shoulder pads' whose gentle curves are made to fit into it exactly.[26]

349

The very recent rings made in 1995 by Michael Becker (b. 1958), like his brooches, have explicit classical and modern architectural references: a simple, broad hoop, its surface punctuated with small quadrangular windows, topped with a bezel, enclosing as in a tower the coloured stone which may be aquamarine or tourmaline (Fig. 349). This jeweller, who was taught by Peter Skubic in Cologne (1982–87), is mainly interested in geometrical proportions and the rhythms of his jewellery in precious metals. He usually bases his work on the conception and production of brooches, which are real hymns to the buildings of two great architects – Palladio (1508–80) with his 'Italian Renaissance' villas, and Mies van der Rohe, with his 'modern' Pavilion for the 1929

346 ANGELA HUBEL *'Between two fingers' rings in cast and/or gilt silver, 1993.*

347 ANGELA HUBEL *'Between two fingers' ring as worn, in cast silver plated with 18-carat gold.*

348 ANGELA HUBEL *'Ansserirdicher' and 'Perlennete' rings in 18-carat gold and cultured pearls, 1995.*

351

352

353

354

351 SABINE KLARNER 'Alien'
ring in silver, 18- and 22-
carat gold and semi-
precious stones, photo of
Sigourney Weaver, 1993.

352 SABINE KLARNER 'Brazil'
ring in silver, 18- and 22-
carat gold, and semi-
precious stones, photo of
Robert de Niro, 1993.

353 SABINE KLARNER 'Blade
Runner' ring in silver and
18-carat gold, garnet,
citrine and photo of
Harrison Ford, 1993.

355 SABINE KLARNER 'Sissi'
ring in silver, 18-carat and
22-carat gold, garnet, pearl
and zirconium, photo of
Romy Schneider, 1993.

354 SABINE KLARNER Idem.

355

Barcelona exhibition[27] – and whose structure he
always develops in a flat manner. The ring, through its
bodily constraints, enables him to construct this architecture in space. (See also Fig. 350.)

The rings of Ulo Florack (b. 1958) are usually made
of gold, silver and enamel, and are also sculptural and
always highly-coloured. They provide a pretext for this
painter-jeweller to express his most personal and
intimate emotions, but they act as reminders of
symbolic and eternal feelings associated with faith,
worship, love and commitment. These non-figurative
compositions – usually enhanced with very bright

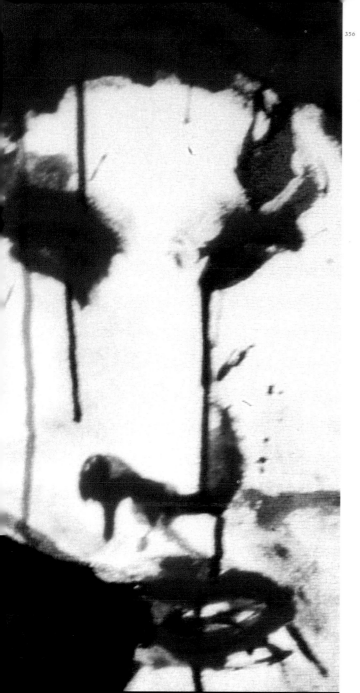

356

358

356 ULO FLORACK *Photograph of paintings.*

359 ULO FLORACK *Ring in silver and gilt enamel, 1995.*

360 ULO FLORACK *Sets of rings in silver and gilt enamel, no date.*

357 ULO FLORACK *Idem.*

361 ULO FLORACK *Designs.*

358 ULO FLORACK *Workshop view.*

enamels – are dreamlike, playful references; as much for their creator as for their recipient. The narrative, sometimes playful – and sometimes troubling – energy and extreme vitality that emanates from these objects make them highly intense. Ulo Florack, who was taught by Hermann Jünger[28] and then Jörg Immendorf at the Munich Academy of Art from 1983-89, is also very active as a painter. (See Figs. 356–361.)

359

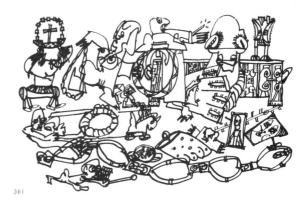

361

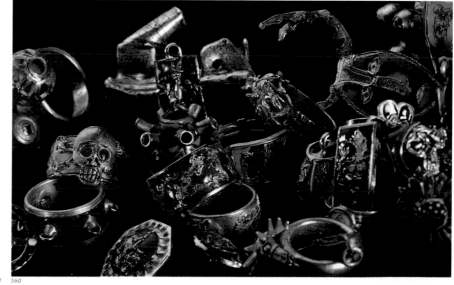

357   360

363 DETLEF THOMAS
18-carat gold ring, 1992.

362 DETLEF THOMAS *Idem.*

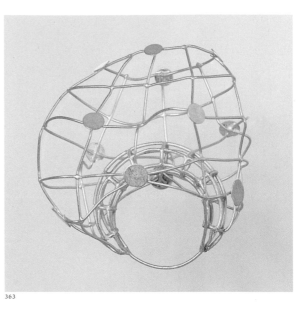

363

Detlef Thomas (b. 1959) made the two rings in Figs. 362 & 363, in 1992 from a gold wire articulated quite freely. Like those of Dutch jeweller Annelies Plandeydt, they too take shape graphically in space, but here in a more demonstrative and narrative manner. They develop their intertwined, fluid and almost transparent – yet suggestive – design with restraint and delicacy. Detlef Thomas was also a pupil of Hermann Jünger in Munich from 1983 to 1988.

Barbara Seidenath (b. 1960) designed and made a series of rings whose metal hoops bear a bezel very delicately illustrating a rosebud in coral and/or enamel. Without wishing to reinvent the concept of the ring, this former pupil of Hermann Jünger demonstrates a great deal of finesse in execution (See Figs. 364–366). She now lives in Providence in the United States.

Because of the very patterned jagged structure, the treatment of the volumes and the metal, and the organisation and rhythm of the planes and surfaces of the rings made from 1991 to 1993 by Anette Wohlleber (b. 1962), they may be likened to fragments of architecture. Her preparatory drawings reveal the motifs and scenes which form the basis for her designs

362

365 BARBARA SEIDENATH
'Rose' ring in 18-carat gold, enamel, pink coral and brilliants, 1995.

364 BARBARA SEIDENATH
'Eyes' ring in 18-carat gold, enamel and coral, 1995.

366 BARBARA SEIDENATH
'Dornröschen' ring in silver, enamel and pink coral, 1995.

367 ANETTE WOHLLEBER
'Mitten durchs Herz' rubber rings, 1994.

364

365

366

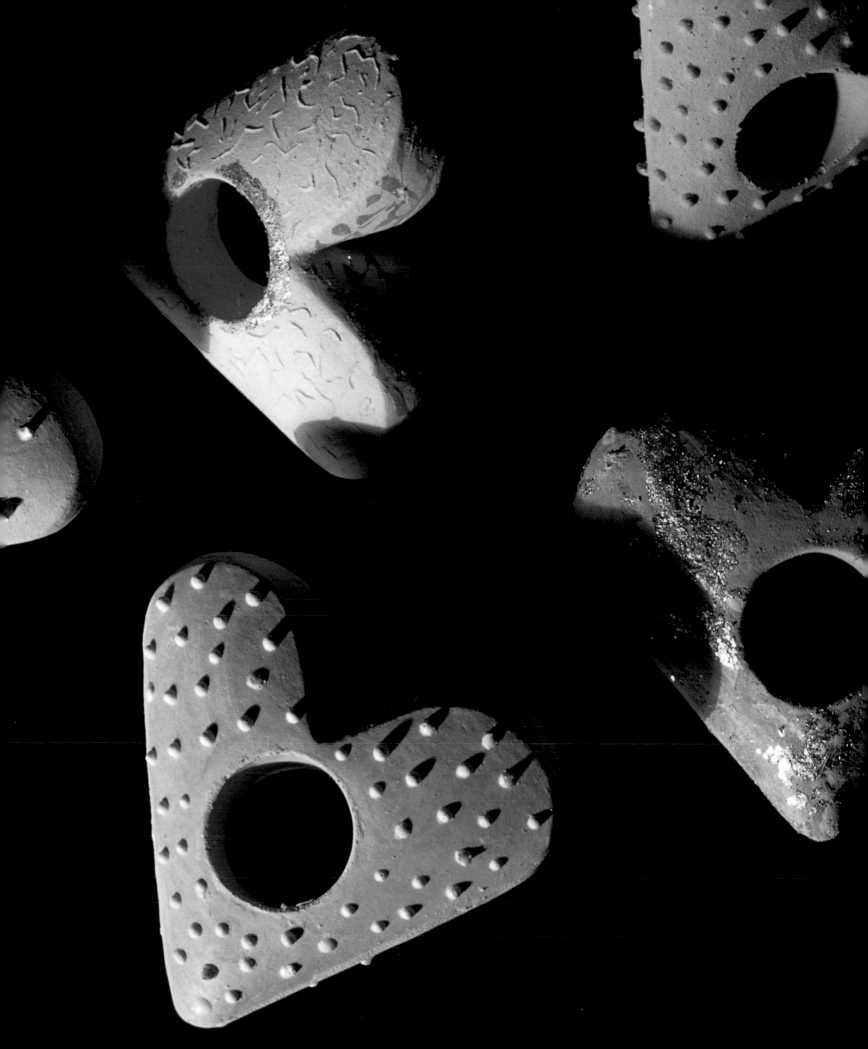

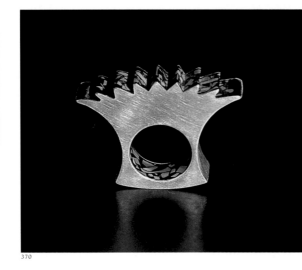

369

368 ANETTE WOHLLEBER
Silver and gold leaf ring,
1990.

370 ANETTE WOHLLEBER
Silver and synthetic material
ring, 1991.

369 ANETTE WOHLLEBER
Ring designs, 1991.

368

370

(b. 1942) at the Fachhochschule für Gestaltung in Pforzheim. They were eminent professors who had themselves developed an independent and personal body of work in the field of jewellery. However, it is undoubtedly Hermann Jünger, a charismatic professor at the Munich Academy of Art from 1972-90, who most deserves our attention here, bearing in mind the large number of jewellers (from Gerd Rothmann and Otto Künzli through to Ulo Florack) who openly claim to have followed his teaching.

As of 1950, the jewellery of Jünger was characterised by its predominantly visual formal approach and its spiritual aesthetic, meaning and resonance. It is therefore not surprising that this jeweller-professor's freedom of formal expression, as well as his spiritual references, should continue to be decisive for a whole generation of German artists, who strive to rediscover a personal, suprasensitive aesthetic approach, by means of sensual, expressive jewellery.

Italy

Between 1975 and 1992, the rings of Diego Piazza (1950-95), mainly made in precious metals, adopted forms and overall structures that were both rigorous and more rounded. They prove that the designer was interested, above all, in the tension between geometric and curved figures and lines, seeking the rhythmic balance between them and their plastic, sculptural complementarity. (See Figs. 371–373 & 376.)

(Fig. 369): these feature bridges, towers, cloisters and temples, amongst other things. It is therefore space that concerns her and is expressed in her somewhat bulky, impressive jewellery. In 1994, this former pupil of Klaus Ullrich and Jens-Rudigen Lorenzen at the Pforzheim Fachhochschule für Gestaltung from 1983-1988, began to direct her work towards the symbolism of her objects. Starting with a gold wedding ring, she made a whole series of heart-shaped rings. She is not the first jeweller to work on this deceptively simple symbolic form, but she has used it as an opportunity to study other spheres of interest in more detail.

This rapid survey of some of the younger jewellers reveal the artistic and aesthetic inclinations of the German 'school'. All of them remain much influenced by their training and their respective teachers, such as Friedrich Becker at the Fachhochschule in Düsseldorf from 1973 to 1982, Reinhold Reiling from 1922 to 1983, Klaus Ullrich (b. 1927) and Jens-Rudigen Lorenzen

371

372

373

373 DIEGO PIAZZA
Ring in white and yellow
gold, 1977.

371 DIEGO PIAZZA
Ring in white gold and
ivory, 1978.

372 DIEGO PIAZZA
Ring in 18-carat gold and
niello, 1992.

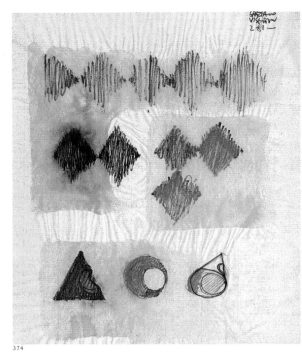

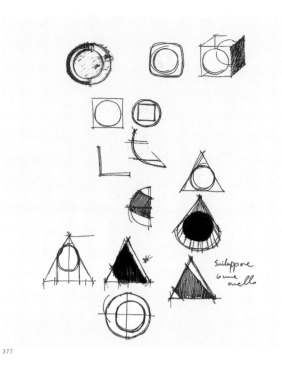

378

Since 1981, the rings made in precious metals by Graziano Visintin (b. 1953) have been construed as a conflict or contrast between lines and forms: that is, straight or curved elements and the actual object or body. His favourite geometric figures are the circle, triangle and square, as well as all their derivations. He deliberately draws on all these formal resources in an attempt to renew their effect once they are placed and worn on the body; thus releasing, with a maximum of 'simplicity' and desire for transcendence, a kind of

375 GRAZIANO VISINTIN
Yellow gold rings, 1981
Photograph by Trento.

378 GRAZIANO VISINTIN
White and yellow gold ring,
1985.

374 GRAZIANO VISINTIN
Illustrations of ring designs.

377 GRAZIANO VISINTIN
Idem.

376 DIEGO PIAZZA
Ring and stand in gold and
iron, 1986.

379

380

381

379 GIOVANNA GIANINAZZI
*'Infinity' ring in 22-carat
gold, no date.*

380 GIOVANNA GIANINAZZI
Illustration of ring design.

381 GIOVANNA GIANINAZZI
Illustration of ring design.

382

382 GIOVANNA GIANINAZZI
*'Ziqqurat' ring in 22-carat
gold, 1990.*

spirituality and purification of matter. A 1973 graduate of the Pietro Selvatico Institute, who then spent two years with Giampaolo Babetto from 1973 to 75, this jeweller has been able to find his own formal and symbolic language. He succeeds magnificently in placing all his experience and technique in the field of precious metals at the service of his thinking about the very essence of geometry. (See Figs. 374, 375, 377 & 378; also 307 & 308).

The 'infinity' rings of Giovanna Quadri Gianinazzi (b. Switzerland in 1957) are fashioned in such a way that the gold wire in these objects – which vary in length and cross-section from 0.9 mm to 2 or 3 mm – coiled up and soldered at both ends, can always take on different appearances and sizes. In the case of 'Ziqqurat' (Fig. 382) – still within this idea of fusion of gold – the effects of lamination and coiling create broad hoops whose surfaces and textures leave distinct strips. In the case of the 'four elements' (Fig. 384) and 'four seasons', there are four rings in one, since all the formal, coloured and symbolic elements are adjustable and inter/independent. For earth, there is a square and a cube in black jade; for air, there is a circle and arch in white jade; for water, there are wavy

383

383 GIOVANNA GIANINAZZI
*'Elements' ring: 'Fire', in
22-carat gold, 18-carat
gold and coral, 1996.*

384

385

384 GIOVANNA GIANINAZZI
*'Elements' ring in 22-carat
gold, 18-carat gold and
semi-precious stones (black
and green jade and coral),
1996.*

385 GIOVANNA GIANINAZZI
*Diagram of 'Elements' ring
design.*

lines and a downward-facing triangle in green jade; for fire, there is an upward-facing triangle and a pyramid in coral, since it was impossible to find orange jade. (See Figs. 379–381, 383 & 385.)

The rings of this jeweller, who now lives and works in Italy, are thus quite symbolic. She refers more particularly to Greek mythology and the myth of Penelope for her gold hoops.

In the case of the 'four elements' rings, each element, material or stone has been rigorously selected for its arrangement and harmony – but also and especially for its spiritual and oriental echoes.

We should remember that jade is charged with cosmic energy (yang) and endowed with solar, imperial and indestructible eternal – as well as alchemic – qualities.[29]

After serving an apprenticeship as a goldsmith in Florence from 1980 to 1986 and then spending a year

386

388

387

at the Massana School with Ramon Puig Cuyas from 1986 to 1987, Giovanna Quadri Giannazi's enquiry into rings demonstrates a great deal of knowledge and maturity.

The rings of Alberto Zorzi (b. 1958), in metal and precious stones, offer all their roundness and voluptuousness to the light, accentuated by the always polished treatment of the gold, as well as reflections and polychromatic effects produced by using materials like onyx, quartz and spinel. This play on roundness and the search for brilliance, sparkle or

386 ALBERTO ZORZI *Ring in gold and red spinel, 1996.*

387 ALBERTO ZORZI *Ring in gold and onyx, 1994.*

388 ALBERTO ZORZI *Ring in gold and brown quartz, 1995.*

389 ANNA MARIA ZANELLA
Iron and glass ring, 1993.

refraction is characteristic of the work of this 1978 graduate of the Pietro Selvatico Institute.[30] He has, nevertheless, retained from his training a taste for the geometry of forms in space, as well as irreproachable technique and mastery of matter. His rings, with their softened contours and multi-coloured reflections are thus much more organic than those of Visintin, another former pupil of Selvatico. Nor do these two jewellers share the same artistic or aesthetic approach. Alberto Zorzi remains much drawn towards design and fashion. His jewellery is also less 'cerebral' and more 'sensual'. (See Figs. 386–388.)

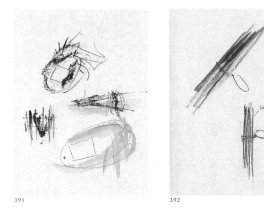

391   392

the world of Italian jewellery with her personal, emotive and poetic style, as if liberated from the line taken by the Padua School. (See Figs. 389–392.)

In 1992, the rings of Giovanni Corvajà (b. 1971) were made up of fine, delicate networks or very close weaving of precious metals. This work on an entanglement of gold (Fig. 395), deliberately circumscribed within a definite general shape – a hollowed circle or square – appears to channel the extraordinary energy inherent in this material. Still working on gold (Fig. 396 shows it coiled and with a matt finish), this artist made a gold hoop of very sober design in 1995. After studying at the Pietro Selvatico Institute from 1985 to 1990 and the Royal College of London from 1990 to 1992, this young jeweller seems to have found his own personal artistic dynamics, imbued with sensory refer-

390 ANNA MARIA ZANELLA
Ring in wood, iron, brass, pure gold, wax colour, 1990, Fond Bevilacqua la Masa, Cà Pesaro Modern Art Museum, Venice.

391 ANNA MARIA ZANELLA
Ring designs.

392 ANNA MARIA ZANELLA
Idem.

393 JACQUELINE RYAN
18-carat gold and enamel ring, 1996.

394 JACQUELINE RYAN
18-carat gold and enamel ring, 1996.

393

The unexpected assemblies of gold, iron, glass and other materials used by Anna Maria Zanella (b. 1966) make up rings in which the different materials confront each other. The contrasts or conflicts between the expressive 'primitive' treatment of these forms and materials and their different origins and histories give these objects a great deal of emotional resonance. This artist, who was taught by eminent professors and jewellers, such as Francesco Pavan, Giampaolo Babetto and Graziano Visintin at the Pietro Selvatico Institute from 1980-85, has enriched

394

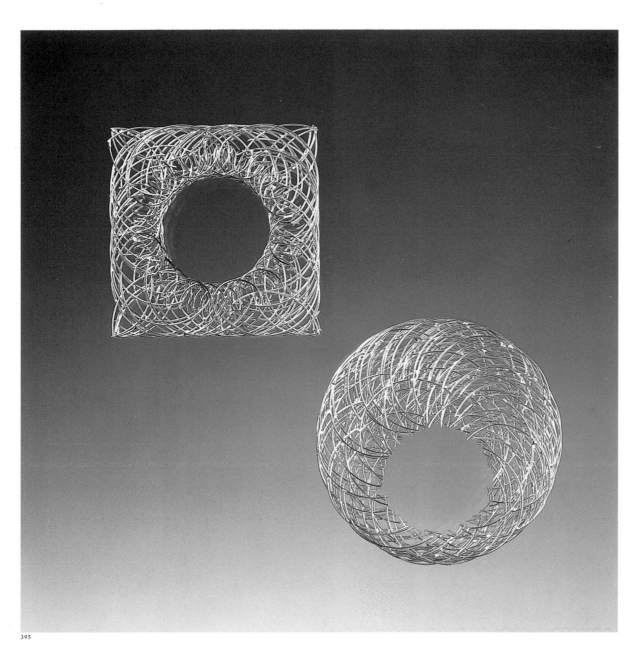

395

396

397

ences. He is currently living and working in Padua with the English jeweller Jacqueline Ryan.

Rings made by the latter (b. London, 1966) include a geometrical structure in gold in or on which tiny white or blue pieces of enamel form or settle, resounding with the movements of the hand (Figs. 393 & 394). As in her brooches, this jeweller works on planes and volumes, with the addition of small beads of colour representing fragments of life. In 1994, one year before her partner Giovanni Corvajà, she made a matt gold hoop of very sober design. Jacqueline Ryan is a graduate of the Royal College of London, where she studied from 1989 to 1991. (See also Fig. 397.)

This young generation of Italian jewellers aims to prove that, through exchanges and contacts with foreign schools in Barcelona or London, as well as adopting other ways of looking at jewellery and objects through the disciplines of fashion and design, it has been able to challenge and enrich the specific training in the techniques of goldworking and geometry received at Padua. The work of Graziano Visintin is probably the most magnificent and representative illustration of this. (See Fig. 308.)

Spain

The series of 'message' rings by Ramon Puig Cuyas (b. 1953) is structured on the basis of a circle of metal sometimes attached to a very fine, long stalk. These objects have tiny tips – fashioned in the image of a

398 RAMON PUIG CUYAS
*'Anell per un navegant
perdut' in silver, alpaca,
wood, plastics, cork and
lead, 1991, and 'Anell per
un dia de boira' in silver,
cork, aluminium, wood, lead
and alpaca, 1991.*

399 RAMON PUIG CUYAS
*Designs for 'Anell per un
navegant perdut' ring and
stand.*

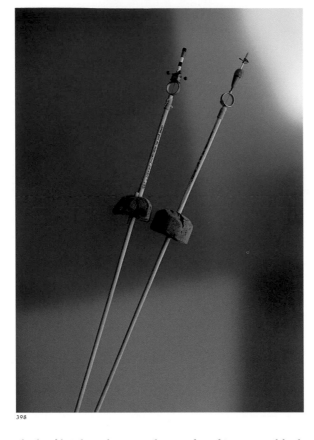

398

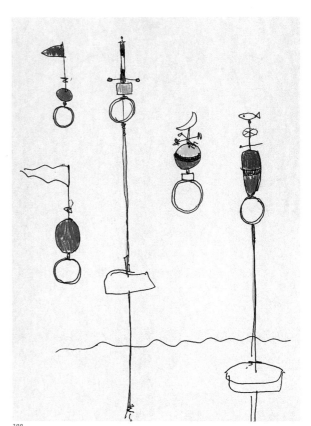

399

400   401

slash of bright colours such as red and/or green, black
or white – which seem to shoot into space. Designed
in 1990 while the artist was staying on an island in the
Baltic Sea, these rings were subsequently made with a
stand and were meant to be seen as little buoys or
bottles thrown anonymously into the sea, at the mercy
of the whims of the wind and the currents.

These graphic and poetic marine objects do not in
any way claim to illustrate a precise story, still less to
channel the emotions that may emanate from them.
These 'lifebelt' rings are thus intended to carry the
recipient as far away as possible, placing in them
whatever interpretation they choose – in short, to give
free rein to the imagination. (See Figs. 398 & 399.)

These rings are thus very representative of the
research and creative work of this great Spanish
jeweller: he approaches jewellery as a composition
that is at once pictorial and sculptural.

His dreamlike and mythological markers are infinite: it is what human beings collectively or individu-
ally convey – stories, fears, feelings and so on – that
interests him, since it is this invisible world that brings
his work to life.

His rings, like his other jewellery, are objects with
multiple meanings; 'open-ended' works. We may see
and feel his whole approach as a marvellous voyage,

in order to rediscover that lost experience of adven-
ture within ourselves. It is this meeting that Ramon
Puig Cuyas is undoubtedly seeking to embody in his
jewellery: a shadow, a fragment of light, a bottle or a
sail on the sea.

After having studied at the Massana School in
Barcelona from 1969 to 1974, Ramon Puig Cuyas has
been teaching there since 1977 and now co-ordinates
the jewellery department. He is the sponsor and
organiser of many events involving jewellery and the
author of many critical articles.

Using precious materials and very simple shapes,
Carles Codina Armengol (b. 1961) designs and makes
rings that refer, through metonymy, either to the
primordial energy of nature, or to the heavenly world
and spirituality, for example, a golden cherub who
may be standing upright to form a bezel or lying,

stretched out on the hoop. This jeweller, who studied at the Massana School from 1980 to 1986, considers the ring to be the piece of jewellery that has the richest and deepest roots and he therefore conceives of it in the most intimate, symbolic and spiritual way possible. He has been teaching at the Massana School since 1996 and also organises exhibitions in the field of adornment. (See Figs. 400–402.)

400 CARLES CODINA ARMENGOL *Ring in gold, silver and red coral, 1995.*

401 CARLES CODINA ARMENGOL *Gold leaf ring, 1996.*

402 CARLES CODINA ARMENGOL *Oxidized silver rings, 1996.*

The rings of Carmen Roher Casselas (b. 1962) must be grasped in an abstract symbolic spirit. With their interplay of different metals and materials such as gold, silver, copper and coral, her rings have a broad hoop on which a bezel develops, bearing a pattern of shapes with marine or natural reference points. A student of Ramon Puig Cuyas from 1983-89, she has been exhibiting regularly since 1987. (See Figs. 403, 404, 406 & 408.)

embedded, standing out against a coloured background (Figs. 405 & 407). Functioning like small icons, these objects are reminiscent of talismans. After studying design in Germany at the Fachhochschule Hildesheim from 1985 to 1991, and at the Massana School, this jeweller has been exhibiting very regularly. (See also Figs. 409 & 410.)

The 'small squares' rings of Xavier Ines Monclus (b. 1966) are objects with metal hoops each topped with a

403

406

404

408

403 CARMEN ROHER
Ring in gold, silver and coral, 1992.

404 CARMEN ROHER
Ring in gold, silver and coral, 1992.

406 CARMEN ROHER
Ring in gold, silver and coral, 1992.

408 CARMEN ROHER
Gold and silver ring, 1993.

405

407

The rings of Silvia Walz (b. Germany in 1965) have here a circular, compact form in silver, in, on and/or under which a tiny image with a gold pattern is

small square box. Small, interchangeable 'childish' images appear to settle on the surface: such as a parrot, apple, fish or frog. In his very humorous objects, this jeweller is questioning and challenging the concept of seriality and multiplicity so dear to the Pop Art movement. A student of Ramon Puig Cuyas and Hans Leicht from 1986-92, he has been exhibiting since 1992. (See Figs. 411 & 412.)

The ring-objects made in 1996 by Dharma Soriano Rodriguez (b. 1975), which combine metals, plastics and photo-engraving, are relatively large-sized spheres; little worlds in interdependent motion and turmoil. Like the frightened planets of Saint-Exupery's 'Little Prince', they all explicitly feature individuals,

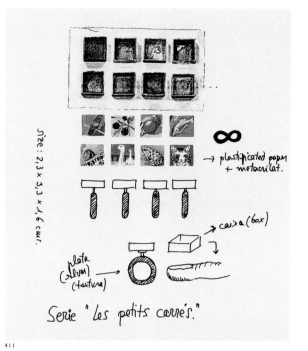

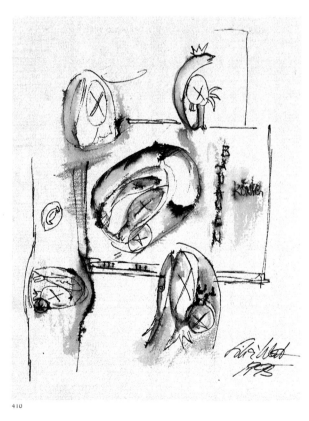

407 SILVIA WALZ *Three rings in gold and silver, no date.*

405 SILVIA WALZ *'Bananenkönig' ring in gold and silver, no date.*

409 SILVIA WALZ *Illustrations of ring designs.*

410 SILVIA WALZ *Illustrations of ring designs.*

412 XAVIER INES MONCLUS
Eight 'Small squares' rings in silver, plasticised paper and 'metacrilat', no date.

411 XAVIER INES MONCLUS
Design for 'Small squares' rings.

objects, animals and items taken from nature or towns. This very coherent set of poetic objects was even designed to be exhibited on stands in the shape of forearms and hands, on the fingers of which the whole 'madness' of these galaxies comes to life. (See Figs. 413–414, 417 & 418.)

This very young jeweller, a student at the Massana School from 1991-95, produces very personal, broad and thoughtful work that goes far beyond pure form and the function or design that the ring may take on or invent: Dharma Soriano Rodriguez links and binds it to – and involves it in – metaphysics. He has been exhibiting since 1992. (See also Figs. 415–418.)

These younger Spanish jewellers have a genuinely dynamic process and creative richness which can be connected to a single ornamental theme. It involves specific work on the patina of metals, the construction and arrangement of forms, the importance of

413

413 **DHARMA SORIANO RODRIGUEZ** *'La prinesita con Boba' ring in silver, bronze, copper and plastics, 1996.*

414 **DHARMA SORIANO RODRIGUEZ** *'Lite' ring in silver, bronze, photograph and plastics, 1996.*

417 **DHARMA SORIANO RODRIGUEZ** *'Set pommates te un pomer' ring in silver, bronze and photograph, 1996.*

418 **DHARMA SORIANO RODRIGUEZ** *Ring in silver, bronze, photograph, plastics and 'pastelina', 1996.*

416 **DHARMA SORIANO RODRIGUEZ** *Designs for the 17 'Galaxy' rings.*

415 **DHARMA SORIANO RODRIGUEZ** *Ring design.*

415

416

417

418

contrasting colours, the explicit and almost systematic figurative references – which are often humorous and playful – and the strong evocations of nature, as well as intuitive and spiritual resonances.

Though remaining as individual as possible, each of these jewellers is seeking a balance between the rational and the intuitive, which is characteristic of their entire training at the Massana School.[31] It should also be stated now that they all see the ring as a privileged, revealing link between the person who designs it and the person who wears or looks at it, as well as a real object that has a life of its own.

419

422

423

424

419 ZELIA NOBRE *Silver rings, 1990-91.*
421 ZELIA NOBRE *Two rings in polished oxidised silver, 1995-96.*
420 ZELIA NOBRE *Ring in polished oxidised silver.*

420   421

Portugal

The 'objects to be handled' and the 'white' series in silver by Ana Campos (b. 1953) – sensual volumes whose surfaces are streaked all over – are objects made to be manipulated and caressed by the hand. A professor in jewellery design at the ESAD (Art and Design School) in Oporto, she approaches jewellery in a conceptual way, and as tactile pieces or objects.

The rings made by Zélia Nobre (b. 1965) between 1990 and 1991, have bezels in the form of small, simple silver pieces of architecture. This jeweller sees them as true reliquaries, containing dialogues held between and with what may be hidden, real or invisible. In 1995, she designed and made a pair of broad, simple hoops in polished and oxidised silver, whose inner parts – rising and hoisting themselves up – resembled a crown. In her rings, this artist seems to be much attracted by the idea of suggesting a possible link that someone might have with an object, feeling or being. After studying jewellery at the Ar. Co. in Lisbon from 1984 to 1988, she now teaches jewellery,

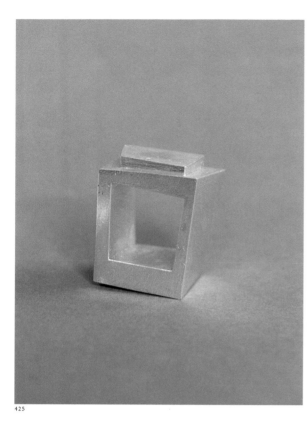
425

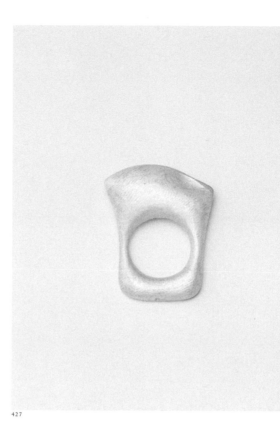
427

428

429

426

amongst other things, at the same school. (See Figs. 419–424.)

For her silver rings dating from 1992, with their cubic lines and inverted forms, Alexandra Lisboa (b. 1966) reveals and hides in turn the motifs of her objects. In 1995, she tackled the infinite on the basis of a sheet of metal tightly coiled up on itself. A student at the Ar. Co. from 1984 to 1988 and then at the Massana School in 1988, she also attended the classes of Peter Skubic at the Fachhochschule in Cologne. (See Figs. 425 & 426, 428–430.)

The rings made by these few Portuguese jewellers prove the creative dynamics of the teaching given by ESAD and Ar. Co. in Lisbon, along with the obvious desire of that country to compete with the jewellery from neighbouring countries.

430

428 ALEXANDRA LISBOA *Ring design.*

429 ALEXANDRA LISBOA *Ring design.*

430 ALEXANDRA LISBOA *'One thousand sheets' ring in silver, 1995.*

426 ALEXANDRA LISBOA *'Interiores Exteriores' ring in silver, 1992.*
425 ALEXANDRA LISBOA *Idem.*
427 ANA CAMPOS *'White' ring in silver, 1995.*

United Kingdom

The rings of Anne Finlay (b. 1953), with their very simple circular shapes, in acrylics of all colours and tinted aluminium, were specially designed and made for a travelling exhibition, the 'Ring Exhibition 1983' (for the Aspects Gallery in London, the Spektrum and Ventil Galleries in Munich and the Mattar Gallery in Cologne). This jeweller is also an industrial designer and only makes rings occasionally. Her ornaments

431

rather like small pierced containers – seem to explore the conceptual boundaries of this small item of adornment. In their deliberately simplified shape, these rings play on 'opening' and/or 'closing', as in the case of the ring in Fig. 432, which allows its flowing threads to run free, or those in Fig. 431 with their narrowing, shrinking forms. All these objects are, above all, tactile rings. They are designed to cover and encompass – but especially to liberate and open up the

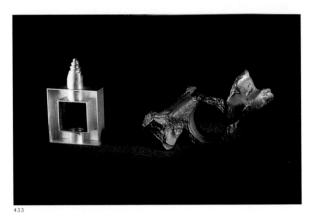

433

and other mechanically produced objects such as alarm clocks and calendars, mainly using plastic, have purified and always colourful lines. This artist immersed herself in the design of objects through her studies at Grays School of Art and Design in Aberdeen, and only specialised in jewellery at the end of her studies in 1976. She has been exhibiting since 1979.

The gold, silver and platinum rings of Cynthia Cousens (b. 1956), dating from 1992/93, form a perfectly coherent whole. Seen by the artist as, amongst other things, receptacles for symbols, all these objects – here annular in shape and looking

433 CHRISTOPHE ZELLWEGER *Ring in 22-carat gold and tool, 1992; and 'bone' ring in steel, 1993.*

432

431 CYNTHIA COUSENS
Group of stacking silver rings, 1992.

432 CYNTHIA COUSENS
'Cocoon' and 'Encircling' rings in silver, 1993. Photographs by Joël Degen.

phalanx, the finger and, by extension, the hand and even the whole body of the wearer towards a freer interpretation of meaning and function. Having studied design and then attended the Royal College of Art from 1979 to 1982, this jeweller approaches ornaments from a very intuitive, sensory and 'natural' angle. She has been exhibiting regularly since 1978.

The ring-objects or 'hand ornaments' of Christophe Zellweger (b. 1962, Switzerland) are usually designed by juxtaposing materials of different origins, such as animal or plant materials, with more traditional materials such as iron, wood, metal, or found objects used as they are.

These objects with their always impressive and sculptural dimensions have a prominent shape that is to be placed above or in the hollow of the palm of the hand. Because of the way the material is treated, these objects still give the impression that they have been

436

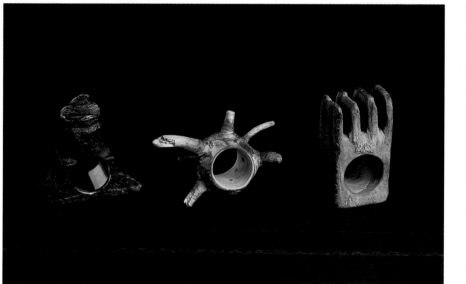

434

434 CHRISTOPHE ZELLWEGER *Three rings in steel, wood and found objects, 1991.*

435 CHRISTOPHE ZELLWEGER *Ring in steel, bone and found object, 1992. Anger Museum Collection, Efurt (Germany).*

436 CHRISTOPHE ZELLWEGER *Ring in steel, bone and found object, 1992. Anger Museum Collection, Efurt (Germany).*

435

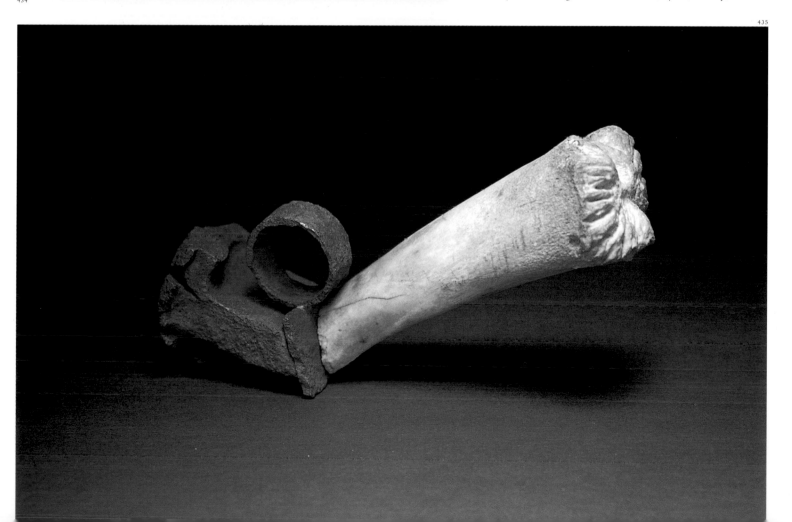

437

439

439 SUSAN CROSS *Rings in 18-carat gold and ring in steel, bonded and rolled metal, 1996.*

439 SUSAN CROSS *Rings in 18-carat gold and ring in steel, bonded and rolled metal, 1996.*

437 SUSAN CROSS *Three rings in lacquered, coloured and crocheted copper, 1993.*

438

found and are in their original state. Their shapes and materials also give these rings a strong aesthetic presence. The intervention of the artist is revealed in his choices – of forms, materials and techniques – but also through deep artistic, analytical and conceptual thinking.

His ring-sculptures deliberately hark back to 'primitive' or 'archaeological' themes. In order to understand this impact, which is sometimes violent and startling, they demand to be touched and worn. (See Figs. 434–436.)

By means of a combination of materials and forms, as well as an artistic, conceptual approach to jewellery, Zellweger seeks to redefine human perception of – and communication with – jewellery; the way people are transformed by objects or visa versa, as well as their influence on the environment and nature and their place in history.

He studied at the Kunstgewerbeschule in Zurich

from 1987 to 1991, followed by two years at the Royal College of Art from 1991-93.

The high bezel and the hoop in the rings of Susan Cross (b. 1964) are carefully woven in gold, oxidised silver, steel and copper. This jeweller has freely adapted needlework to metal using an artistic standpoint and not simply to show technical prowess. These objects, with their delicacy, poetry and femininity, sometimes have natural or figurative connotations. With a 1982 diploma from the Herefordshire College of Art and Design and a degree in jewellery

441

440 MARY PRESTON *'Josie' ring in silver, braid and lace, 1995.*

441 MARY PRESTON *'Endeared' ring in silver, fabric and mother-of-pearl buttons, 1995.*

438 MARY PRESTON *Illustration for ring design.*

440

442 ANNE FINLAY
Rings in acrylics and tinted aluminium, no date.

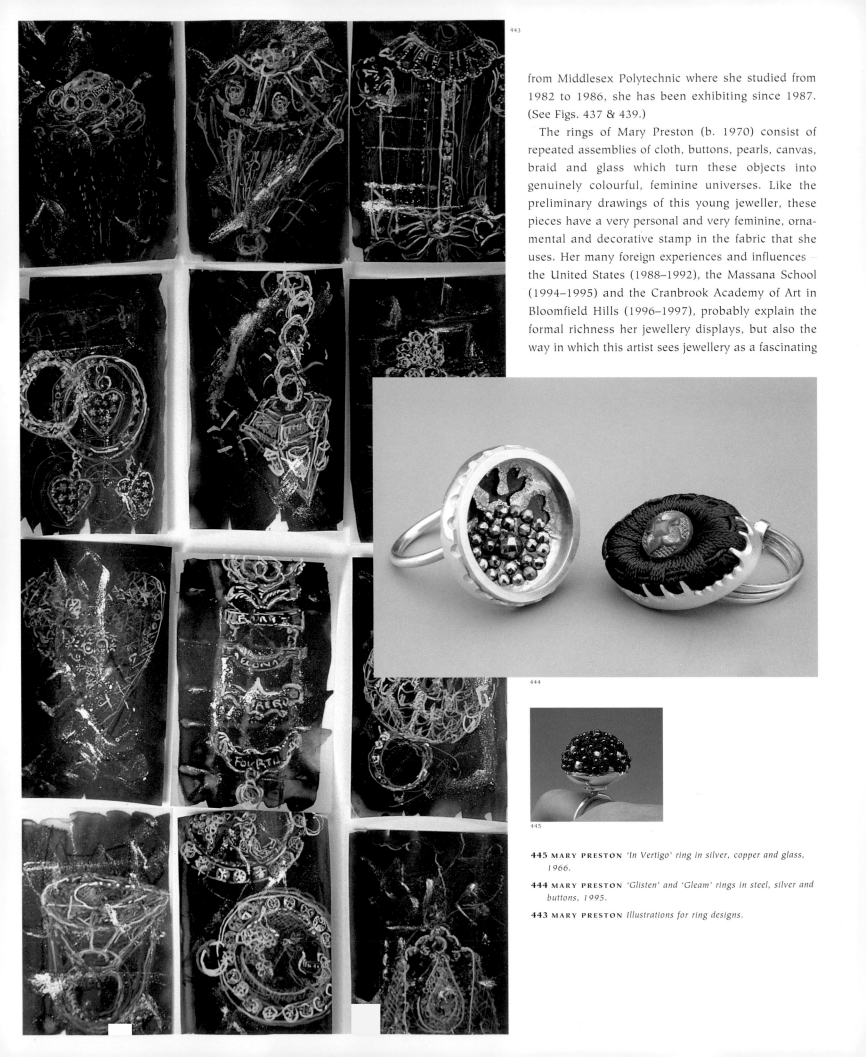

from Middlesex Polytechnic where she studied from 1982 to 1986, she has been exhibiting since 1987. (See Figs. 437 & 439.)

The rings of Mary Preston (b. 1970) consist of repeated assemblies of cloth, buttons, pearls, canvas, braid and glass which turn these objects into genuinely colourful, feminine universes. Like the preliminary drawings of this young jeweller, these pieces have a very personal and very feminine, orna- mental and decorative stamp in the fabric that she uses. Her many foreign experiences and influences — the United States (1988–1992), the Massana School (1994–1995) and the Cranbrook Academy of Art in Bloomfield Hills (1996–1997), probably explain the formal richness her jewellery displays, but also the way in which this artist sees jewellery as a fascinating

445 MARY PRESTON '*In Vertigo*' *ring in silver, copper and glass, 1966.*

444 MARY PRESTON '*Glisten*' *and* '*Gleam*' *rings in steel, silver and buttons, 1995.*

443 MARY PRESTON *Illustrations for ring designs.*

individual, social and historical indicator. The Hypotesi Gallery held an exhibition of her work in 1996. (See Figs. 438, 440, 441 & 443–445.)

The rings of Catherine E. Hills (b. 1968) – made of silver or steel, sometimes oxidised or gilded with gold leaf – have round, smooth bezels with a biomorphic appearance, which are sometimes interchangeable. In the design of her lifelike, somewhat futuristic objects, this English jeweller draws on sources of inspiration as disparate as gardens, flowers, insects, birds, toys and sex. She studied at the Royal College of Art from 1991 to 1993. (See Figs. 446–448.)

In studying the rings of these jewellers, it is clear that their work possesses a very British quality; certainly still under the influence of the training given at the Royal College of Art by David Watkins,

447

447 CATHERINE E. HILLS
Three 'Flower' rings in oxidised silver, green plastic and 18-carat gold, 1992.

448

448 CATHERINE E. HILLS
'Bird' ring in silver and gold leaf, 1991.

446 CATHERINE E. HILLS
Three rings in 18-carat gold, silver and oxidised silver, 1993.

446

but also through a very design-orientated approach to jewellery. This school is still today the point at which university teaching of fine arts and the so-called 'decorative' arts converges.

Austria

449

The rings of Anna Heindl (b. 1950), designed and made between 1995 and 1996, are very structured, like little sculptures, and narrative, as reflected by their figurative titles, such as 'Sky' (Fig. 449), 'Near the Storm' (Fig. 451), 'Sunday morning' (Fig. 450)

or 'Drop in the Net' (Fig. 452). From an annular base of precious metal – a simple divided or open-work hoop – they all deploy their high bezels from which the brightly sparkling stone shoots out in an upward movement. These rings, which all come under the 'Horizon 1' theme, are more particularly concerned with the sky and light.

The ring-sculptures of this great Austrian jeweller are always designed on the basis of an initial concept involving apparently contrasting themes, such as 'Ears and tears', 'Framing and ornaments' or 'Land-scape and garden'.[32] She tackles this basic constraint

451

and overcomes it magnificently with perfect technical mastery, a great deal of formal research, renewal and finesse, as well as femininity, poetry and references that are as much historical and cultural as personal and intimate. She has been involved in collective exhibitions since 1972 and has held solo exhibitions since 1977.

Most of the younger generation of Austrian jewellers seem to work on the basis of a much more analytical, fragmentary and non-descriptive aesthetic: Melitta Moschik (b. 1960) prefers to take this line. The series of rings in Fig. 454 is relatively representative of her research and her carefully analysed, logical and realistic experiments involving constructions and compositions made by assembling simple, adjustable mechanical elements.

The concept of the multiple ring as addressed by Michael Ramharter (b. 1961) is demonstrated by the variety of forms his silver objects take, with their cylindrical design and volume. These nevertheless retain a natural, stylised reference, often using leaf and flower forms (Fig. 453). In 1991 this jeweller designed and produced several copies of a very beautiful aluminium ring, bearing a red rose in full bloom,

453 MICHAEL RAMHARTER
Five silver rings, 1990.

from a baroque and 'kitsch' viewpoint (Fig.458). Ramharter studied at the Hochschule für Angewandte Kunst in Vienna from 1987 to 1993 and has been exhibiting since 1988.

In the series of 'satellite' rings, in bronze and gold leaf, Andrea Halmaschlager (b. 1961) seems to be more interested in working on matter – thus fitting in with a more spiritualist aesthetic. Another former pupil of the Hochschule für Angewandte Kunst in Vienna from 1980 to 1986, she also gained a wealth of experience from a whole year spent at the Gerrit Rietveld Academy in Amsterdam from 1986-87, under the guidance of Onno Boekhoudt. Her work, which draws much inspiration from the colours and shimmer of fabrics, has been affected by this.[33] She has been exhibiting since 1986. (See Fig. 455.)

The rings made by Florian Lädstätter (b. 1967), in gilt wood and steel, are impressive monumental structures. This very productive and creative jeweller produces a variety of work using simple, basic shapes such as cylinders, squares and rectangles, arranged in a pattern. He too studied at the Hochschule für Angewandte Kunst in Vienna from 1986 to 1992. (See Figs. 456 & 457.)

The round, very sensual and tactile ring-objects of Bernhard Fink (b. 1970) are designed and made in a spirit of continuity, tightly embracing the finger, hand, body and, more generally, the environment: 'Eis' (Fig. 459) is an ephemeral ring made of ice, while 'Chicken egg' (Fig. 460) is made of synthetic resin and 'Quail's egg' (Fig. 461) of silver. This young and very original artist, who has worked with Anna Heindl, amongst others, from 1992 to 1994, constructs his work with the aid of materials that are sometimes fragile or ephemeral, but uses primordial, eternal and material forms, such as the circle or the shape of an egg. The recipient is free to wonder about the vulnerability of his or her surroundings or to take the time to dream about what a ring or ornament could more

454 MELITTA MOSCHIK
Three rings in 14-carat gold and silver, no date.

449 ANNA HEINDL *'Sky' and 'Star' rings in gold, silver and semi-precious stones, 1996.*

451 ANNA HEINDL *'Near the storm' ring in silver and semi-precious stone, 1996.*

450 ANNA HEINDL *'Sunday morning' ring in gold and semi-precious stone, 1995.*

452 ANNA HEINDL *'Drop in the net' ring in silver and semi-precious stone, 1995.*

456

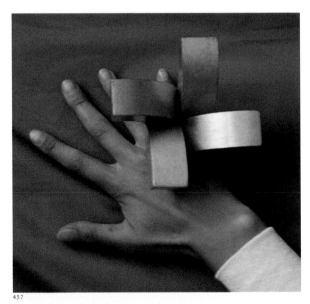

457

458

455 ANDREA HALMASCHLAGER *'Satellites' rings in bronze and gold leaf, 1995.*

456 FLORIAN LADSTATTER *'Stories' ring in gilded wood and steel, 1994.*

457 FLORIAN LADSTATTER *Ring in gilded wood and steel, no date.*

458 MICHAEL RAMHARTER *Rose ring in tinted aluminium, 1991.*

profoundly represent. He held his first, solo exhibition at Galerie V&V in Vienna in 1996.[34]

There seems to have been a unified style in Austria during the 1980s and 1990s, probably as a result of the training received from the Hochschule für Angewandte Kunst in Vienna by Verena Scharzinger (b. 1953), Sonja Bischur (b. 1966) and Florian Lädstätter, which was characterised by simple and effective design. Patricia Todosze (b. 1964), who did not undergo this training and yet still works in a similar perspective, is undoubtedly proof of the very strong influence of the Hochschule's school of thought; from which only jewellers with a strong personality who are very expressive and indeed very original, such as Anna Heindl or, more recently, Bernhard Fink, could really succeed in escaping.

Switzerland

The circular, almost flat gold rings made by Alban Hürlimann (b. 1953) were designed to be arranged or adjusted when positioned in the centre of their stands. These resemble astrological charts, with the network of coloured graphics representing the interplay of positions of the stars or planets (mysteriously orchestrated around the date of 26th April 1969) radiating out from the ring, which is both solar and lunar.

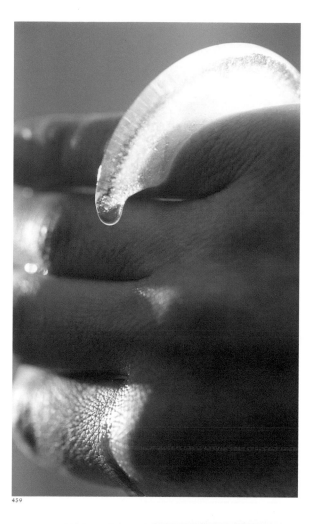

459

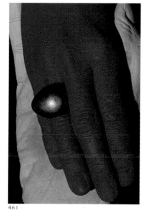

461

460

459 BERNARD FINK
'Eis' ring in ice, 1996.

460 BERNARD FINK
'Chicken egg' ring in synthetic resin, 1995.

461 BERNARD FINK
'Quail's egg' ring in silver, 1995.

462 ALBAN HURLIMANN
Ring in 18-carat gold with its box, no date.

463 ALBAN HURLIMANN
Idem.

462

463

and hand with which they resonate. This jeweller works on the physical, living presence that this small object imposes on the wearer, involving play on the senses and a kind of metamorphosis. Greatly attracted to working with metal and to the raw energy that emanates from it, she deliberately reveals all stages in the transformation of the material. It is the change in an individual's behaviour brought about by a specific object or the move from the (visible) exterior to the (invisible) interior – as well as the traces left by this secret metamorphosis – that interests this artist. After studying at the School of Decorative Arts in Geneva

After studying jewellery in Lucerne from 1969 to 1973, this Swiss artist saw jewellery from a conceptual angle, much influenced by the artistic approach of Joseph Kosuth. His passion for metaphysics led him to reflect on the meaning and evolution of this ornament for the hand; in its simplest form and in its relationship with space and the universe. He has been exhibiting since 1976 and opened his own gallery, Schmuck Forums, in Zurich in 1984. (See Figs. 462 & 463.)

The single and double rings made in forged, hammered metal such as gold and/or silver, iron and anodised aluminium, or wood, by Esther Brinkmann (b. 1953) are 'recipients for the finger' supplied with their own stand (Figs. 464–467). Designed using basic forms, images and concepts such as that of the vase, the bell, sphere or ball, her rings show off the finger

466

465

465

464

464 ESTHER BRINKMANN
'Recipient for finger' ring, hammered gold bell and silk, 1995.

465 ESTHER BRINKMANN
Idem.

466 ESTHER BRINKMANN
'Recipient for finger' ring, hammered gold ball, 1992.

467 ESTHER BRINKMANN
Idem.

468

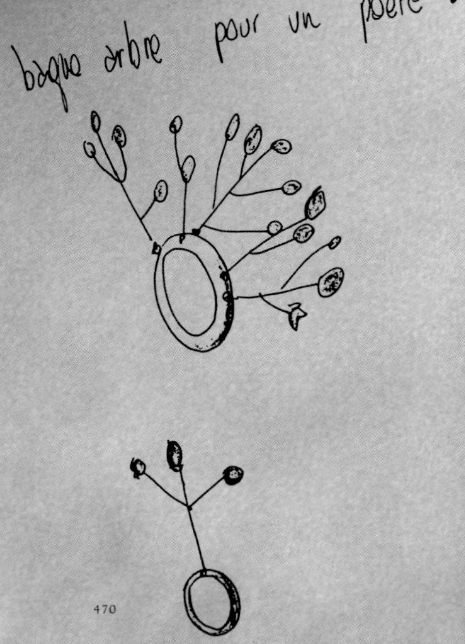

bague arbre pour un poète.

470

from 1974-78, she taught there from 1983 to 1987. In 1987, she took charge and was probably the instigator of the famous workshop of the same school where jewellery and other objects are designed, and has since lectured abroad on her approach. She has been exhibiting since 1984.

Until 1988, the rings of plastic (coloured Plexiglas®) and/or rubber made by Carole Guinard (b. 1955), with their light, simplified component shapes, designed to be interchangeable (Figs. 473 & 474), were designed for mass production. After that, this jeweller's designs returned to the unique 'amulet' pieces with spiritual, historical and more intimate references. Examples of these are the 'tori' or circular stands in silver, made in 1991, on which a small, full mobile circle slides (Fig. 475).

After studying at the School of Decorative Arts in Geneva from 1973 to 1977 and gaining experience

468 SOPHIE BOUDUBAN
Gold ring, 1990.

469 SOPHIE BOUDUBAN
Design for ring.

469

abroad, in Boston particularly, this jeweller set up her workshop-gallery, *Noblesse-Oblique*, in Lausanne (1979-95). While continuing with exhibitions and creative work, she developed a modernist, minimalist concept of designer jewellery in which the materials are the pretext for technical research into lighter, effective forms. Mass production then obliged her to develop her prototypes to perfection. A short while ago, Carole Guinard began to devote herself entirely to her own creative work.

The rings of Sophie Bouduban (b. 1967) seem to establish an intimate relationship with the wearer.

This younger jeweller, who works mainly in metal such as bronze, blackened silver, patinated brass, steel and sometimes gold gives her jewellery mobile reference points and resonant echoes. The 'Flowerpot' (Fig. 471), 'Tree' (Fig. 470) or 'Fingerprint' rings are made up of removable, independent pieces such as the small pivoting wheels or the five spirals turning on themselves and around the finger in Fig. 468, constantly reminding the wearer of their presence. Seen in relation to the moving body and the intimate history of their recipients, these small objects thus have a life of their own and are irrevocably linked to

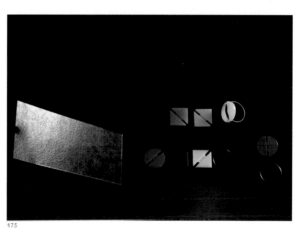

473

474

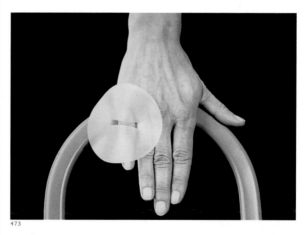

175

473 CAROLE GUINARD *Ring in plasticised tracing paper, 1987.*

475 CAROLE GUINARD *Rings in Plexiglas® and rubber, 1985.*

474 CAROLE GUINARD *Rings in gold and silver, 1991. Photographs by Magali Koenig (Lausanne).*

471   472

470–472 SOPHIE BOUDUBAN
Illustrations for ring designs.

476

477

478

477 SOPHIE HANAGAERT
'Floral cage' ring in iron, no date.

476 SOPHIE HANAGAERT
Three 'Heaven's vault' rings in iron and chased mother-of-pearl, no date.

478 SOPHIE HANAGAERT
'Sixth finger' ring in iron, no date.

479

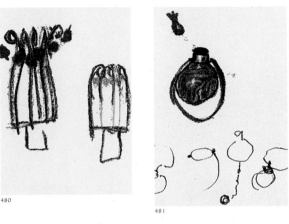

480

481

481 SOPHIE HANAGAERT *Design for 'Parasite' ring.*
480 SOPHIE HANAGAERT *Design for 'Bud' ring.*
479 SOPHIE HANAGAERT *Design for 'Sixth finger' ring.*

482

483

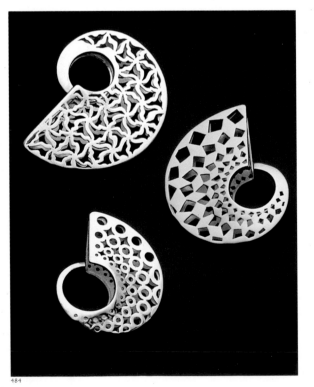

484

temporality. She studied at the School of Decorative Arts in Geneva from 1988 to 1991 and has been exhibiting regularly since 1989. (See also Fig. 472.)

The rings of Brune Boyer-Pellerej (b. 1967, Toulouse) explicitly echo architecture. In the 1992 'solari' series (Fig. 484), her objects spread out like open-work silver and vermilion shells reminiscent of the typical wooden partitions of Arab buildings. Shadows are east on the hand, just as they are on the walls of those buildings. In the case of 'Message' (1992), a rectangular rosewood structure clasps interlaced words made from a metal wire in gilt brass (Fig. 483). Yet these literary, philosophical illuminations remain illegible and secret, as they are too close together and superimposed on each other to allow their secret to be revealed. In 'Castle in the air' (1995), a 'medieval', open-work weaving of silver wire is to be slipped onto a silver base that bears an aquamarine (Fig. 482). This jeweller thus prefers to work on dual complementary themes in creating rings with a mysterious, sacred appearance. After gaining her diploma from the School of Decorative Arts in Geneva in 1990 and obtaining first prize for her 'Nautilus' bracelet, made in co-operation with the House of Bellon in 1989, she went to live and work in Spain.

Since 1991, Sonia Morel (b. 1968) has been working on a series of mobile silver and brass rings of variable sizes. This jeweller designs pieces that, by means of a manual mechanism, can expand or shrink and go up or down. After training under Esther Brinkmann at the School of Decorative Arts in Geneva (1989 to 1991),

484 BRUNE BOYER-PELLEREJ *'Solari' rings for the little finger in silver and vermilion, 1992. Photograph by Pascal Canedi.*

483 BRUNE BOYER-PELLEREJ *'Message' ring in rosewood and brass gilded with gold leaf, 1992. Photograph by Pascal Canedi.*

482 BRUNE BOYER-PELLEREJ *'Castle in the air' ring in silver and aquamarine, 1995. Photograph by Alfredo Rosado.*

she conceived of the ring as a fragile, constantly changing object, alternately protecting or freeing the finger, the hand and the body. (See Figs. 485 & 486.)

Sophie Hanagaert (b. 1968) lengthens and stretches out her long rings that often feature a light, airy bezel made out of fine, delicate iron and/or gold, ebony, mother-of-pearl, rubber or latex graphics. However, these 'Parasite' (Fig. 481), 'Bud' (Fig. 480), 'Floral cage' (Fig. 477), 'Heaven's vault' (Fig. 476) or 'Sixth finger' (Fig. 478 & 479) rings may also include a piece to be held and kept in the hollow of the hand, representing a bud, flower or message. All of them are thus conceived as anthropomorphic and secret pieces, amulets, votive objects, resonant fetishes or sexual emblems. In the final analysis, it is the owner who has the semantic freedom to interpret this jeweller's pieces – by turn parasites and lucky charms – which are

487

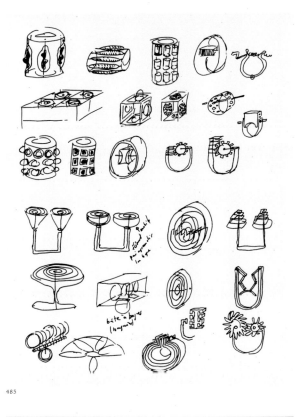

485

486

always playful, natural, sensual and lifelike. A 1995 graduate of the School of Decorative Arts in Geneva, Sophie attempts to free the ring from its simple annular or circular constraint. Her very personal and formal functional aim, linked to the imaginary and intuition, speaks of what is shown or hidden; of the relationship to be found between body and soul. She has been exhibiting since 1994.

The French jeweller Christine Maréchal (b. 1968) has done very little work on the ring motif, but she should be listed here as she is also a graduate of the School of Decorative Arts in Geneva from 1990. Although diversity of form, materials and techniques seem to characterise her work, the 'Garden' ring (Fig. 487) with its six sides in gold, blackened bronze and gold wire, accompanied by a boxwood and wire container, was made as part of research into 'French-style gardens'. She is interested in presenting matter as revealed by an appropriate form.

487 CHRISTINE MARÉCHAL *'Garden' ring in gold, blackened bronze and gold wire with boxwood container, no date.*

486 SONIA MOREL *Rings in silver and brass, 1996.*

485 SONIA MOREL *Ring designs.*

Needless to say, Switzerland, particularly Geneva, has traditionally been a leading centre for jewellery and clockmaking. It was not until 1987 that a real course on jewellery-object design was opened at the School of Decorative Arts or Applied Arts in Geneva, at the instigation of the jeweller-teacher Esther Brinkmann. This high-flying workshop, with its international meetings and exhibitions, has now become a place of experimentation and a centre for reflection on the art of jewellery that cannot be ignored. It has the ambition to train jewellers and designers of objects who are able to develop a free, original language.[35]

Denmark and Norway

488

Small coloured volumes in anodised aluminium are sunk or fitted (Fig. 489) on to the rectangular silver stand of an object by Kim Buck (b. 1957). The creative concept in the work of this Danish jeweller has remained almost unchanged since the ring was made in 1986. In fact, fascinated by formal simplicity and rigour, as well as the irreproachable technical execution of the decorative and functional items which usually go with clothing, such as buttons and pins, she gives pride of place to the ring which strikes an effective and simple balance between form and function. The forms, planes and volumes – coloured or otherwise – have strong geometric and abstract tendencies. Their execution is fine and sophisticated, and uses the body as a reference or interchanging integral part. Since completing her studies at the

489 KIM BUCK *Ring in silver and anodised aluminium, 1986.*

489

Danish College of Jewellery in 1982, Kim Buck has lived and worked in Copenhagen.

The rings made by Sigurd Bronger (b. 1957) since 1994 have been very substantial pieces of jewellery in metals like gold, silver and steel and/or hardened meerschaum, rubber and painted acrylics: his pieces are noteworthy for their very characteristic and monumental organic forms, as well as the perfect mastery shown in their technical execution. These objects with their impressively high bezels have a humorous and theatrical side. After studying jewellery and design in the Netherlands, this Norwegian jeweller now lives and works in his native town of Oslo. He exhibits in many countries. (See Figs. 488 & 490.)

490 SIGURD BRONGER
Ring in silver, steel, hardened meerchaum, rubber and painted acrylic, 1995, Ra Gallery, Amsterdam. Photograph by G. Dahl.

488 SIGURD BRONGER
Ring in 18-carat gold, hardened meerchaum and painted acrylic, 1994, Vestlandske Craft Museum collection, Bergen, Norway. Photograph by Sigurd Bronger.

491   492

493

The minimalist, austere hoop of the 1995 rings in oxidised silver and copper by Janicke Horn contrasts strongly with the luxuriant, generous coloured flowers on the bezel. This Norwegian jeweller seeks to achieve and communicate emotional tension through this firm, open, formal and symbolic contrast.

A ring in silver and enamel (Fig. 493) by Synnove Korssjoen (b. 1949) illustrates the approach of this Norwegian artist to the technical treatment of matter, and her symbolic view of jewellery. The coloured enamel, treated again after fusion, and the volume, with its natural, organic references give this ring-object a tactile, expressive, sensual, and indeed, sexual presence. She lives and works in Oslo.

The philosophy of the Scandinavian countries, which we have already mentioned in connection with the 1970s, needs some explanation here. With regard to Denmark, Kim Buck can be seen to embody the 'functionality' and approach to forms and materials traditionally associated with design in her country. The Norwegian jewellers, like Liv Blavarp (b. 1956) or Toni Vigeland (b. 1938) pursue their experiments into

491 JANICKE HORN
Ring in oxidised silver and yellow copper, 1995.

492 JANICKE HORN
Ring in oxidised silver and red copper, 1995.

493 SYNNOVE KORSSJOEN
Ring in silver and enamel, 1995.

the limits of matter (Korssjoen), forms (Bronger) or the symbol (Horn). Scandinavian jewellery is thus characterised by this ever 'elegant' and functionalist aesthetic, with a deferential and reverent link to Nature, creating the connection 'forms–matter–environment'.

France

The abstract, conceptual approach of Christophe Burger (b. 1950) is captured in a broad silver hoop with a strip of sandblasted glass across it (Fig. 496), and a hand ornament in cold-galvanised bronze and brass (Fig. 495). Aware of the difference in form, function and meaning between a 'ring' (as in a hoop or a circlet) and a finger ring, this jeweller has set out to redefine the two concepts. The strip of glass that prevents the finger from slipping into the inner space of the ring makes that empty space all the more present. In the case of the hand ornament, this jeweller has gone beyond the form of the 'finger ring', since the circle or hoop that traditionally bears the bezel and fits onto the finger has been supplanted by the intersecting structure. (See also Fig. 494.)

We have already observed the use of this plastic solution by the Dutch jewellers Ruudt Peters and Hermann Hermsen, amongst others. However, the

way the body is treated and approached by the French jeweller is perhaps more abstract. More recently in 1996, Christophe Burger attempted to further his investigation of the ring in 'pure' or 24-carat gold, showing the forging marks, which traditionally remain hidden, on the outer surface. This gold hoop, with its strong symbolic connotations, is said to condense within it the genesis and *raison d'être* of all the others.

Having studied at the School of Decorative Arts in Strasbourg from 1973-76, Christophe Burger had already opened his own gallery, the Héliodor, in Colmar, from 1977-81. He took part in setting up the Corpus Group in 1991. In 1995, he opened another gallery in Colmar, where he now lives and works.

494 CHRISTOPHE BURGER
Gold hoop, 1994.

495 CHRISTOPHE BURGER
Hand ornament in cold-galvanized bronze and brass, 1992.

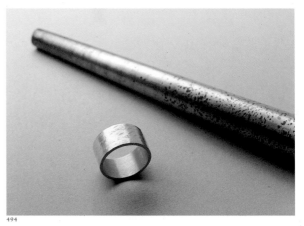
494

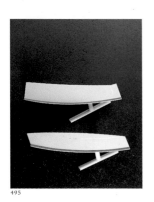
495

496 CHRISTOPHE BURGER
Ring in silver and sandblasted glass, 1994.

496

236

497

498

499

500

501

502

497 ASTRID MEYER *Ring for two fingers in stainless steel and steel, 1992.*

500 ASTRID MEYER *Gold hand ornament, 1994.*

501 ASTRID MEYER *Idem.*

499 ASTRID MEYER *Hand ornament in copper, stainless steel and steel, 1993.*

498 ASTRID MEYER *Idem.*

502 ASTRID MEYER *Hand ornament.*

The rings of Astrid Meyer (b. 1955), in stainless steel, steel and/or copper, gold and nickel, are hand ornaments, since they are designed and made with reference to that specific part of the body. Constructed in all cases by the addition of different elements, they deliberately go beyond the annular circle, either by being worn between the fingers or through a system of adjustable (or otherwise) lines or planes to be passed between the fingers. They can be understood as architectures, sculptures or autonomous objects, but their

503

504

graphic game, mystery or power of fascination is only apparent when worn. This jeweller, who has deliberately moved away from the 'imprisoning' circle, is interested in the intimate relationship between object and wearer. She thus dresses, transforms and plays with space and light by means of the hand. (See Figs. 497–502.)

Meyer is a graduate of the School of Decorative Arts in Strasbourg where she studied from 1974 to 1979, and also the co-founder of the Corpus Group in 1991.

505

The rings made by Hervé Ducruet (b. 1957) in metal such as gold, silver and bronze, and cabochon precious stones such as amethyst, tiger's eye and lapis lazuli, are often one-off pieces using the lost wax technique. Whether based on figurative inspirations (like the serpent in Fig. 507 & 508) or not, they seek to translate aspects of the inner reality of the artist or of an invisible world. After studying tribal art and ethnology, this jeweller was trained as a sculptor in metal at the multi-disciplinary arts workshops in Fontblanche from 1982 to 1984. He approaches the ring like a master of plastic arts seeking to embody an emotion or energy.

The very elaborate rings by Michael Greschny (b. 1960) – always made in gold and precious stones such as tourmaline, pearls and sapphires – have a medieval appearance. In his jewellery, he calls upon his vast knowledge of the traditions and skills of his trade. He uses casting, chasing, engraving, enamelling and niello effects, but also has deep respect for family practices relating to icons and frescoes. For this artist, these are techniques revealing love of matter and colour that, while perpetuating custom, enable him in his turn to tackle the ring with his own sensitivity as an aesthete. Great nobility and something of a sacred presence emanate from his jewellery. Trained by his father in icon and fresco-painting techniques from 1970-74, he only learned the jeweller's trade a few years later in 1978. His creative activity is mainly directed towards the liturgy. (See Figs. 503–506.)

The series of gold rings by Ann Gerard (b. 1963) shown in Fig. 509 is sensual and tactile. This jeweller has developed an interesting concept through her jewellery: the idea of 'touching in order to communi-

507

508

507 HERVE DUCRUET *Silver ring with cabochon amethyst, one-off creation, 1992.*

508 HERVE DUCRUET *Idem.*

cate' has inspired this collection she intends for the blind and everyone who can decipher or appreciate Braille. The rings are thus punctuated with little messages, words of love or friendship to be caressed and touched with the fingertips. Since 1981, this artist has studied jewellery at various Belgian and Parisian schools: the Jewellery School in Liège, the Brussels Arts and Crafts School and then the BJO (Bijouterie-Joaillerie-Orfèvrerie School) and AIS (Académie Internationale de Stylisme) in Paris.

503 MICHAEL GRESCHNY *Gold ring with rubellite, 1995.*

504 MICHAEL GRESCHNY *Gouache drawing.*

505 MICHAEL GRESCHNY *Ring in gold, sapphires and nielloed engravings, 1994.*

506 MICHAEL GRESCHNY *Idem.*

506

509

509 ANN GERARD *'Treasure' ring in 18-carat gold, no date. Photograph by Sabine Hartl.*

510 ANN GERARD *Braille design plate.*

510

A series of rings on the theme of 'life through rose-tinted glasses' (Fig. 511) consists of objects displaying tall, conical structures. Since 1989, the rings of Florence Lehmann (b. 1964) have been intended to be worn on a particular finger. They are already impressive because of their large size and volume – round, simple forms shown off by working metal to a matt or brushed surface, softened by points of colour in tinted resins; and there is charm in their poetry and symbolic word plays.

'Heart of marble' (Fig. 513), 'Heart of metal' (Fig. 522), 'Multi-coloured heart' (Fig. 521), 'Heart of clover' (Fig. 517), 'Heart as a fragment of love-talk (Roland Barthes)' (Fig. 523), 'Heart in love', and 'Heart on the hand' in transparent or coloured Plexiglas, cut from the solid, sometimes with letters or clover leaves inserted – these are all rings belonging to the 'hearts' series, designed from 1990-91 and made for the little finger of either hand. The last ring in this series, 'Shared hearts', consists of a pair of rings in black Plexiglas® inlaid with two chrysoprases, to be worn on the little finger but which can also be separated and used as earrings. This suite of rings once again constitutes a very coherent formal and symbolic whole.

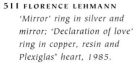

511

512

513

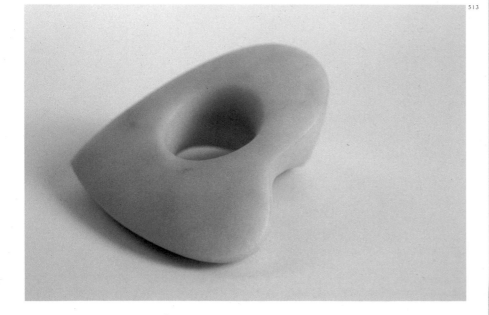

In contrast, 'Bits of paper' and, 'Yes/no' rings (Fig. 519), for the little finger of either hand, consist of an annular form in ivory and transparent Plexiglas®. In the 'Rattle ring' (Fig. 518), the artist has even ousted the circle, since the object is worn between the middle and ring fingers. It also has two functions, being a ring for the mother and an object-rattle for the child.

515

516

Through more recent pieces produced in 1994 and 1996, Florence Lehmann continues to explore references other than the circle: 'Hidden heart' (Fig. 512) is a mysterious object in silver and inlaid Plexiglas® which can open and shut; 'Reason and passion' (Fig. 516) is a resonant silver ball that oscillates between a white pole (a small meerschaum head) and a red one (a Plexiglas® heart), two objects rendering fear, ultimate questioning or introspection; and finally, 'Waltz' (Fig. 514), in leaded white resin, which draws two profiles in photographic negative, seeming to dare to look each other in the eye or even to love each other. These creations are ambivalent hand ornaments, to be worn between the middle and index fingers, the essential quality of which is undoubtedly the movement inherent in their conception, and especially their very strong symbolism of the search for loving equilibrium.

515 FLORENCE LEHMANN
'Heart on the hand' ring: 'Multi-coloured heart' and 'Transparent heart' in Plexiglas® cut from the solid, 1990.

516 FLORENCE LEHMANN
'Reason and passion' ring, silver ball filled with shot, meerschaum and red Plexiglas®, for the middle finger, 1996.

514 FLORENCE LEHMANN
'Waltz' ring in enamelled white resin to slip between two fingers, 1996. Photographs by Zvardon.

520

520 CATHY SPECHT *Hand ornament in horn and pearls, 1992.*

520

Attracted by objects with round, soft shapes, Florence Lehmann thus approaches rings from a resolutely volumetric, sensual and allegorical angle. On top of this, she is lyrical and poetic, redefining her jewellery in accordance with the symbolism of the fingers: the index finger designates the finger of life, judgement, balance and silence; the middle finger, the largest on the hand, symbolises the assertion of personality; the ring finger for its consonance with the engagement and wedding ring, the symbol of a senti-mental bond and commitment; and finally the little finger, resonating with the most secret desires and the occult powers of divination.[36] This jeweller seems to invite us to an initiation in love in which story and legend alternate. These references are undoubtedly autobiographical, but sufficiently allegorical and universal for everyone to be able to read into them their own emotions and feelings, and their most personal and secret histories.[37]

Following her studies at the School of Decorative Arts in Strasbourg (1984–87) under the guidance of Henri-Morand Boltz, she learned glass-making tech-niques from 1987 to 1988 and has been exhibiting regularly since 1987. She has even produced a collec-

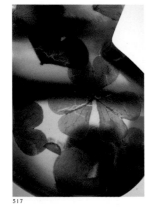

517

517 FLORENCE LEHMANN *'Heart of clover' (detail) in Plexiglas® and trefoil clover, cut from the solid, 1990.*

518 FLORENCE LEHMANN *'Rattle' ring in coloured Plexiglas® discs, pierced and threaded onto a stalk of fluorescent Plexiglas® to be wedged between two fingers, 1991. Photographs by Zvardon.*

519

519 FLORENCE LEHMANN *'Yes/No' ring in transparent white Plexiglas® and ivory ('Yes' ring for the little finger of the left hand, 'No' ring for the little finger of the right hand), 1991.*

521 FLORENCE LEHMANN *'Multi-coloured heart' ring in different coloured Plexiglas®, hot-pressed then cut from the solid, 1990.*

522 FLORENCE LEHMANN *'Heart of metal' ring for the little finger of the left hand, in hollow silver, 1990.*

523 FLORENCE LEHMANN *'Love Talk' ring in Plexiglas®, stamped, glued and cut from the solid. Photographs by Zvardon.*

518

tion of rings and jewellery with the Bellon company and is also the co-founder of the French jewellers' group, Corpus. Through the consistency of her artistic progression and commitment in the field of rings, she takes her place amongst the most admired jewellers of her generation.

The rings made by Géraldine Luttenbacher (b. 1965), in gold and precious stones, draw inspiration from the mysterious, unreal, natural or spatial worlds: poetry, legend, leaves and flowers, cinema and inter-stellar space are the creative media for jewellery with a matchless finish. After gaining her vocational

521

training certificate in jewellery using precious metals, this jeweller worked for six years in workshops producing for the leading Parisian fine jewellery houses. A teacher in jewellery at the AFEDAP in 1995, she now devotes herself to designing and making her own jewellery. (See Fig. 526.)

The ergonomic rings made by Cathy Specht (b. 1967), in wood or horn and silver 'stars', are hand ornaments or sculptures with generous, sensual lines that wrap around the fingers and stand out from them. (See Figs. 520, 524 & 525.) Objects of relaxation, with a symbolic or sentimental value, they are made also to be touched and thus to be in contact with the skin itself. These rings – which may have also aquatic, plant or animal motifs – are imbued with the great mystery of living.

A graduate of the School of Decorative Arts in Strasbourg, where she studied from 1985-90 and much attracted by ethnology, zoology and botany, this jeweller now works with Lalique and since 1991 she has been able to develop her research into the vital link between forms, fauna and flora.

The hand ornaments, with their rough, unfinished appearance, in the 1996 'showcase' series by Maud

525

Rottier (b. 1969) are made up of bits of wood picked up in the countryside. Left as far as possible in their natural state, these noble, tactile pieces of jewellery can be worn on the hand thanks to a fastener, hook or ring. Making use of nature – in the form of a branch – as the starting point for her research, this jeweller has sought to establish a balance between jewel and material; between culture and nature. A playful, poetic and somewhat nostalgic game, her plastic approach, which is very close to that of Arte Povera, examines areas in which man impinges on nature. Her Master's degree in the plastic arts from 1988-94, and diploma from the School of Decorative Arts in Strasbourg where she studied from 1992-95, have opened up a broad field of artistic enquiry to this jeweller. She has been a member of Corpus since 1995. (See Figs. 527–529.)

In a country that has, despite everything, retained a strong degree of classicism, the rings of the few French jewellers of this latest generation provide us with a broad range of fresh artistic and aesthetic options. The artists trained by the jewellery workshop of the School of Decorative Arts in Strasbourg produce work of very high quality, rivalling that of neighbouring countries. The designers who passed through that workshop show how magnificently the teaching given by Henri-Morand Boltz and Eric Vandemeulebroecke succeeded, amongst other things, in freeing them from an overly traditional approach to jewellery. In France today, this workshop has become an experimental laboratory that cannot be ignored.

The Corpus Group was set up in 1992 in the spirit of vitality, continuity and creativity in the field of contemporary jewellery, bringing together eighteen artist-jewellers, almost all of whom are former pupils of the School of Decorative Arts in Strasbourg.[38] Following on from the experience of the Héphaistos Group, artists belonging to the Corpus Group now share a field of investigation into jewellery that is perhaps better thought-out and more extensive with regard to jewellery than that of their predecessors.[39] With the avowed aim of taking a new look at objects that are worn, they are working together with a great deal of originality and commitment. Their travelling exhibition 'Jewellery and the Sacred', held in 1993 – whose starting point was the Chéret AAM Gallery in Paris[40] – magnificently demonstrated the troubling relationship that a piece of jewellery can have with the sacred. Artists from Fontblanche and elsewhere had been invited for the occasion; these included Olivier

526

526 GERALDINE LUTTENBACHER *'Snow White' ring in gold-plated brass and Swarosky crystal, 1991.*

524 CATHY SPECHT *'Star' ring in silver, 1989. Photograph by Yves Bérard.*

525 CATHY SPECHT *'Coral couple' ring in horn, 1992. Photograph by Bernard Jaspar.*

Bouchard, Xavier Domenech, Isabelle Imbert, Patricia Lemaire et Suzanne Nègre.

The Fontblanche Workshop in Nîmes is a centre for research and training in the plastic arts with a jewellery section. Hervé Ducruet, Joël Faivre-Chalon (who is now a lecturer there) and especially Gilles Jonemann (a founder member of this research and design unit) are the three best representatives, considering themselves to be both sculptors and creators of jewellery. This very broad training tackles jewellery from a resolutely plastic angle, emphasising the relationship between body and object.

Finally, the BJO private technical college in Paris and the many vocational training courses in jewellery offered throughout France and in all European countries have curricula with a strong professional orientation, though only the most individual and original graduates, such as Ann Gerard or Géraldine Luttenbacher, have become genuinely independent artist-jewellers.

527

In addition to the three-year international jewellery fairs held in France since 1987, the Museum of Modern and Contemporary Art in Nice plays a fundamental role. In mounting exhibitions or retrospectives such as those devoted to Robert Smit in 1994 or Henri Gargat in 1995, Pierre Chaigneau has become the first French museum curator to defend and display contemporary jewellery on such an artistic stage.

and meanings. This begs the question of whether or not the artist-jewellers who attend these schools get more assistance and are thus more favoured than the others. The answer must be no, since far from these specific teachings regarding jewellery, there are also those who have learnt through personalised transmission or initiation (as in the case of Michael Greschny in France), as well as those who, entirely self-taught, unorthodox and very original, have come to jewellery through a passion for ornament: Agate Saint-Girons is probably the best example as far as France is concerned.

In this way, following on from the modernist era, with its utopian and somewhat revolutionary ideology, the rings of this latest generation are noticeably less idealistic and rigorist; turning more towards eclecticism, with its many avowed references. This considerable growth in the potential for reproduction and communication has certainly provoked and accentuated a broadening of knowledge amongst artists, as well as amongst the public. These changes have irreversibly altered artistic attitudes and favoured postmodern introspection and questioning of art. This should perhaps be seen as less 'evolutionary' and thus less optimistic, but is undoubtedly much more personal and expressive.

IN SUMMARY

It is relevant to point out that the number of jewellers in this generation has increased considerably. Developments on the social scene (especially in 1968), as well as the development of real 'jewellery' sections within some of the art schools of European cities, very clearly lie behind this phenomenon. However, these different schools are often establishments in which specialist collective teaching is given around a single theme and where specific techniques are learned. It is possible to see them as not so much 'schools', as groups or associations of artists calling themselves disciples of the same master or the same sort of training.

This is far from being the case, since even though there are some similarities or formal and semantic characteristics shared amongst jewellers who have followed the same curriculum, this study has shown that jewellers of the same age and with similar training are able to make objects with radically different design

528

528 MAUD ROTTIER *First branch of the tree.*

529 MAUD ROTTIER *Knot and ring, 1996.*

527 MAUD ROTTIER *Hand ornaments in boxwood, silver and 'mocumé', 1996.*

Notes

[1] For this section, we have relied in particular on specialist works, some of them more recent than others:

BOOKS

Arlette Barré-Despond (ed.), *Dictionnaire International des Arts Appliqués et du Design*, Editions du Regard, Paris, 1996.

Barbara Cartlidge, *Les Bijoux au XX ème Siècle*, Payot, Paris, 1986, pp74–200.

Peter Dormer and Ralph Turner, *Le Nouveau Bijou*, Flammarion, Paris, 1985.

Helen W. Drutt-English and Peter Dormer, *Jewelry of Our Time. Art, Ornament and Obsession*, Thames and Hudson, London, 1995.

Martine Elzingre, *Femmes habillées, la mode de luxe: style et image*, Austral Essais, Paris, 1996.

Toni Greenbaum, *Les Messagers du Modernism. Bijoux Artistiques aux Etats-Unis de 1940 à 1960*, Flammarion, Paris, 1996.

Anny Tailli Nencioni, *Robert Smit*, Aurum, Zurich, 1992.

Marta Pietribiasi, *Giampaolo Babetto*, Aurum, Zurich, 1991.

Ralph Turner, *Jewelry in Europe and America. New Time, New Thinking*, Thames and Hudson, London, 1996.

David Watkins, *The Best of Contemporary Jewellery*, Rotovision, Mies, 1993.

CATALOGUES

Europea Contemporaria Joeria, Fondacio Caixa de Pensions, Barcelona, February-March 1987.

Ornementa 1, Schmuckmuseum Pforzheim, Prestel Verlag, Munich, 1989.

Qu'est ce que la Sculpture Moderne?, Centre Georges Pompidou, Musée d'Art Moderne, Paris, 3 July to 3 August 1986.

Ring, Galerie Michèle Zeller, Bern, 8 July to 12 September 1992.

Zeit Genossiche Schmuckkunst aus der Bundesrepublik Deutschland, Institut für Auslandsbezizehungen, Stuttgart, 1989.

[2] It is important to mention here that Bauhaus, established in 1919, set itself the task of 'building the future' with the firm intention of bringing all artistic fields into that splendid venture. Beyond academic specialisation, Bauhaus thus endeavoured to train a new type of artist. The founder of this German art school, Walter Gropius, did not just believe in new teaching methods applied to arts and crafts. Apprenticeship and production led by artist-craftsmen thus began in Weimar and immediately challenged the traditional separation between arts and crafts; between the 'fine arts' and the so-called 'applied arts'. When the realities of an increasingly technical civilisation necessitated a few readjustments and redefinitions of the programme, industrial techniques were, as of 1923, turned to even greater effect in objects, from lamps to houses.

While these modernist conceptions and claims regarding life and the environment were not always successful, the image of the Bauhaus has remained as the symbol of experimental work. Its history and experience were, moreover, marked by different internal movements and revivals, as remarkable masters and teachers like Johannes Itten, Paul Klee, Wassily Kandinsky and Moholgy-Nagy, with their different influences and policies, took over from each other. Despite all this, this issue of uniting aesthetic and functional aspects in the same object is still very much alive in our day.

This geometric, abstract language was a possible plastic response for those artists who sought to reflect in their work their faith in the values of pure (optimistic and idealistic) thought, as well as in progress, science and technology. It was also embodied in various movements such as Suprematism, De Stijl and Constructivism, as well as kinetic art after the Second World War.

[3] Catherine Francblin, 'Qu'est-ce-que la sculpture moderne?', interview by Margit Rowell in *Art Press*, No. 104, June 1986, pp16–23.

[4] Yvonne Deslandres and Florence Müller, *Histoire de la Mode au XX ème Siècle*, Somagy, Paris, 1986, pp234–271.

[5] Ibid., pp.263.

[6] Jean-Marie Schaeffer, *Les célibataires de l'art, pour une esthétique sans mythes*, Gallimard Essais, Paris, 1996, and Philippe Dager, *L'Art d'Aimer les Arts* in Le Monde des Livres, 8 March 1996, p.9.

[7] Ibid., p.199.

[8] Catalogue *Der Kosmos des Peters Skubic*, Museum fur Kunsthandwerk, Leipzig.

[9] The Royal College of Art, set up in 1837 in the heart of London, is the only institution in the world entirely devoted to the study of art, design and visual communication. The technical courses given in goldsmithing, jewellery and design, as well as theoretical courses in the history of art, prepare and train students from all over the world. Many internationally famous artist-jewellers, such as Onno Boekhoudt, Bruno Martinazzi, Fritz Maierhofer, Robert Smit, Giampaolo Babetto, Georg Dobler and Daniel Kruger, are invited every year to teach and lead workshops. A few of their pupils may be mentioned here: Elizabeth Callinicos, Giovanni Corvaja, Felix Fury, Catherine Hills, Zsuzsanna Morrison, Gordon Stewart, Clara Vichi, Esther Ward, Christoph Zelleger and Maria Wong.

[10] Catalogue *Wendy Ramshaw Jewellery*, April 1989, Eve France, Texas, 1989. Marina Vaizey, in catalogue *Wendy Ramshaw Picasso's ladies*, Dacs, 1989. Catalogue *Wendy Ramshaw. From paper to gold*, South Bank Centre, 1990. Anna Beatriz Chadour, in catalogue *Wendy Ramshaw Rings*, 1994.

[11] The 100 pieces purchased by the museum were sold for 25 Swiss francs.

[12] Hans Dieter Zwirchmaier, in catalogue *Uber Deinen Schatten. Schmuck Aloïs Bauer*, Fläx, 1993.

[13] Jean Chevalier and Alain Gheerbrant, *Dictionnaire des Symboles*, Robert Laffond, Paris, 1969, pp.165–169.

[14] Catalogue *Living Design in Denmark*, Kjeld Ammundsen, May 1995, pp.92–95.

[15] Tapio Periänen, *Soul in Design. Finland as an Example*, Kirjayhtymä, Helsinki, 1990, and exhibition catalogue Living Design in Denmark., op. cit.

[16] Ramon Puig Cuyas, 'Jewellery in Barcelona', in *Art Aurea*, No. 8, 1988, pp.46–48.

[17] Catalogue *Exposicio de Joieria Contemporania. Un Art Intim*, Centre Cultural Can Mulà, 26 April to 30 June, 1996.

[18] Marcel Paquet, *Michel Journiac. L'ossuaire de l'Esprit*, La Différence, Paris, 1977, p.104.

[19] Pascale le Thorel-Daviot, *Petit Dictionnaire des Artistes Contemporains*, Bordas, Paris, 1996, p.129.

[20] Jan Hein Sassen, in catalogue *Ouroboros. Ruudt Peters*, Uitgave, Amsterdam, 1995.

[21] Heide Hinterthür, in catalogue *Echo. Rian de Jong*, October 1992, Zoo Produkties, The Hague.

[22] Catalogue *Philip Sajet. 'Achttien Ringen'*, Stedelijk Museum Amsterdam, 4 July to 31 July 1996.

[23] Marjam Unger, in catalogue *Philip Sajet. 'Elf Colliers'*, Amsterdam, 1994.

[24] Liesbeth den Besten, in catalogue *Ted Noten*, Amsterdam, 1996.

[25] Hermann Jünger, in catalogue *Daniel Kruger*, Schmuckmuseum Pforzheim, 14 January to 11 March 1984.

[26] Hermann Jünger, 'Zwischenfingerring und Schulterstück', in *Art Aurea*, Ebner-Verlag, Ulm, 1990, pp.74–75.

[27] Tom Berens, in catalogue *Michael Becker. Works on Architecture*, München, 1990.

[28] Hermann Jünger, in catalogue *Ulo Florack Schmuck, 1987–1995*, Ulo Florack, 1996.

[29] Jean Chevalier and Alain Gheerbrant, op. cit., pp.527–530.

[30] Catalogue *Alberto Zorzi. Schmuck-Skulptur-Graphik, 1971–1990*, Deutsches Goldschmiedenehaus Hanau, 4 March to 16 April 1990.

[31] Catalogue *Exposicio de Joieria Contemporania. Un Art Intim*, op. cit., and Ramon Puig Cujàs, op. cit.

[32] Wolfgang Kos, in catalogue *Landschaft und Garten. Schmuck Anna Heindl*, Vienna, 25 November to 23 December 1987. Plus catalogue *Rahmen und Ornament. Schmuck Anna Heindl*, travelling exhibition from 1989 to 1990.

[33] Verena Formanek, in catalogue *Andrea Halmaschlager. Arbeiten 1993–1994*, Vienna, Galerie V & V, 2 March to 9 March 1994.

[34] Eva S. Sturm, in catalogue *Wodurchschmuck. Bernhardt Fink*, Galerie V & V, Vienna, 16 March to 4 May1996.

[35] 'Panorama', in *Craft Council Suisse*, September 1990.

[36] Jean Chevalier and Alain Gheerbrant, op. cit.

[37] Catalogue *L'Europe des Créateurs. Utopies 89*, Ecole des Arts Décoratifs,

Strasbourg, 24 November to 10 December 1989. Catalogue *Florence Lehmann Bijoux*, Société Bellon, Bourg-Lès-Valence, 1991. Catalogue *Le Bijou et le Sacré*, Corpus, Strasbourg, 1993.

[38] Since 1992, the Corpus Group has been made up of former students from the School of Decorative Arts in Strasbourg: Christophe Burger (graduated 1976), Véronique Buri (graduated 1989), Olivier Daunay (graduated 1978), Marie Ivonne Dos Santos (b. Brazil in 1958), Joël Faivre-Chalon, Isabelle Fustinoni, Florence Lehmann (graduated 1987), Marie-Josèphe Lesprit (graduated in 1985), Astrid Meyer (graduated 1979), Véronique Oshé (graduated 1977), Marie-Juliette Pailler (graduated 1988), Christine Schoetel (graduated 1986), Anne Silbermann (graduated 1983), Laurent Stoll (graduated 1985), Christine Walter (graduated 1985), Maud Rottier (graduated 1995) and Brune Boyer-Pellerej, who is a graduate of the School of Decorative Arts in Geneva. See also catalogue *L'Europe des Créateurs*. Utopie 89, op. cit.

[39] In 1982, in an attempt to check the feeling of monopoly, suffocation and frustration felt in France in the field of jewellery, Francine Sixou decided to bring together 22 jewellers to form the Héphaistos Group: Goudji, Catherine Noll, Roland Schad, Bonnie Anderson, Marc Boisonnet, Claude and Françoise Chavent, Alicia Moï Orban, Elisabeth Riveiro, Suzanne Nègre, Gérard Chacun, Christophe Burger, Roland Tschiegg, Eve and Denis Verel, Jiri Ledecky, Hervé Lanternier, Dominique Favey-Blackmore, Jean-Claude Bonillo, Joël Faivre-Chalon, Thérèse Sudre, Martine Ruegg, Emmanuel Ricard and Francine Sixou. The purpose of this group, which was subsidised by the Ministry of Cultural Affairs and Crafts, was to promote contemporary jewellery at national and international level (holding exhibitions and salons in Switzerland, the United Kingdom, the United States and so on). The desire of Francine Sixou, followed by Marc Boissonnet, to show off the artistic personality of each member above all undoubtedly lay behind the difficulties in co-ordination of the group and its subsequent dissolution. Since then, these French jewellers have worked on a more individual basis and only the most talented amongst them have gone on successfully to make a living from their creations: the late Catherine Noll, the Chavents, Goudji, Alicia Moï Orban, Christophe Burger and Joël Faivre-Chalon.

[40] *Le Bijou et le Sacré*, op. cit.

4

Conclusions

Avant-garde and towards the year 2000

Since the 1960s, a certain degree of technical, formal, functional and semantic diversity has expanded and thrown off its shackles. Added to this there are similar, recurrent artistic themes and the emergence of strongly individual features, which can help to identify the initial characteristics of this period. So far this book has shown how, moving between two fairly loosely-defined poles (cultural and natural), the creation of modernist rings could be divided into two phases.

In the third phase, covering the 'post-modern' rings of today and the future, the lack of critical distance prevents us from setting precise boundaries and classifying the rings finally into one or other category. However, the creative process discernible in the work of these jewellers suggests the need for some clarification. Within the broad structure of two general phases, there are four distinct reference points: technique, form, function and meaning.

The technical aspect relates to the particular features of the materials used and the way they are handled – it is the transmutation from and around matter that may first have caught the artists' attention, and sometimes they could be described as alchemists (for example, Peter Skubic, Robert Smit and Giovanni Corvajà). We should also note that their knowledge and irreproachable technical and technological mastery permit this transformation of materials: through procedures such as direct cutting, sculpture, moulding, melting, electroforming, compression and assembling, as well as all stages in processing plastics such as extrusion, injection, calendering, rotary moulding, coating, heat forming, transfer moulding and pressing.[1] Secondly, greater concentration on form, as in aesthetic criteria, may take pride of place (for example, as in the work of Emmy van Leersum, Giampaolo Babetto and Graziano Visintin). Thirdly, a consideration of function and use leads to the adaptation of rings to the body (for example, as in the work of Gerd Rothmann, Angela Hübel and Lucy Sarneel). Lastly, the semantic aspect, with its mechanistic, geometric and conceptual emphasis (as demonstrated by Friedrich Becker, Claus Bury and Ted Noten) or the more sensual, poetical and metaphorical one (for example, as in the work of Hermann Jünger, Ramon Puig Cuyas and Bernhard Fink), shows the role of symbolism.

Even though all these artists have striven to achieve a subtle balance between these four fields, nevertheless, classification along these lines would have proved to be problematical, reductionist and probably less easy to understand. In fact, the jewellers of the first, and indeed second, generation tended to develop their work around a substantially constant set of problems. Those of the latest generation, on the other hand, seem to be more attracted by alternative ways or styles.

With this necessary clarification out of the way, we can now tackle some other constant themes that have recurred amongst these artists from the 1960s onwards. In fact, their personalities have led all of them to prize creativity in rings over their pure market value. Since they imagined rings that function and can exist as 'autonomous' objects, they were sometimes able to go far beyond the concept of 'wearability'. Despite everything, however, it is the relationship between the artist, object and recipient that has been the preferred area of study since the 1960s. Rings continue to include the constraints and references that are specific to an item adorning the hand, namely the particular dimensions required for a volume that is to be slipped on to a finger and the variation in the way it is handled and seen.

A ring is defined as a 'small, circular band' placed on the finger, which may be decorated with a bezel of, for example, a solitaire, signet or marquise.[2] In addition, unlike architecture which encompasses mass and space, and painting, which is a flat, impenetrable surface, the finger ring is a volumetric object that occupies and suggests space like sculpture. With its significants (its materials and forms), the ring also plays a role as the receptacle of signifieds or mean-

ings, and acts on the recipient, who projects upon it their own dreams, beliefs, ideas and so on. It is thus in this unceasing, ambiguous movement back and forth between creator, ring and recipient that the artistic and aesthetic intentions of jewellers today seem to focus on the relevance of the object as a sign or sense. Because of the way the materials, forms, semantic resonances and usual references are handled, these rings will only rarely leave someone indifferent.

From a diachronic point of view, far from the traditional approach to rings, artist-jewellers have thus always sought to express their emotions. By emphasising the essential concerns specific to this small item of adornment, they link it magnificently to the artistic expression, as well as the individual and social activity, of the whole 20th century. In this way, the use of 'natural' materials, such as wood, bone or stone, refers to and includes the artistic and philosophical references of primitivist and expressionist art as found in the work of Rian de Jong and Bernhard Schobinger. In the simplification and interplay of surfaces and planes of the same tone, some plastic and intellectual echoes of Cubism may be seen (shown for example, in the work of Francesco Pavan).

The manual or mechanical use of plastics has links with the modernist and futuristic avant-garde movement based on rhythm and the expression of movement and light, seeking the continuity between the object and the body or between the object and surrounding space. For example, this is shown in the work of Peter Chang and David Watkins. Linking elements and materials from different realities echoes Constructivism (as in the work of Fritz Maierhofer). As far as challenging and acknowledging the status of the ring is concerned, the Dadaist attitude tends to show that, if placed in a particular context, the object acquires another meaning (as demonstrated by the work of Otto Künzli and Gerd Rothmann). The influence of surrealism or Pop Art shows in the playful, dreamlike and sometimes ephemeral associations with allegorical scope, as can be seen in the work of Pierre Degen.

As far as forms are concerned, Cubism, Constructivism, archaic configuration and organic abstraction, as well as gestural energy, are also movements that have greatly influenced the rings made by modern and contemporary jewellers – for example, Wendy Ramshaw, Wilhem Mattar and Claus Bury. Minimal art and Arte Povera both brought a new sense into the close, dependent and reciprocal relationship that the recipient maintains with the finger ring; this is reflected in the work of Gijs Bakker and Hermann Jünger.

Thus, the creation of rings closely follows art, in addition to the discoveries and progress of the 20th century. It has already been established that, from the end of the 19th century, a few jewellers of the time succeeded in escaping from mass production, which was much less interesting from a formal and semantic point of view. Lalique and Desprès, for instance, were able to take judicious advantage of technological advances and to continue to introduce elements of art and aesthetics into the lives of ordinary people. However, generally accepted ideas persisted, since the technical aspect remains dominant in making a piece of jewellery.

The distinction between art and technology is not a given, but rather a comparatively recent social phenomenon that gradually came about in the 18th century during the industrial revolution in western Europe. From the linguistic point of view, it was also around the same time that languages began to distinguish the word 'art' (from the Latin 'ars'), designating processes of natural creation (from the Greek word 'techne') applied to processes of more methodical or scientific creation. This systematic dichotomy was then crowned by the appearance of the concept of 'fine arts', the sole aim of which was to be beautiful, as distinct from the technical nature of the work of production. These conceptual gains and substantial slippages in meaning resulted in a radical opposition between art and technology. One of the reasons why jewellery is still not seen as an art probably lies in the long-lived myth that artistic objects are in opposition to objects issuing from technology.

The Cubists, Constructivists, Futurists, Dadaists, Surrealists, Minimalists and the rest, had already rejected this Manichean opposition by openly declaring that artistic creation could not be separated from the technical discoveries and processes of transforming matter. As polemicists, they had themselves integrated mechanical and scientific elements into their respective creations. It is therefore logical that jewellers should also have adopted the same approach in the design of their rings since, like the blacksmith, the jeweller has always worked on technical transformation of matter. Today, many of them continue to work with materials considered as more traditional, and yet the range of possibilities offered by increasingly sophisticated technology opens up to them an infinite sphere of activity.

Since the industrial era, the potential for mass-producing jewellery has irreversibly altered the relationship with rings that individuals had maintained until then, as the unique object transmitted from generation to generation gave way to a piece of jewellery that could be produced in unlimited quantities. The unique object gradually lost ground in favour of an object that could be reproduced at a lesser cost. These objects accompanied individuals to a lesser and lesser extent during their lives, as they were now exchanged, recycled or simply thrown away. This was a response to the frenetic and endless system of style and fashion, or the more pernicious system of consumption. The ring was itself unable to escape this gradual change in status, linked as it was to the sectors of fine jewellery, industry, fashion and, broadly speaking, fancy goods. The creation of artist-jewellers was thus aligned with either the production of nostalgic luxury or the reproduction, at lower cost, of objects with forms that were barely innovative, or with fashion accessories, reflecting ephemeral trends.

However, more generally, the change in the status of objects has also been reflected in art. While Picasso, Duchamp and the Dadaists were the first to bring industrial and ordinary objects into a space conventionally set aside for so-called 'unique' objects, artists like Warhol, Yves Klein, Rauschenberg, Kosuth or Dan Flagging have more recently taken this line. All their playful, ironic 'placing in context' thus conceptually challenged the very definition of the *objet d'art*, as well as the relationship between the object and its environment. Whatever the approach adopted by these artists, they all seek to show that the immanence of works of art is such that it is more the circumstances of their appearance – or where they are placed – that really establishes semantic innovations. It is by placing objects from everyday life in a specific context, that these artists make their individual statements.

The object has certainly invaded art, but things are more complicated because the converse proposition is also true. Art has also influenced the object since art became a consideration at the beginning of the century in the production and design[3] of everyday objects: this occurred in the movements such as Art Nouveau, Arts and Crafts, Bauhaus, De Stijl and the Ulm School. Aesthetic considerations relating to everyday industrial objects are a historical fact and contemporary concern, and these pose problems today since the debate on the subject has never been resolved. What role do these everyday objects – with their effective, 'aesthetic' design – play? What is their relationship with art? Can they be considered as artistic objects? The democratisation and 'aestheticisation' of objects have made artistic classification extremely delicate and indeterminate.

This raises the question of whether jewels can be considered as art, since the jeweller uses both technology and mechanics. Whether we are talking about fine or mass-produced jewellery, or the fancy goods sector, jewellery remains one of the expressive forms of 20th-century art. Artist-jewellers continue to endeavour to give it dimensions proportionate to the part of the body for which it is destined, to give it a degree of uniqueness and thus to preserve all its specific features and complexity as an ornament. Like art, some rings have followed the aesthetic, social or political concerns of their period of reference and have adopted more or less relevant techniques, forms and meanings.[4]

Finally, with regard to the artistic status of the ring, it is in the 'subjective' relationships that connect us to works of art that the entire legitimacy of their existence and their artistic appreciation lie. Aesthetic quality is not, therefore, a property of objects, but rather a part of how we view them. Following the *ad hoc* challenging that was characteristic of the modernist years, today's jewellers have definitely decided to work on the basis of aesthetic pleasure, thereby continuing to give this small ornament its whole – formal and semantic – richness.

Circulation

Since the 1960s, and especially the 1970s, the concept of the ring has gradually been redefined in accordance with the general utopianism of that time, during which the world itself was also transformed. More generally, the artists of that generation saw jewellery as an experimental field, in reaction to Pop Art and a rather conservative state of mind present in society in general. In categorically refusing the past and traditional society and history, avant-garde jewellers drew on the same sources. While positions that were almost as 'extreme' existed at the very beginning of the 20th century, the idea that jewellers should devote themselves exclusively to designing and making jewellery of a different type was, on the contrary, entirely new.

Fortified by these avant-garde and idealistic stances and convictions, events organised around artistic jewellery as from the 1970s onwards tried to show the diversity of these contemporary trends: these included institutions, exhibitions, galleries and publications, which meant that jewellery was more widely circulated and understood.

This may suggest that contemporary jewellery was inevitably going to be absorbed into society's commercial values, which tend to place a market value on objects which, in previous times, would have had a sacred one. It should be noted that knowledge and circulation of contemporary jewellery are fundamental issues that touch on both the artistic and commercial fields: this is an area that can be damaged as much by considerations of short-term profit as by inappropriate artistic straitjackets or criteria. Jewellery is a product, and therefore needs to be advertised, circulated and consumed following the pace of fashion. Its methods of design and production, which are very carefully thought out, are today increasingly one step ahead and effective. Moreover, the public is perpetually encouraged to speed up this race towards frantic, endless consumption. Here, jewellery is only picking up on the general ideological dynamics that can be seen in clothing, objects and accessories, and also in art – which above all seeks satisfaction in perpetual change. This is a reality. Therefore it is helpful and more relevant to approach ornaments from an artistic angle rather than as objects of consumption.

The fact that the world of contemporary jewellery continues to bring together only a limited number of people proves that artistic jewellery has apparently remained on the periphery of social life, having little or no connection with economic constraints. Collections, institutions and galleries certainly ensure its existence and give it a place, but it needs to be encompassed within a more general artistic and social context. Jewellery undoubtedly impinges on many fields and contributes to the personality of a collector or the image of a gallery, but its influence on society is minimal, since even those artist-jewellers who have acquired a firm reputation reach only a very limited number of the initiated.

When, by happy chance, their work succeeds in interesting a wider public – as was the case for example in Pforzheim with the Ornamenta 1 Exhibition in 1990, or in Paris with the three-yearly jewellery fairs in 1987, 1990 and 1992 – it is still too often described as cranky, overly dramatic or unwearable. But the fact that this field of artistic expression is still outside the traditional dominant currents also 'protects' artists, allowing them to remain almost entirely free to create as they wish.

Since the 1980s, there has been a quickening of interest in contemporary art, an enthusiasm sometimes resulting in fads which have profoundly and irrevocably altered the overall artistic context, and indeed seem to be taking over creative work and artists. There has also been a change in attitude on the part of the youngest generation of jewellers, in their almost systematic preference for precious metals and 'softened' overall shapes. However, this does not mean that they are beginning to share the prevailing values of the public and society. They constantly question the essence of the ring itself to determine its single dominant motif. The constant challenges they have made to the techniques, forms, customary references and meaning of the rings within the last fifteen years enable them to take their place in the fascinating history of this ornament.

However, in comparison with what is happening in contemporary art,[5] the number of galleries, museums, exhibitions and publications relating to jewellery has remained almost unchanged over the last fifteen years. Jewellery thus seems to have entirely escaped the general trivialisation and 'snobbery' which has permeated the art world. The contemporary ring is not completely excluded from this phenomenon, since when buying this ornament, which continues to mark a particular event, those concerned seem to prefer an object with the most traditional techniques, forms and references. This may or may not be a good thing. In any event, whatever the changes or developments that may come in this field, this type of jewellery – or indeed art in general – can never be genuinely integrated, created simply for society's demands. 'True' works of art are always essentially outside or just at the edge of the frame. When integration has occurred or is occurring, art loses specific features and becomes 'something else'. This is why the process of raising awareness of contemporary jewellery still seems to be motivated by quite 'pure' pleasure in participating in the ongoing history of jewellery, as well as by a genuine desire to support jewellers and not to see their craft as a means of speculation or immediate enrichment.

Despite the aura that surrounds the artistic profession, becoming a jeweller today can therefore seem to be a very profound, almost anti-social choice; a committed desire to work as a 'researcher', rather than becoming attached to fame, success or mere financial achievement. It should be noted also that these artists are not working from the perspective of 'pure' art or art for art's sake, but are seeking through this medium to formulate an aesthetic link with the wearer.

Under the circumstances, and with the example of Pforzheim in mind, perhaps it is possible to envisage a museum of contemporary jewellery. Certainly, exhibiting contemporary jewellery, whilst retaining great respect for artistic and aesthetic considerations, can be a formidable catalyst for an entire society, rather than being merely an economic or financial affair. Jewellery is not an easy art, and the problem lies in measuring and understanding its intensity so that the knowledge may be shared and the art may progress.

Hermeneutic references

The ring has always conveyed strong mythical and legendary resonances, although, in the West, the general democratisation of art and objects has gradually led to the loss of their spiritual and magical references and functions. Even studied with a strongly scientific approach, the ring has nevertheless retained occult and esoteric values – implicitly, but none the less intensely, present. Proof of the extent to which this item of jewellery has retained its sacramental value can be found in the way a bride and groom exchange rings as part of a religious or lay wedding ceremony.

The ongoing success of *The Lord of the Rings*, the three-volume saga by J.R.R. Tolkien, published in 1954-55, shows that this ornament continues to fascinate and to be the stuff of dreams. This book, which was adored by protesting youth in the 1960s, does, in fact, recount a quest for the Holy Grail in reverse: and tells of recovering a magical ring in order to destroy it. The ring thus continues to mark a bond.[6] A study of mythical and legendary rings shows how beliefs and superstitions can still persist and be effective in our day.

Solomon, the King of Israel in the 10th century BC, wore a ring (a gold hoop engraved with a moon and the esoteric inscriptions, '*Dabi Habi Haben Alpha Omega*', and bearing an emerald engraved with a sun) on his right index finger, marked with the seal of his domination over the demons and giving him wisdom, power and intelligence. On the day he lost it while bathing in the River Jordan, he was deprived of these faculties until a fisherman brought it back to him, thereby restoring them. According to legend, anyone who got hold of this talisman would become master of the world.

According to the two Greek versions, the more traditional one (from the 8th century BC) and that of Plato (from the 4th century AD), it was thanks to his silver ring with its double bezel (one with a topaz representing the sun and an emerald representing the moon, the other with a heliotrope or opal, bearing engraved cabalistic inscriptions) that the shepherd Gyges was able to ascend the throne of Lydia and marry the wife of King Candaule: this mysterious ring had the power to make him invisible. While there is a description extant of the stages in manufacture and conjuration of this object,[7] perhaps its properties of invisibility lie more in its power to charm (taken in the primary sense of the term to mean distracting the attention). At a higher level, this ring symbolised the power offered to everyone to withdraw from the world and to seek the real powers within themselves. Through its mere materialisation, the ring embodies mysticism itself.

Another Greek legend has it that Prometheus, delivered by Heracles, had to keep an iron ring set with a splinter of stone from the rock to which he had been chained on his finger as a sign of submission to Zeus and of his own heroic greatness.

King Polycrates, aware of how lucky he had been and feeling guilty at his good fortune, decided one day to sacrifice some of his most precious objects, including a ring bearing an emerald, and throw them into the sea. The ring was constantly thrown back on to the shore and given back to the king. Some time later, Darius declared war on Polycrates and he was crucified. We can understand that Polycrates's gesture of compensation was somehow rejected by the Gods, who did not accept anyone usurping their powers of decision. The ring thus symbolises destiny, which man must accept because he cannot change it. Abandoning goods cannot equal either inner sacrifice, or the pact with destiny. In the Christian religion, the ring can be seen as a symbol of faithful, freely accepted attachment. The first rings from the early Christian period bore religious images or symbols on their bezels. Bishops' rings and especially the 'Fisherman's Ring' superimposed two symbols: one of temporal power and the other of spiritual submission. According to the very strict sumptuary laws of the

time, a knight was authorised, amongst other things, to wear a gold ring.

However, throughout the Middle Ages, a whole host of rings with magical powers also existed: such as the so-called 'travellers rings', with their power to transport an individual effortlessly to somewhere else; the Byzantine rings, which protected against the evil eye; or all the rings designed and made under the influence of the planets. Molière does, in fact, refer to these 'star-studded' rings in his play L'Amour Médecin.[8]

The power of talismanic or amuletic rings was said to lie in the properties inherent in the precious and semi-precious stones that were used, probably known since pre-history and specific to each civilisation. An example of this is the 'Alpha' ring (in copper or lead engraved with its Greek letter, to be worn on the little finger of the right hand), which is the jewel of businessmen, assuring them of financial success. The 'Omega' ring, in the shape of that letter, facilitates creativity and all intellectual activity. The ring of fortune designed and made in the metal corresponding to the planet ruling the owner was to protect him from evil spirits, bringing wealth and prosperity. In order to be infallible, the ring of friendship (the fede ring shape) must also bear an engraved closed circle and also an incomplete circle. A ring in gold or silver, either convex or concave and worn on the right-hand little finger, is a spur to action. Like the Ouroboros (a snake biting its tail), any ring using this motif is a symbol of life; a promise of longevity and happiness.

Stories linking the amorous destiny of historical and legendary figures to that of a ring are also very common. For example, Charlemagne was said to have mysteriously fallen in love with each person taking turns to wear a strange ring. One day, the enchanted object was thrown to the bottom of the lake near Aix-la-Chapelle. Charlemagne fell in love with this place too, to the extent that he built a town and a monastery there.

In the 14th and 15th centuries, there was a ring that, it was believed, had the power to attract love. The Duke of Touraine (brother of Charles VI), Diane de Poitiers, Louise de Burdos (the second wife of Henry I) and Madame de Demizieu, amongst others, are said to have taken full advantage of this power of attraction and fascination in their love life.

The symbolism of the ring of the Niebelungen in the famous opera by Richard Wagner can be understood at different levels. Illustrating the desire for power, the ring is certainly the sign of man's possible omnipotence over nature, but also of his painful subservience in the face of so many responsibilities.

Popular and country beliefs are also rich in anecdotes and superstitions, which cannot be listed comprehensively here. To mention just one of them, breaking or losing a ring, especially a wedding ring, is a sign of ill-omen, presaging a break, separation or death. The husband or partner must ward off this evil destiny by replacing the lost object.

Since deepest antiquity, the circle as seen in a ring, bracelet, necklace, belt or wreath – has invoked a picture of perfection and eternity. It also symbolises the heavens with their immutable, circular movements. As an enveloping, closed form, the circle has a function of protection and insulation. Its magical function is seen when, for instance, a magician marks out on the ground the circular field in the centre of which he will be calling up demons or spirits. Once outlined, this shape serves to protect and isolate him. This link is also found amongst the fairy stories and many of the rites of the Celtic people especially concerned with healing and dancing, as well as in many traditional architectural features such as enclosures, apses, arches and domes.

We can see how the circular form almost always takes on a double meaning: the circle joins together, but also isolates. This perfect, finite, immutable, indivisible, divine form – a sign of strength and power – can also hold, grasp and enclose a particular part of the body and, by extension, the entire individual, certainly to protect, but also to hinder, and indeed prevent that individual from undertaking any real or spiritual action, thus ensuring his submission. Putting a ring on one's own or someone else's finger is simultaneously to accept the gift of eternal love from the other, but also to submit oneself to it. It is probably for this reason that, according to Roman custom, priests serving a particular god (Flamen Dialis) had to wear a broken ring with no stone, and possibly also why jewellery is still removed from a woman on the point of giving birth. However, the ring bearing a seal, such as a signet ring, is a symbol of domination and not of submission. This ambivalent symbolism of the ring calls to mind the dialectical master-slave relationship, in which the apparent and true master may be different. At a magical and esoteric level, it may also bring to mind the symbolism of the belt (a circle with a buckle), which connects through its protective function and binds, because it ensures submission, man to the Great Whole.

The ring has played a role of adornment for all peoples since antiquity, glorifying the person wearing it, but making sacred a feeling or magical, spiritual, political or social power.

Mention should be made here of the particular case of engagement and wedding rings. The Greeks, who placed the wedding ring on the left ring finger in the 3rd century BC because the 'vein of love' linked that finger directly to the heart, were not apparently the first civilisation to adopt this meaning. The Egyptians (around 2800 BC) were probably the first to give a ring on the occasion of marriage.

For its part, marriage was instituted and decreed throughout the Christian kingdom unified by Charlemagne (in AD 800), who was alarmed by the number of children of incestuous parenthood. The union between man and woman is said to be a receptacle; a transitional channel forming part of the ritual of regarding life as sacred. Symbolically, marriage as the union of two principles must preside over the transmission of life. In the western world, the idea of an engagement with a ring (preferably in gold in order to represent a financial sacrifice for the young man) being customarily given to the fiancée dates back to a decree issued by Pope Nicholas I in AD 860. Rings set with a diamond were introduced around 1503. Two centuries later, it had become the most popular model in Europe to mark an engagement. Like the wedding ring, it was placed on the left ring finger.

Since antiquity, the ring has also played the role of stabilising energy, ensuring balance between body and soul. This may perhaps explain the fact that warriors in ancient times used to cover themselves with ornaments and why, generally speaking, all jewellery is taken from a dead person so that their spirit and soul may leave the body.

Looking further afield, in China the ring is a symbol of heaven and the infinite cycle, the central hole or void being the place through which its influence passes. In contrast to the medallion, which is traditionally a full circle, this space signifies the emptiness at the centre of being into which the celestial influx must descend.

The ring also plays a role in protecting the fragile, vulnerable fingers, since they are – like the hands – the place where 'power' is emitted and received. Moreover, during a session of hypnosis, it is recommended that all jewellery be taken off, since it could interfere with the vibratory circuit. Conversely, some stones, crystals and metals are said to help in protecting the overall body-energy system.[9] Since pre-history, in all civilisations and at all times,[10] the hands have expressed ideas of action, power and links with the spiritual. The right hand is related to beneficial authority in action (Justice) and the left to non-action (Wisdom), but also used for wrong-doing and curses. Like the circle or the eyes, the hands play an important role in magic, as in laying on of hands, indicating a manifestation and a transfer of power or energy fields in Buddhist and Hindu iconography and in dance, especially Chinese and Indian, as well as Flamenco. Caught up in such a symbolic net, the ring must inevitably play a key role.

Symbolism also plays a part in the making of these usually metal objects, which introduces the ambivalent image of the jeweller, or the more mythical image of the blacksmith. In many mythologies and civilisations, the blacksmith – the creator of the weapon of the Gods (thunder) – is a symbolic figure – almost a midwife – in the creation of the world. According to the Romanian religious historian, Mircea Eliade,[11] the blacksmith's close links with magic and metallurgy made him a magician and alchemist. The gifted holder of secret powers that he could turn against the divinity and against men, he could be as malefic as he was beneficent. His enigmatic, initiatory activity was linked to the transformation of matter and mainly of metals: he made tools, weapons and objects used in religious worship.

The symbolism of metals also has two aspects, one malefic (metals belonging to the underworld, to fire and to hell), and the other beneficent (providing transformation and purification), which the blacksmith himself transforms. This is why those involved in working metals have often been associated with magic or alchemy, as if able to extract their spirit or essence. According to Jung, metals are also – as symbols of solidified cosmic and underground energies – living, sexual substances associated with desire and libido, so that they are to be sublimated.

Gold, born from the earth, is undoubtedly the most precious and the most 'perfect' amongst the metals. The first metal discovered (in its native state) by man, it was probably not used initially as a tool or weapon – symbolic of solar, spiritual, sovereign and immortal power, as well as the actual flesh of the gods and pharoahs, with protective and curative powers – its 'impure' value as money could also make it a symbol of perversion or degradation. Furthermore, in the Masonic initiation rite, the stripping away of metals

(the initiate must remove all metallic objects or jewellery), symbolising material detachment, relates to this 'impure' side of metal that is connected with its solidification or hardening.

Apart from metals, precious stones have also been linked with sex, fertilisation and gynaecology.[12] In a universe regarded as sacred and sexualised, the blacksmith's secret knowledge of matter and role as a 'mediator' (minerals are said to have alternately male and female qualities) allowed him to speed up the 'birth', 'growth', or 'marriage' of metals. This master of fire – able to substitute himself for the processes of Nature and Time – was often feared but highly respected; driven into exile and frequently into becoming a nomad. A civilising hero, he was thus the main agent in disseminating mythological rites and mysteries.

By analogy, the sacred activity of the blacksmith may be related to that of master goldsmiths and, therefore, to jewellers. They too 'knew how to calculate the quantities and direct the physical-chemical processes of smelting and alloy' and they 'sought, in their own transmutation, an experience of death and initiatory resurrection'[13] – in short, immortality. By perfecting matter as much as themselves, by perpetually creating new forms, they took on the responsibility of altering nature; of substituting themselves for and accelerating time.

Yet it is difficult and perhaps futile in today's world, excelling in experimental science, to try to reconstitute these practices of a time in history 'when the world was not just "living", but also "open", [when] an object was never just itself (...), but the sign of or receptacle for something else, the reality that transcended the level of being of the object'.[14] Although modern science prefers to ignore these ancient hermetic or hermeneutic traditions, the semantic proximity of the word 'blacksmith' with that of 'craftsman', 'artist' or 'one who makes', remains, nevertheless, somewhat troubling.[15]

Today, as the ring is the most popular piece of jewellery, artist-jewellers continue to see it as a means of exploring the notion of the body, its many codifications, beliefs and appearances. Indeed, the gradual and almost total disappearance since the middle of the 20th century of the custom of wearing gloves has revealed a new eroticism of the hand. An emblem of authority (the privilege of the nobility) and liturgy (the investiture of bishops), gloves have, in fact, always symbolised a desire for purity because they provide a way of avoiding all impure contact. Yet the glove was also a sign of seduction and allegiance. Now, the hand is completely exposed, revealed to everyone's gaze and desire. This game, in which immodesty eventually wins at the expense of modesty, also seems paradoxically to have coincided with the appearance of a determined struggle for total control over anatomy and behaviour.[16] While the feminine appearance may still look to traditional models of elegance, another type of silhouette is nevertheless tending to make its mark: spindly, rangy, almost androgynous, where clothes become increasingly close-fitting so that they show without showing.

Jewellery, which is also becoming lighter, must continue to adorn without hindering (those large earrings or very broad necklaces, so characteristic of the 1980s, are hardly ever seen in the last years of the twentieth century). It must hug the lines and movements of a body that has apparently been 'liberated'. As its forms become larger and its materials more diverse, the ring becomes an aesthetic meeting point. In concentrating their artistic approach on the very essence of this item of jewellery, today's artist-jewellers become the splendid heirs of mythology, reviving and linking it once again to its original meanings and images. The ring remains a powerful mediator between the artistic and aesthetic desire to transform Nature, and the desire to link body and spirit together.

CONCLUSION

The history of the ring should not be seen as one of rigid divisions or a linear series of styles or currents of opinion, but as a perpetual interweaving, alternation and movement of sociological, aesthetic and artistic endeavours and influences, occurring in response to new situations. Yet while the techniques, materials and forms of rings have been constantly brought into question over the centuries, the need for the existence of this small object of adornment seems scarcely to have changed. It is still based on the sensitive, fragile desire of men and women to change their appearance, to differentiate themselves and to symbolically capture the spirit of a close relationship with the immaterial. What then seems to persist, beyond any attempt at analysis or discursive explanation, is the full intensity of the artistic approach, as well as the profound and sincere feeling which links the artist, the recipient and these always personal and entirely orig-

inal artistic rings. Far from being predetermined by each other, form and function seem to respond to each other, carried along by the same momentum, for their mutual and reciprocal enrichment.

In terms of design, the quest for the ring – the perfect circle – will never reach a conclusion. Discoveries are made, and then repeated and modified by new generations of artist-jewellers. This constant process of renewal – evidence of an ongoing dialogue and interdependency between makers throughout the ages – is, in itself, a reflection of the eternal.

Notes

1. Catalogue *Magie des Plastiques*, Ecole Nationale Supérieure des Beaux-Arts, Paris, 20 September to 10 November 1996.

2. Chambers Dictionary.

3. The English word 'design', apart from meaning intention or purpose, corresponds to two slightly different French words when referring to the artistic or industrial fields. 'Dessin' refers to the arrangement of forms in space with no concern for their function, while 'dessein' indicates all ideas, aims and functions attributed to an industrial object before it is made and which cannot be changed (unlike craftwork where manual alterations are possible as the object is being made).

4. Jean-Marie Schaeffer, op. cit.

5. Catherine Millet and Seth Siegelaub, in *Art Press*, 69/96, Special issue No. 17, 1996.

6. In this section, we have relied in particular on the following two bibliographical references: Jean Chevalier and Alain Gheerbrant, op. cit., pp.49–52; Eloïse Mozzani, *Le Livre des Superstitions*, Robert Laffont, Paris, 1995, pp.77–85.

7. Eloïse Mozzani, op. cit. p.79.

8. Act III, scene 6.

9. Barbara Ann Brennan, *Le Pouvoir Bénéfique des Mains*, Tchou, Paris, 1993.

10. Leroi-Gourhan, *Le Geste et la Parole, Technique et Langage*, Albin Michel, Paris, 1964. J. Piveteau, *La Main et l'Humanisation*, Masson, Paris, 1991. D. Champault and A.R. Verbrugge, *La Main, ses Figurations au Maghreb et au Levant*, catalogues du Musée de l'Homme, 1965. Various authors, *La Main*, Heurasie, L'Harmattan, Paris, 1993.

11. Mircea Eliade, *Forgerons et Alchimistes*, Flammarion, Paris, 1977.

12. Ibid., pp. 29–36.

13. Ibid., pp.122 and 126.

14. Ibid., p.120.

15. Ibid., p.83.

16. Philippe Perrot, *Le Travail des Apparences. Le Corps Féminin, XVIII ème-XIX ème Siècles*, Seuil, Paris, 1984, pp.199-208.

Annular An adjective meaning ring-shaped. The equivalent French word – *annulaire* – is also a noun meaning 'ring finger', the fourth finger of the hand counting from the thumb, on which the ring is traditionally worn.

Symbolically, referring to the microcosm's planetary connections, traditional astrology matches the ring finger with the sun. According to myth, belief and legend, it is also the luckiest finger. The engagement and/or wedding ring is slipped onto the ring finger of the left hand. Greek doctors in the 3rd century BC thought that a vein linked this finger directly to the heart: 'the vein of love'. This belief, which persisted amongst Roman doctors – who also credited the ring finger with healing power – has come down through the centuries to us.

Architectonic An adjective referring to the art and/or technique of architectural construction.

Bevel An edge cut slantwise. The technique of cutting at an oblique angle.

Bezel The oblique faces of a cut gem.

Cameo Semi-precious stone (e.g. agate, amethyst or onyx) sculpted in relief.

Carat The unit of measure for gold. It also refers to the fine gold content of an alloy divided into twenty-four parts or carats.

Chalecdony A type of quartz that occurs in several different forms, including onyx and agate.

Chrysoprase Apple green chalcedony.

Collet The projecting flat rim, collar or rib that keeps the stone of a ring in place. It is the setting for the stone.

***Fede* ring** A ring with the motif of two clasped hands. The design first appeared in the 12th century and was more symbolic than formally innovative. The fede ring was very common in the 16th century when it was used to mark an engagement and/or wedding.

Gimmel ring A ring constructed so that it may be divided into two or sometimes three separate parts.

Intaglio An engraving technique whereby the design is hollowed out of a semi-precious stone; this is the reverse of a cameo. An intaglio may be used as a seal or stamp.

Lapidary A craftsman who cuts, polishes and engraves precious stones.

***Memento mori* ring** This type of ring was very common in the 16th century and evoked death, displaying, for example, a coffin, death's head or skeleton. It was intended both stylistically and symbolically to recall the fragility and vanity of life.

Niello Black enamel (silver sulphide) used for inlays.

Opus Interrasile A highly-skilled gold-cutting technique that was introduced in Roman times. Intricate shapes were traced onto sheets of gold and then precisely cut out using a hammer and chisel. The delicate shape was then welded onto a separate sheet of metal giving an almost three dimensional appearance to the finished design.

Paste A hard vitreous composition of fused silica, potash, white oxide of lead, borax, etc., used in making imitations of precious stones.

Phalange The general meaning implies an ordered group that is ranged in a line. In an anatomical context, a phalange refers to each of the bones that are arranged in series or rows that form the last, distal segment of a limb skeleton. These are the bones of the digits or the finger bones.

Phalanx This has the same meaning as Phalange.

Stirrup (-shaped) ring A type of ring characteristic of the 12th century. The stirrup ring is made up of a hoop and a bezel set with a precious stone.

General Bibliography

BOOKS

Black Anderson, *Histoire des Bijoux*, Grange Batelière, Paris, 1974.

Jacques Arax, *Le Guide Pratique des Bijoux et des Pierres Précieuses*, Sand, Paris, 1988.

Arlette Barré-Despond (ed.), *Dictionnaire International des Arts Appliqués et du Design*, Editions du Regard, Paris, 1996.

Jean Baudrillard, *Le Système des Objets*, Gallimard, Paris, 1968.

Jean Baudrillard, *La Société de Consommation*, Gallimard, Paris, 1970.

Michel Baxandall, *L'œil du Quatrocento*, Gallimard, Paris, 1989.

R. Bianchi-Bandinelli, *Rome, le Centre du Pouvoir*, L'Univers des Formes, Gallimard, Paris, 1977.

R. Bianchi-Bandinelli, *Rome, la Fin de l'Art Antique*, L'Univers des Formes, Gallimard, Paris, 1971.

Alain Bonfand, *L'Art Abstrait*, PUF, Paris, 1994.

François Boucher, *Histoire du Costume en Occident*, Flammarion, new edition, Paris, 1996.

Barbara Ann Brennan, *Le Pouvoir Bénéfique des Mains*, Tabou, Paris, 1993.

Pierre Cabanes, *Introduction à l'Histoire de l'Antiquité*, Armand Colin, Paris, 1992.

Roger Caillois, *L'Ecriture des Pierres*, Skira, Flammarion, Paris 1970.

Jean Carpentier and François Lebrun (eds.), *Histoire de l'Europe*, Seuil, Paris, 1987.

Barbara Cartlidge, *Les Bijoux au XX ème Siècle*, Payot, Paris, 1986.

Giuliano Centrodi et al., *Gio Pomodoro. Ornamenti 1954–1996*, Artificio, Florence, 1996.

André Chastel, *Renaissance Méridionale en Italie 1460–1500*, L'Univers des Formes, Gallimard, Paris, 1965.

Jean Chevalier and Alain Gheerbrant, *Dictionnaire des Symboles*, Robert Laffond, Paris, 1969.

Créateurs de Bijoux Contemporains, Société d'Encouragement aux Métiers d'Art, Paris, 1986.

Marie Noël de Gary, *Anneaux et Bagues. Dessins*, Musée des Arts Décoratifs, Réunion des Musées de France, Paris, 1992.

Anne de Tugny, *Guide des Pierres de Rêve*, Flammarion, Paris, 1987.

Maximin Deloche, *La Bague en France à Travers l'Histoire*, Didot, Paris, 1929.

Taisen Deshimaru, *L'Anneau de la Voie*, Albin Michel, corrected edition, Paris, 1993.

Yvonne Deslandres and Florence Müller, *Histoire de la Mode au XX ème Siècle*, Somogy, Paris, 1986.

Christiane Desroches-Noblecourt, *Vie et Mort d'un Pharaon*, *Toutankhamon*, Hachette, Paris, 1963.

Christophe Domino, *L'Art Contemporain*, Scala, Centre Georges Pompidou, Paris, 1994.

Christophe Domino, *L'Art Moderne*, Scala, Centre Georges Pompidou, Paris, 1991.

Peter Dormer and Ralph Turner, *Le Nouveau Bijou*, Flammarion, French edition, Paris, 1987.

Magdalena Droste, *Bauhaus 1919–1933*, Taschen, Cologne, 1993.

Helen W. Drutt-English and Peter Dormer, *Jewelry of our Time. Art, Ornament and Obsession*, Thames and Hudson, London, 1995.

P.-M. Duval, *Les Celtes*, L'Univers des Formes, Gallimard, Paris, 1977.

Ernst A. and Jeanne Einiger, *Le Grand Livre des Bijoux*, Edition Lausanne, 1974.

Mircea Eliade, *Le Mythe de l'Eternel Retour*, Gallimard, Paris, 1969.

Mircea Eliade, *Forgerons et Alchimistes*, Flammarion, Paris, 1977.

Martine Elzingre, *Femmes habillées, la mode de luxe: styles et images*, Austral Essais, Paris, 1996.

Deanna Farneti Cera (ed.), *L'Art du Bijou*, Flammarion, French edition, Paris, 1992.

Fédération Française BJOC, *Bijoux de France. La Garantie Française*, Azur, Paris.

Caroline Fullée, *Bijoux du XX ème Siècle*, Celiv, French edition, 1992.

Melissa Gabardi, *Les Bijoux de l'Art Déco aux Années 40*, Editions de l'Amateur, Paris, 1986.

Melissa Gabardi, *Les Bijoux des années 50* (french edition), Les Editions de l'Amateur, Paris, 1987

Gilberte Gautier, *Rue de la Paix*, Paris, 1980.

Ernst Gombrich, *Histoire de l'Art* (French edition), Flammarion, Paris, 1982.

Gori and Zucchi, *Sessanta Anni di Arte Orafa*, Grifo, Montepulciano, 1986.

H. Graham, *Modern Jewellery*, London, 1965.

Toni Greenbaum, *Les Messagers du Modernisme. Bijoux Artistiques aux Etats-Unis de 1940 à 1960*, Flammarion, Paris, 1996.

Françoise Hamon and Philppe Dagen (eds.), *Histoire de l'Art Epoque Contemporaine XIX-XX ème Siècles*, Flammarion, Paris, 1995.

Peter Herion, *La Parure, Instinct et Art Populaire*, Hans Schöner, Königsbach-Stein, 1985.

Hugues Honour and John Fleming, *Histoire Mondiale de l'Art*, Bordas, Paris, 1992.

Georges Jehel, *La Méditerranée Médiévale de 350 à 1450*, Armand Colin, Paris, 1992.

Claudette Joannis, *Les Bijoux des Régions de France*, Flammarion, Paris, 1992.

Bertand Lançon, *Le Monde Romain Tardif III-VII ème Siècle ap. J.C.*, Armand Colin, Paris, 1992.

Pascale Le Thorel-Daviot, *Petit Dictionnaire des Artistes Contemporains*, Bordas, Paris, 1996.

Maurice Leloir, *Dictionnaire du Costume et de ses Accessoires*, Gründ, Paris, 1951.

Jacques Lenfant, *Bijouterie-Joaillerie*, Chêne, Paris, 1979.

André Leroi-Gourhan, *Les Racines du Monde*, Pierre Belfond, Paris, 1982O

André Leroi-Gourhan, *Préhistoire de l'Art occidental*, Mazenod, Paris, 1965.

Les Bijoux Anciens et Modernes, Société d'encouragement du Livre d'Art, Paris, 1887, pp.15–84.

L'Or et les Bijoux, World Gold Council, 1994.

Robert Maillard (ed.), *Le Diamant, Mythe, Magie et Réalité*, Flammarion, Paris, 1979.

Jean Marcadé, *Bijoux*, Nagel, Hachette, Geneva, 1973.

Anni Talli Mencioni, *Giampaolo Babetto*, Aurum, Zurich, 1991.

Catherine Millet, *L'Art Contemporain en France*, Flammarion, Paris, 1987.

Eloïse Mozzani, *Le Livre des Superstitions*, Robert Laffont, Paris, 1995.

Robert Muchembled, *Société, Cultures et Mentalités dans la France Moderne XVI–XVIII ème Siècle*, Armand Colin, Paris, 1990.

Jane Mulvach, *Fantaisies. Les Bijoux Chic et Choc*, (French edition) Chêne, Paris, 1989.

Hans Nadelhofer, *Cartier*, Editions du Regard, Paris, 1984.

Gilles Néret, *Ces Bijoux qui font Rêver*, Solar, Paris, 1990.

Charles Oman, *British Rings 800–1914*, B.T. Batsford, London, 1974.

Erwin Panofsky, *L'œuvre d'art et ses significations. Essais sur les arts visuels*, (French edition) Gallimard, Paris, 1969.

Erwin Panofsky, *La Renaissance et ses Avant-Courriers dans l'Art d'Occident*, Flammarion, Paris, 1976.

Marcel Paquet, Michel Journiac. *L'Ossuaire de l'Esprit*, La différence, Paris, 1977.

A. Parrot, *Sumer*, L'Univers des Formes, Gallimard, Paris, 1960.

Tapio Periänen, *Soul in design. Finland as an Example*, Kirjayhtymä, Helsinki, 1990.

Philippe Perrot, *Le Travail des Apparences. Le Corps Féminin, XVIII–XIX ème Siècles*, Seuil, Paris, 1984.

Philippe Perrot, *Le Luxe, une Richesse entre Faste et Confort, XVIII–XIX ème Siècle*, Seuil, Paris, 1995.

Philippe Perrot, *Les Dessus et les Dessous de la Bourgeoisie*, Fayard, Paris, 1981.

Petite Bibliothèque des Symboles, Editions du Chêne, Paris, 1994.

Marta Pietribiasi, *Robert Smit*, Aurum, Zurich, 1992.

Jean-Marc Poinsot, *L'Atelier sans Mur*, art éditions, Villeurbanne, 1991.

Frank Popper, *L'Art Cinétique*, Gauthier-Villars, Paris, 1970.

Evelyne Possémé, *Bijouterie. Joaillerie*, Massin, Paris, 1996.

Emma Pressmar, *Indian rings*, Insel Verlag, Frankfurt, 1982.

Barbara Radice, *Gioielli di Archtetti*, Electra, Milan, 1987

Sylvie Raulet, *Bijoux des Années 1940–1950*, Editions du Regard, Paris, 1987.

Herbert Read, *Histoire de la Peinture Moderne*, Arted, French edition, Paris, 1985.

Herbert Read, *Histoire de la Sculpture Française*, (french edition) Arted, Paris, 1985.

Maurice Sartre and Alain Tranoy, *La Méditerranée Antique IV Siècle av. J.–C–/III ème Siècle ap. J.–C.*, Armand Colin, Paris, 1990.

Diana Scarisbrick, *Les Bagues: Symboles de Richesse, de Pouvoir et d'Amour*, Céliv, French edition, Paris, 1993.

Jean-Marie Schaeffer, *Les célibataires de l'art. Pour une esthétique sans mythes*, Gallimard Essais, Paris, 1996.

H.J. Schubrel, *Pierres de Lumière et Objets*, Arthaud, Paris, 1987.

Karl Scollamayer, *Art Contemporain du Bijou*, Dessain et Tolra, Paris, 1975.

Seven Thousand Years of Jewellery, Hugues Tait, British Museum Press, London, 1995.

Yvette Taborin, *La parure en coquillage au paléolithique*, 29th supplement to Gallia Préhistoire, CNRS, 1993.

V. Tapié, *Baroque et Classicisme*, Librairie Générale Française, Le Livre de Poche, Paris, 1980.

Anne de Tugny, *Guide des Pierres de Reve*, Flammarion, Paris, 1987.

Ralph Turner, *Jewelry in Europe and America. New Times, New Thinking*, Thames and Hudson, London, 1996.

Dora Vallier, *L'Art Abstrait*, Librairie Générale Française, Le Livre de Poche, Paris, 1980.

Ouvrage collectif, Emmy Van Leerwsm, Broken Livres c/o Beeldrecht, Amsterdam, 1993.

Various authors, *Art du Bijou*, Société d'Encouragement aux Métiers d'Art, No. 22–23 September 1983.

Various authors, *Joaillerie 'Le Livre'. Chefs d'œuvre de l'Art du Bijou de l'Antiquité à Nos Jours*, Florilège, French edition, Paris, 1990.

Various authors, *La Main*, L'Harmattan, n°4, Paris, 1993.

Various authors, *L'Art du Bijou*, Flammarion, Paris, 1992.

Henri Vever, *La Bijouterie Française au XIX ème Siècle*, 3 vol., H. Floury, Paris, 1906–08.

A. Ward, J. Cherry, C. Gere, B. Cartlidge, *La Bague. De l'Antiquité à Nos Jours*, Office du Livre, Bibliothèque des Arts, Paris, 1981.

David Watkins, *The Best of Contemporary Jewellery*, Rotovision, Mies, 1993.

Donald Willcox, *Evolution du Bijou*, Dessain et Tolra, Paris, 1974.

Dyfri William and Jack Ogden, *Greek Gold Jewellery of the Classical World*, British Museum Press, London, 1994.

B. Zucker, *Gemmes et Joyaux*, Zaphir, Geneva, 1988.

CATALOGUES

Alberto Zorzi. Schmuck-Skulptur-Graphik, 1971–1990, Deutsches Goldschmiedenehaus Hanau, 4 March–16 April 1990.

Andrea Halmaschlager. Arbeiten 1993 to 1994, Vienna, Galerie V&V, 2 March-9 March 1994.

Artiste-Artisan, Musée des Arts Décoratifs, Paris, 25 May to 5 September 1977.

Daniel Kruger, Schmuckmuseum Pforzheim, 14 January to 11 March 1984.

Der Kosmos den Peters Skubic, Museum für Kunsthandwerk, Leipzig.

Deuxième Triennale du Bijou Contemporain, Musée du Luxembourg, Paris, 18 September to 18 October 1990.

Echo. Rian de Jong, October 1992, Zoo Produkties, The Hague.

Europea Contemporaria Joeria, Fondacio Caixa de Pensions, Barcelona, February to March 1987.

Exposicio de Joieria Contemporaria. Un Art Intim, Centre Cultural Can Mulà, 26 April to 30 June 1996.

Florence Lehmann Bijoux, Société Bellon, Bourg-Lès-Valence, 1991.

La main, Musée de l'Homme, 1965.

Landschaft und Garten. Schmuck Anna Heindl, Vienna, 25 November to 23 December 1987

L'Art de Cartier, Musée du Petit Palais, 20 October 1989 to 28 January 1990.

L'Europe des Créateurs. Utopies 89, Ecole des Arts décoratifs, Strasbourg, 24 November to 10 December 1989.

Le Bijou et le Sacré, Corpus, Strasbourg, 1993.

Les Arts du Métal, Bibliothèque Forney, Paris, 1976–77.

Les Métiers du Métal, Bibliothèque Forney, Paris, 17 December 1976 to 14 March 1977.

Living Design in Denmark, Kjeld Ammundsen, May 1995.

Magie des Plastiques, Ecole Nationale Supérieure des Beaux-Arts Paris, 20 September to 10 November 1996.

Ornementa 1 Internationale Schmuckkunst, Schmuckmuseum, Pforzheim 30, Prestal Verlag, Munich, 1989.

Ouroboros, Ruudt Peters, Uitgave, Amsterdam, 1995.

Philip Sajet. 'Achttien Ringen', Stedelijk Museum Amsterdam, 4 July-31 July 1996.

Philip Sajet. 'Elf Colliers', Amsterdam, 1994.

Première Triennale du Bijou Contemporain, Hôtel de Sens, Paris, 8 September-12 November 1987.

Qu'est ce que la Sculpture Moderne?, Centre Georges Pompidou, Musée d'Art Moderne, Paris, 3 July to 13 August 1986.

Rahmen und Ornament. Schmuck Anna Heindl, travelling exhibition from 1989 to 1990.

Ring, Galerie Michèle Zeller, Bern, 8 July to 12 September 1992.

Ted Noten, Amsterdam, 1996.

Troisième Triennale du Bijou Contemporain, Musée des Arts Décoratifs, Paris, 20 October to 20 December 1992.

Uber Deinen Schatten. Schmuck Aloïs Bauer, Fläx, 1993.

Ulo Florack Schmuck, 1987–1995, Ulo Florack, 1996.

Wendy Ramshaw Jewellery, April 1989, Eve France, Texas, 1989.

Wendy Ramshaw Picasso's Ladies, Dacs, 1989.

Wendy Ramshaw Rings, 1994.

Wendy Ramshaw. From Paper to Gold, South Bank Centre, 1990.

Wodurchschmuck. Bernhardt Fink, Galerie V&V, Vienna, 16 March to 4 May 1996.

Zeit genossiche Schmuckkunst aus der Bundesrepublik Deutschland, Institut für Auslandsbezizehungen, Stuttgart, 1989.

Museums and Galleries

GERMANY

Galleries

Die Werkstattgalerie
Meierottostr. 1
1000 Berlin 13

Galerie Treykorn
Savignyplatz 13
1000 Berlin 12

Galerie am Fischmarkt
Fischmarkt 7
5020 Erfurt

Galerie Werkstatt
Reinsburgstr. 154
7000 Stuttgart

Galerie für Angewanddte Kunst des
Bayrischen Kunstgewerbevereins
Pacellistr. 7
8000 München 2

Galerie Spekrum
Tükenstr. 37 Rgb
8000 München 40

Der 4 Konig
Grosse Brinkgasse
5000 Köln 1

Museums

Schmuckmuseum
Reuchlinhaus
Jahnstrasse 42
D-75173 Pforzheim

Württembergisches Landesmuseum
70173 Stuttgart
Altes Schloss

Stadtmuseum München
St. Jacobsplatz 1
8000 München 2
Bayern

Neue Sammlung – Staatliches Museum
für Angewandtekunst
Prinzregentenstr. 3
80538 München

Bayerisches Nationalmuseum
Prinzregentenstr. 3
80538 München

Deutsches Goldschmiedehaus
Alstädter Markt 6
6450 Hanau
Hessen

Badisches Landesmuseum
Sclossplatz 1
76131 Karlsruhe

Kestner Museum
Trammplatz 3
30159 Hannover

Museum für Kunsthandwerk Leipzig,
Grassi Museum
Johannisplatz
04103 Leipzig

Museum für Kunst und Gewerbe
Hamburg
Steintorplatz 1
20099 Hamburg

Kunstgewerbemuseum SMPK
Tiergartenstr. 6
1000 Berlin 30

Museum für Angewande Kunst
An der Rechtschule
5000 Köln 1

Museum für Kunsthandwerk
Schaumainkai 17
60594 Frankfurt

Museen der Stadt Nürnberg
Verwaltung
Hirschelgasse 9–11
90317 Nürnberg

AUSTRIA

Galleries

Galerie V+V
Bauernmarkt 19
1010 Wein

Galerie Slavik
Himmelpfortg. 17
1010 Wien

Galerie E L
Elsa Drobny
Altstadt 2
4020 Linz

Museums

Österreichisches Museum für
Angewandte Kunst
Stubenring 5
1010 Wien

Kunsthistorisches Museum
Privatwirtschaftlicher Bereich
1010 Wien
Bugring 5

Keltenmuseum Hallein
Pflegerplatz 5
A-5400 Hallein

BELGIUM

Galleries

Que Van
Dumortierlaan 112
Knokke

Galerie Muylaert-Hofman
Nieuwstraat 36
Aalst

Museums

Museum voor Sierkunsten en Industriele
Vormgeving
7, de Coninck Mansion
Jan Breydelstraat 5
9000 Gand

Provincial Museum voor Modern Kunst
Romestraat 11
Ostende

DENMARK

Galleries

Galerie Metal
Nybrogade 26
1203 Copenhagen

Tactus
Ny Ostergade 13
1101 Copenhagen

Museum

Kunstindustrimuseet
Bredgade 68
1260 Copenhagen

SPAIN

School

Escola Massana
C. Hospital, 56
08001 Barcelona

FINLAND

Design Forum Finland
Fabianinkatu 10
00130 Helsinki

Museum

Museum of Applied Art
Laivurinkatu 3
00150 Helsinki

FRANCE

Galleries and Shops

Aurus
88 rue Quincampoix
75003 Paris

Hélène Porée
31 rue Daguerre
75014 Paris

Roxane de Saule
6 rue Malher
75004 Paris

Marie Zisswiller
61 rue d'Auteuil
75016 Paris

Cheret
9 rue Madame
75006 Paris

Naila de Monbrison
6 rue de Bourgogne
75007 Paris

Arthus Bertrand
6 Place St-Germain-des-Prés
75006 Paris

Mybrose Cabrilhac
Carré d'Or
46 avenue Georges V
75008 Paris

Look 16
16 rue Vavin
75006 Paris

Galerie Artcurial
Centre d'Art Plastique Contemporain
9, avenue Maignon
75008 Paris

Museums

Musée du Louvre
32 Quai du Louvre
75058 Paris

Musée des Arts Décoratifs
Palais du Louvre
107 rue de Rivoli
75001 Paris

Musée des Arts Décoratifs
39 rue Bouffard
33000 Bordeaux

Musée Réattu
10 rue du Grand-Prieuré
13200 Arles

Musée d'Art Moderne et d'Art
Contemporain
Promenade des Arts
06300 Nice

Musée National des Arts et Traditions
Populaires
Centre d'ethnologie française
6, avenue du Mahatma Gandhi
75116 Paris

Musée des Antiquités Nationales
Château - BP 3030
78103 St-Germain-en-Laye

Library

Bibliothèque Nationale – Estampes
Photographic library
58 Rue du Richelieu
75084 Paris

UNITED KINGDOM

Galleries

Contemporary Applied Arts
2 Percy Street
London W1P 9FA

Crafts Council Shop
Victoria & Albert Museum
Cromwell Road
South Kensington
London SW7 2RL

Scottish Gallery
16 Dundas Street
Edinburgh EH2 6HZ

Oxford Gallery
23 High Street
Oxford OX1 4AH

Craze Two
35a Clerkenwell Green
London EC1R ODU

Electrum Gallery
21 South Molton Street
London W1Y 1DD

Argenta
82 Fulham Road
London SW3 6HR

Museums

Victoria & Albert Museum
South Kensington
London SW7

British Museum
Great Russell Street
London WC1B 3DG

Ashmolean Museum
Beaumont Street
Oxford OX1 2PH

Bodleian Library
University of Oxford
Broad Street
Oxford OX1 3BG

ITALY

Museums

Galleria Nazionale d'Arte Moderna
Viale delle Belle Arti 131
Rome

Musee Nationale
Piazza Museo
8000 Napoli

NORWAY

Galleries

Kunstnerforbundet
Kjellstubsgt 3
0160 Oslo

Gallery Ram
Kongensgt 3
0135 Oslo

Format
Vesthanepl 1
0250 Oslo

Museums

Kunstindustrimuseet i Oslo
St Olavsgate 1
0165 Oslo

Nordenfjeldske Kunstindustrimuseum
Munkegaten 5
7013 Trondheim

Vestlandske Kunstindustrimuseum
Nordahl Brungt 9
5014 Bergen

Tromsø Museum
9000 Tromso

NETHERLANDS

Galleries

Gallerie Marzee
Gansenbeuvel 33
Nijmegen

Galerie Louise Smit
Prinsengracht 615
Amsterdam

Galerie Ra
Vijzelstraat 80
Amsterdam

Museums

Stedlijk Museum
Paulus Potterstraat 13
Amsterdam

Gemeentemuseum
Utrechtseweg 87
6812 AA Arnhem

Museum Kruthruis
Citadellaan 7
Den Bosch

SWEDEN

Galleries

NFS Nutida Svensk Silver
Arsenal gatan 3
10389 Stockholm

Metalluum
Hornsgatan 30
11820 Stockholm

Museums

Röhss Museum of Arts and Crafts
Vasagatan 37-39
41755 Göteborg

Nationalmuseum
Sodra Bläsieholmshamnen
Box 16176
10324 Stockholm

SWITZERLAND

Galleries

Galerie Michele Zeller
Kramgasse 20
3011 Berne

Galerie Farel
Place du Marché 1
1860 Aigle

Museums

Musée de l'Horlogerie
15 route de Malagnou
1208 Genève

Musée d'art et d'histoire
Rue Charles-Galland 2
Case postale 3432
1211 Genève 3

GREECE

Museums

Benaki Museum
1, Koumpari Str.
106 74 Athens

National Archaelogical Museum
44 Patision Str
106 82 Athens

UNITED STATES

Museum

The Metropolitan Museum of Art
1000 Fifth Avenue
New York
New York 10028-0198

EGYPT

Museum

Cairo Museum
15 Kadry Street
Cairo El saida, Zieb
Egypt

Index

Abstract Expressionism 117
Age of the Enlightenment 87
Alexander the Great 41
Am Graben Gallery 162
Apollo 158
Ar. Co. 186
Ark of the Covenant 83
Arman 149
Armengol, Carles Codina 210
Art Brut 157
Art Nouveau 99, 100, 101, 110, 158, 186
Arts and Crafts movement 97, 101
Asclepius, god of medicine 41
Aspects Gallery, London 217
Atrium Gallery 162

Babetto, Giampaolo 179
Bahlmann, Alexandra 179
Bakker, Gijs 152, 167
Bakker, Ralph 195
Bauer, Aloïs 181
Bauhaus 143, 150, 151
Becker, Friedrich 150, 163, 166
Becker, Michael 179, 199
Beeren, Wim 153
Behrens, Peter 101
Berlage 151
Bill, Max 150
Billet, Christiane 176
Bischur, Sonja 227
Bishop Hilary of Chichester 56
Bishop of Marbode 57
Bishop Thierry of Verdun 56
Blavarp, Liv 235
Boekhoudt, Onno 169
Boileau 84
Boltz, Henri-Morand 173
Bordinckx 96
Botticelli 69
Bouchard, Olivier 246

Boucheron, Frédéric 96
Bouduban, Sophie 231
Boyer-Pellerej, Brune 232
Boyvin, René 77
Brancusi, Constantin 176
Brinkmann, Esther 228
Brno man 19
Bronger, Sigurd 235
Brumaire Law 94
Buck, Kim 234
Bulgaria 26
Burger, Christophe 236
Bury, Claus 165, 167
Bury, Pol 155

Calvin, Jean 73
cameo ring 68
Campos, Ana 216
Capdevila, Joaquim 184, 186
Capdevilla, Manuel 186
Caravaggio 83
Cardin, Pierre 159
Carolingian Empire 55
Carthage 46
Cartier, Louis François 96
Cartlidge, Barbara 162
Casselas, Carmen Roher 212
Cato the censor 45
Cave of the Hands 19
Cellini 69, 79, 153
Celtic 51
César 149
Chaigneau, Pierre 246
Chanel 108, 176
Chang, Peter 172
Chavent, Françoise and Claude
    176
Chéret, Claude 162
Christ 50, 51, 69, 71
Christo 149

classical period 37
Conception exhibition 162
Constantine 49
Contacto Directo 186
Cornet, Antoni Gaudi i 186
Corpus Group 242, 245
Corvajà, Giovanni 208
Council of Nicaea 49
Counter-Reformation 89
Courrèges 159
Cousens, Cynthia 218
Crafts Council 162
Cro-Magnon man 20
Cross, Susan 220
Cuyas, Ramon Puig 186, 209
Czachka, Carl Otto 102

d'Alembert 90
Da Vinci 153
Dahm, Johanna 174
Dali, Salvador 111
Davie, Alan 156
de Chirico, Giorgio 155
de Jong, Rian 190
De Kleik 151
De Patta, Margaret 158
de Ruysch 84
de Sousa, Filomeno Peirera 185
De Stijl movement 111, 151
Decree of Villers-Cotterêts 76
Degen, Joël 173
Degen, Pierre 173, 177
Derrez, Paul 162
Desprès, Jean 109, 150
Deutsche Werkbund 101
Diderot 90
Diocletian 49
Dionysius 158
Dior 176
Dobler, Georg 179, 199

Domenech, Xavier 186
Dubuffet, Jean 157
Duchamp 162
Ducruet, Hervé 239
Dudok 151
Dürer 69

Egypt 33-35
Eickhoff, Jürgen 162
Electrum Gallery 162
Emagold 134
emblematic ring 59-60
Emperor Augustus 44
Emperor Justinian 51
Engelhard-Clal 135
Erasmus 74
Eros 39
Exposition Des Arts Décoratifs et Industriels
    Modernes 110
Exposition Internationale Des Arts et
    Techniques dans la Vie Moderne 113

Fahrner, Theodor 101
fede ring 75, 96
Ferdinand I 74
Feuillâtre, Eugène 100
Fink, Bernhard 225
Finlay, Anne 217
Fisch, Arline 158
Fisherman's Ring 57, 69
Flöckinger, Gerda 157, 162
Florack, Ulo 200
Flötner, Peter 77
flower garden rings 88
Fluxus movement 187
Fontana, Lucio 155
Fontblanche Workshops 175
Fouquet, Georges 100
Fouquet, Jean 110
Francis I 76
François, Bernard 162
Fröhlich, Max 177
Froment-Meurice, François-Désiré 95
Front, Anna 186
Frühauf, Anton 153

Gagliardi, Ornella 162
Gaillard, Lucien 100
Galerie V&V, Vienna 227
Galleria Nazionale d'Arte Moderna, Rome
    162
Garbardi, Melissa 113
Gargat, Henri 166
Garrard 96
Gerard, Ann 239
Ghirlandaio 69, 153
Gianinazzi, Giovanna Quadri 206
Gibert, Joseph Jujol i 186
gimmel ring 77, 106
Gothic style 63
Gourhan, Leroi 22
Grassetto, Graziella 162

Greschny, Michael 239
Güell, Euseibi 186
Guinard, Carole 231

Halle School of Art and Design 150
hallmark 132
Halmaschlager, Andrea 225
Hamilton, Richard 157
Hanagaert, Sophie 233
Hardoin-Mansard, J. 85
Hassenplug, Marie and Peter Gallery,
    Düsseldorf 161
Heindl, Anna 224
Heintze, Renate 150
Héliodor Gallery 236
Hellenistic era 37
Henry VIII 74
Herbst, Marion 169
Hercules' knot 40
Hermsen, Hermann 192
Hills, Catherine E. 223
Hoffman, Joseph 101
Holbein, Hans 74
Holy Name 50
Homer 37
Horn, Janicke 235
House of Karl Rothmüller 101
Hübel, Angela 199
Hürlimann, Alban 227

Imbert, Isabelle 246
International Gothic 63-65
Iran 26

Jacob Meyer 74
Jean Calvin 73
Jensen, Georg 103
Jewellers in Revolt 169
Jewellery and the Sacred exhibition 245
Jewish ring 83
Jonemann, Gilles 175
Journiac, Michel 187
Jünger, Hermann 150

Kalf 84
Kamer, Sam 158
Kirchner, Margarita 162
Klarner, Sabine 199
Kleeman, Georg 101
Korssjoen, Synnove 235
Kosuth, Joseph 228
Kounellis 177
Kraen, Annette 182
Kruger, Daniel 198
Krüger, Winfried 179
Kunstgewerbemuseum, Vienna 162
Künzli, Otto 167

La Fontaine 84
Labruyère 84
Lachaert, Sophie 162
Lädstätter, Florian 225

Lalique, Réne 100
Le Mignot, Jean-Yves 246
Le Nôtre 85
Le Vau 85
van Leersum, Emmy 152
Légaré, Gilles 83
Lehmann, Florence 240
Leicht, Hans Erwin 184
Lemaire, Patricia 246
Lichtenstein 149
Lisboa, Alexandra 217
Livrelli, Bruno 162
Lohmann, Jan 175
Lorenzen, Jens-Rudigen 204
Lorrain 83
Louis XIV 84
love, goddess of 39
Lulli 84
Luther, Martin 73
Luttenbacher, Géraldine 242

Mackintosh, Charles Rennie 97
Maierhofer, Fritz 165
Mantegna 153
Map Sauer Gallery 161
Marcel Ficin 71
Maréchal, Christine 233
Marini, Marino 153
Marti, Teresa Capella i 185
Martinazzi, Bruno 154
Marx 93
Marzee 162
Massana School, Barcelona 184
Mattar Gallery, Cologne 217
Mattar, Wilhem 162
Medic wars 38
memento mori ring 75
Mercade, Jaume 186
Merovingian 53
Merz 177
Mesolithic man 25
Mesopotamia 29
Meyer, Astrid 237
Migno, Daniel 77
Mina, Jacqueline 177
Minkkinen, Eila 181
Molière 84
Monclus, Xavier Ines 212
Mondrian 151
Montaigne 75
Montaner, Louis Doménech i 186
Montesquieu 90
Morel, Sonia 232
Morris, William 97
Moschik, Melitta 225
Munch 102
Munich Academy of Art 150
Musée des Arts Décoratifs 162
Museum of Art 162
Museum of Decorative Arts, Lausanne 174
Mycanaean period 37

narrative ring 34
National Gallery of Victoria 162
Neanderthal man 19
Neevincz, Riet 151
Nègre, Suzanne 246
Neolithic period 25
New Images Gallery 162
New Realists 149
Nietzsche 93
Nike 40
Nobre, Zélia 216
Noll, Alexandre 175
Noll, Catherine 175–176
Noten, Ted 194–195

Octavian 44
Of Losse Schroeven 153
Oldenburg, Claus 149, 177
Olympic games 38
Op Art 151
ornamental ring 34

Paccioloi, Lucas 78
Padua School 153
Palaeolithic period 20–23
Pavan, Francesco 179
Pax Romana 44, 50
Peche, Dagobert 102
Perroud, Charles 127
Peters, Ruudt 190
Pforzheim 101
Pforzheim Schmuckmuseum 161–162
Pharaoh 35
Philip of Macedonia 41
Piazza, Diego 204
Picabia 162
Picasso 170–171
Pico della Mirandola 71
Pietro Selvatico Art Institute, Padua 153,
    179, 181
Pinton, Mario 153
Plandeydt, Annelies 193
Plato 40, 71
Platonic Academy of Florence 71
Plotinus 71
Poiret, Paul 107
Pomodoro, Arnaldo and Gio 155
Pop Art 157, 177, 150
Pope Pius 69
Porée, Hélène 162
Poussin 83
Practical Aesthetics College, Ulm 150
Preston, Mary 222
Prospect 69 exhibition 162
Prühl, Dorothea 150
Pseudo-Dionysius 71

Râ Gallery 162
Ra, sun god 33, 35
Rabanne, Paco 159
Rabelais 75
Ramharter, Michael 225

Ramshaw, Wendy 170
Raps, Jean 90
Register of Trends 139
regulation 132
Reiling, Reinhold 150
Rembrandt 83
Rémy de Gourmont 57
Ricci, Nina 176
Rieckert, Frantz 150
Rietveld, Gerrit 151
Rodriguez, Dharma Soriano 212
Roher, Carmen 186
Ronsard 75
Roses, Luis Masriera i 186
Rothmann, Gerd 165, 177
Rottier, Maud 245
Rousseau 90
Rubens 83
Ruskin, John 97
Rupp & Company 101
Ryan, Jacqueline 209

Sajet, Philip 191
Sarneel, Lucy 197
Schaeffer, Jean-Marie 162
Scharzinger, Verena 227
Schiaparelli, Elsa 108
Schick, Marjorie 159
Schliwinsky, Marianne 162
Schmidt-Rottluff, Karl 102
Schmuck aus Stahl 164
Schmuck Forums 228
Schobinger, Bernard 177
Schwarzinger, Veronika 162
Sculpture to Wear exhibition 153
seal ring 29–30
Seidenath, Barbara 202
signet ring 34, 73
Skubic, Peter 163–165
Smit, Louise 162
Smit, Robert 169
Smith, Arthur 158
Soviet Constructivism 150
Specht, Cathy 245
Spektrum Gallery, Munich 161, 217
St Augustine 71
St Barbara 71
St Benedict 71
St John the Baptist 71
St John the Evangelist 71
St Omer 71
Stedelijk Museum, Amsterdam 153
Steenberg, Chris 151
stirrup-shaped ring 55–57
Sumerian era 29–30
sumptuary laws 96
Suntum, Per 182
Sunyer, Ramon 186
symbolic ring 49–53
Syracuse 39
Syria 26

Teixé, Ramo 186
Tendahl, Brigitte 179
Thomas, Detlef 202
Tiffany & Company 103
Tiffany, Louis Confort 103
Todosze, Patricia 227
Toussaint, Jeanne 107
Trinity ring 106
Tudosze, Léa 162
Turkey 26
Turner, Ralph 162
Tutankhamun 35

Ullrich, Klaus 150, 204
Ulm School 143, 151
Union Des Artistes Modernes 110

Van Cleef & Arpels 107
Van der Leck 151
Van Gogh 102
Varna necropolis 26-27
Velasquez 83
Ventil Gallery, Munich 217
Verbeek, Miriam 197
Verrochio 69
Versailles 84
Vever brothers 100
Victoria & Albert Museum 36, 83, 90, 162
Vigeland, Toni 235
Virgin, the mother of God 51
Visintin, Graziano 205
Voltaire 90

Walz, Silvia 186, 212
Warhol, Andy 149
Watkins, David 170
Wesel, Claude 173
What is Modern Sculpture exhibition 158
Wiener Werkstätte 102
Wimmer, Josef 102
Winkelmann 90
Woeiriot, Pierre 77
Woell, Fred 159
Wohlleber, Anette 202
World Gold Council 139
Wytlesey, William 64
Wycliffe, John 64

Yugoslavia 26

Zanella, Anna Maria 208
Zeller, Michèle 162
Zellweger, Christophe 219
Zisswiller, Marie 162
Zorzi, Alberto 207